The
Isle of Wight Railway

by
R.J. Maycock & R. Silsbury

THE OAKWOOD PRESS

© Oakwood Press, R.J. Maycock & R. Silsbury 1999

British Library Cataloguing in Publication Data
A Record for this book is available from the British Library
ISBN 0 85361 544 6

Typeset by Oakwood Graphics.
Repro by Ford Graphics, Ringwood, Hants.
Printed by Cambrian Printers, Aberystwyth, Ceredigion.

Opening the Isle of Wight Railway

Hark! Hark! - I hear a whistle shrill,
And lo! the puffing steam
All over hedge, and through the hill;
What! - am I in a dream?

Strangers at Shanklin well may stare
With joy and admiration
When they behold a Railway there
And also Railway station!

Now all the folk, so fair and fine,
Who visit bustling RYDE,
May take a peep at SHANKLIN CHINE,
And hundred things beside.

Hurrah! for railway and for steam,
That bring us near all places; -
And quickly light with friendship's gleam
A thousand happy faces.

For now the parted soon can meet!
From SANDOWN, BRADING,RYDE;
And pace with light and joyous feet,
Together side by side.

And many now, in hours of need,
Of timely help may tell;
Or haply catch, through Railway Speed,
Affection's last farewell.

Hurrah! for Railroad and for steam -
Which, spite of wind or weather,
Though many miles may lay between,
So soon bring friends together.

Mrs J.C. Westbank
Shanklin, August 1864

Published by The Oakwood Press (Usk), P.O. Box 13, Usk, Mon., NP15 1YS.
E-Mail: oakwood-press@dial.pipex.com
Website: http://ds.dial.pipex.com/oakwood-press

Contents

Abbreviations

Whenever possible, the quotations and wording in minute books, Parliamentary Bills, Acts of Parliament and press reports are exactly as written. The titles 'Isle of Wight Railway' and 'Isle of Wight Central Railway' were repeatedly used by promoters to describe early railway schemes but they had no connection with later companies of the same name. The railway was incorporated in 1860 as The Isle of Wight (Eastern Section) Railway but changed its name in a later Act to The Isle of Wight Railway. Except where the wording was considered significant we have used the abbreviation IWES to denote the name of the company before January 1864 and IWR thereafter. The Brading Harbour Improvement and Railway changed its name in 1896 to the Brading Harbour Railway; the abbreviations BHIR and BHR reflect this. The following companies have been mentioned in this book:

BHIR	Brading Harbour Improvement & Railway Company
BHR	Bembridge Harbour & Railway Company
CNR	Cowes & Newport Railway
FYN	Freshwater, Yarmouth & Newport Railway
IWC	Isle of Wight Central Railway
IWES	Isle of Wight (Eastern Section) Railway Company
IWFC	Isle of Wight Ferry Company
IWNJ	Isle of Wight (Newport Junction) Railway
IWR	Isle of Wight Railway
LBSCR	London, Brighton & South Coast Railway
LCDR	London, Chatham & Dover Railway
LSWR	London & South Western Railway
NGStL	Newport, Godshill & St Lawrence Railway
NLR	North London Railway
REC	Railway Executive Committee
RNR	Ryde & Newport Railway
RPC	Ryde Pier Company
SBRPC	Stokes Bay Railway and Pier Railway
SECR	South Eastern & Chatham Railway
SR	Southern Railway

The plans and drawings are for illustrative purposes and should not be relied upon in all aspects. The early plans are based on drawings in the care of the National Railway Museum, York.

Foreword

The Isle of Wight Railway never truly lived up to the description 'the detestable little railway' bestowed on it by the American author Henry James, but it had its moments. Born with high hopes of becoming the main, if not the only railway in the Isle of Wight, plans for expansion faded away in a financial crisis that dogged its early years. Once the railway opened, however, it had an assured income from passenger traffic during the summer months that grew steadily as the years went by. The IWR suffered accidents typical of those occurring elsewhere in Britain - there was a 'cornfield meet' between two trains, a runaway train and many others. Meanwhile it managed to indulge in a little infighting with other railway companies in the Island as they competed for traffic. Although an independent company, within three decades the company's history came to be shaped more by events in Parliament than in the boardroom. The Great War did the railway no favours and it was with some relief when the Southern Railway took charge. Against the odds, the original line from Ryde to Shanklin has survived, battered but intact.

Acknowledgements

Through the company's Minute books and other documents in the care of the Public Record Office, it has been possible to gain some interesting insights into the history and management of the Isle of Wight Railway Company. The Minutes did, of course, paint the company in the best possible light and some entries were clearly made as a way of setting down the Board's policy for public record. Reports by the Directors to meetings of shareholders proved equally illuminating; those meetings during the company's financial crisis were particularly lively and a verbatim record of the exchanges has survived. Documents from other Island railway companies, the Ryde Pier Company and Joint Committee of the London & South Western and London, Brighton & South Coast Railways were also seen. The relevant Parliamentary papers, Acts of Parliament and Board of Trade files containing companies' returns, reports by the Railway Inspectors and some later material dating from Southern and British Railways' days was also inspected. These sources of information have been supplemented by extracts from contemporary accounts in local newspapers.

The nature of the source material has forced us to concentrate mainly on the management of the railway, whether it be the company's Directors or railway officials with a brief mention of the staff, usually when they broke the rules! A few myths have been exploded and some misconceptions perpetuated in previous accounts have been corrected. The reader may find references to previously unknown events whilst others have been ignored where they could not be validated from surviving records. This is particularly so in the chapters dealing with locomotives and rolling stock, as the engine register and other Ryde Works' documents seen by past authors are now missing. In a book of this size there must be some mistakes for which we apologise in advance.

A number of organisations and individuals have helped in the provision of information, including staff at the Public Record Office at Kew, House of Lords Records Office, National Railway Museum, the Museum of Science and Industry of Manchester, Railtrack Plc, R. W. Kidner and members of the Isle of Wight Steam Railway including Tim Cooper, Dr John Mackett, Roy and Mark Brinton.

Richard Maycock
Roger Silsbury

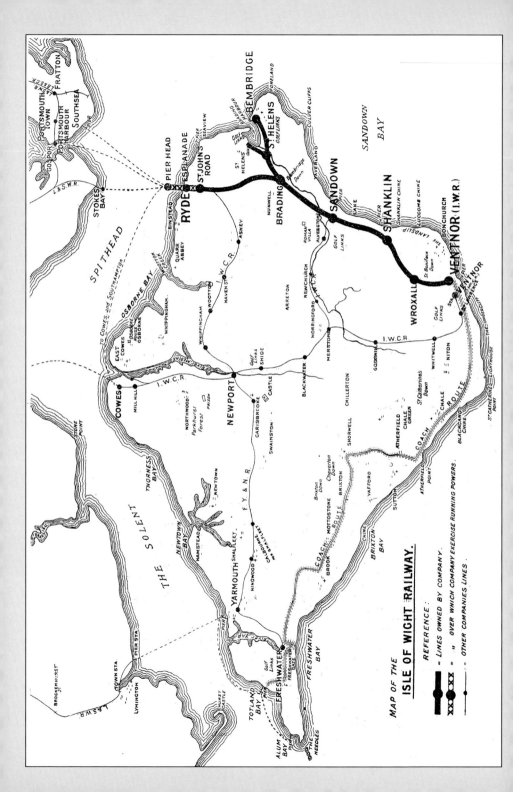

MAP OF THE
ISLE OF WIGHT RAILWAY.

REFERENCE:
= LINES OWNED BY COMPANY.
= " OVER WHICH COMPANY EXERCISE RUNNING POWERS.
= " OTHER COMPANIES LINES.

Introduction

The Isle of Wight Railway (IWR) was one of the first railways in the Island. It secured an Act of Incorporation as the Isle of Wight (Eastern Section) Railway Company (IWES) in 1860 and eventually completed a line from Ryde via Brading, Sandown, Shanklin and Wroxall to Ventnor in 1866.

The IWR had been preceded by the Cowes and Newport Railway (CNR) that opened in 1862. The Isle of Wight (Newport Junction) Railway (IWNJ) obtained an Act in 1868 for a line from Sandown to Newport. Opened in sections, it joined with the Cowes and Newport Company at Newport in 1879. Meanwhile, the Ryde and Newport Railway (RNR) was formed in 1872 and opened from Ryde to a joint station with the Cowes and Newport in 1875. These three companies amalgamated in 1887 to form the Isle of Wight Central Railway (IWC).

In 1880 the Freshwater, Yarmouth and Newport Railway (FYN) obtained its Act of Incorporation. It opened to passengers in 1889, worked by the Isle of Wight Central. Another railway worked by the Central was the Newport, Godshill and St Lawrence Railway (NGStL), originally promoted as the Shanklin and Chale Railway. Its railway opened from Merstone on the Sandown to Newport line to Ventnor in 1900. The IWC operated both until 1913 when the FYN began working their line themselves. The IWC bought the NGStL that year.

At the eastern end of the Island, the Brading Harbour Improvement and Railway Company (BHIR) opened a railway from a junction with the Isle of Wight Railway near Brading to Bembridge in 1882. The IWR worked the line and eventually bought it in 1898. The Ryde Pier Company (RPC) opened its pier in 1814 and extended it on several occasions thereafter. The pier company began operation of a horse tramway along the pier in 1864 and extended it in 1871 through the streets to the IWR station. It was replaced by a railway opened in 1880 by the London and South Western (LSWR) and London, Brighton and South Coast railways (LBSCR); they owned no rolling stock in the Island, services being operated by the IWR and IWC. The LSWR and LBSCR also took over the ownership of the Portsmouth - Ryde ferries in 1880. The pier company retained its pier tramway powered at various times by steam, horse and electricity.

In 1923 the Southern Railway (SR) assumed control of the railways and ferries, followed a year later by the purchase of the Ryde Pier Company's property at Ryde. The new organisation carried out a number of improvements both to modernise the railways and provide a more frequent service. This came to an end at the onset of the 1939-1945 war and in 1948 Britain's railways were nationalised. In 1952 the British Transport Commission closed the line from Merstone to Ventnor, followed a year later by those from Brading to Bembridge and Freshwater to Newport. Newport to Sandown closed in 1956. In 1966 British Railways (Southern Region) ceased running trains from Ryde to Newport and Cowes and part of the IWR main line from Shanklin to Ventnor. The remaining 8½ miles of railway was electrified and since then has been worked using former London Transport tube stock. The pier tramway closed in 1969 and in 1996 the railway became a franchise managed by Stagecoach Plc. A section of the former Ryde and Newport Railway from Smallbrook to Havenstreet and Wootton is operated by the Isle of Wight Steam Railway.

Dates of Opening and Closure of Railways and Tramways
For Passenger Traffic in the Isle of Wight

Railway	Owning Co.	Distance	Date Opened	Date Closed
Cowes to Newport	CNR	4¼	16th June, 1862	21st February, 1966
Ryde St Johns Road to Shanklin	IWR	7¼	23rd August, 1864	E
Ryde Pier Gates to Pier Head *	RPC	½	29th August, 1864	26th January, 1969
Shanklin to Ventnor	IWR	4	10th September, 1866	18th April, 1966
Ryde Pier Gates to The Castle *	RPC	¼	28th January, 1870	5th April, 1880
The Castle to St Johns Road *	RPC	½	7th August, 1871	5th April, 1880
Sandown to Shide	IWNJ	8¼	1st February, 1875	6th February, 1956
Shide to Pan Lane (Newport)	IWNJ	½	6th October, 1875	6th February, 1956
Ryde St Johns Road to Newport	RNR	10	20th December, 1875	21st February, 1966
Pan Lane to Newport	IWNJ	¼	1st June, 1879	6th February, 1956
Ryde St Johns Road to Ryde Esplanade	LSWR & LBSCR	¾	5th April, 1880	E
Ryde Esplanade to Ryde Pier Head	LSWR & LBSCR	½	12th July, 1880	E
Brading to Bembridge	BHIR	2¾	27th May, 1882	21st September, 1953
Newport to Freshwater	FYN	12	11th July, 1889	21st September, 1953
Merstone to St Lawrence	NGStL	5½	20th July, 1897	15th September, 1952
St Lawrence to Ventnor Town	NGStL	1¼	1st June, 1900	15th September, 1952

E - Closed 1st January, 1967 to 19th March, 1967 for electrification works. Reopened 20th March, 1967.

* a tramway - other lines in the Isle of Wight were railways.

	Total Mileage
IWR	14
IWC	28 ¼
FYN	12
LSW/LBSC Joint	1 ¼
Total	55 ½

Chapter One

A Railway Company is Formed

The Isle of Wight was formed during the Ice Age when a rising sea drowned the Solent river. The geology of the resulting Island created large areas of fertile farmland separated by chalk uplands and deep chines (valleys) by the action of water on soft clays. Such was the lush nature of the vegetation that the Island earned a well deserved reputation as the 'Garden Isle'; all this in an area measuring roughly 23 miles east to west and 13 miles north to south.

For centuries the economy of the Isle of Wight was based mainly on agriculture. Much of the land was in the ownership of a small number of gentry who managed their tenants in the same feudal manner as their forefathers. There was fishing and some smuggling whenever the opportunity arose, a healthy disrespect for outside authority, and visitors were not encouraged!

The majority of the towns along the eastern seaboard of the Island did not exist before the coming of railways. Brading was a long-established port but its importance had diminished with the silting of Brading Haven. Ryde grew from a handful of fishermen's cottages and developed further following the introduction of a reliable ferry service to the mainland in the 1820s, Sandown and Shanklin were still hamlets whilst in 1830 Ventnor was no larger; a few scattered houses and a water mill.

Fashionable British society had little interest in taking vacations in their own country prior to the 1790s; they preferred to visit German spas or the French and Italian Rivieras. However, the Napoleonic Wars and the consequential unrest on the Continent led to a search for alternatives away from the pollution of Britain's cities. Several guide books helped to bring the Isle of Wight to public attention. Ventnor was singled out as having a climate helpful for sufferers of chest ailments. Elsewhere in the Island, Queen Victoria bought the Osborne estate in 1845 and eight years later the poet Tennyson moved to Farringford, near Freshwater. Close behind the Queen and Tennyson came more poets, politicians and the middle classes. Twenty years later Ryde had become a major point of entry to the Island, Sandown with its wide and safe beaches benefited from the new fashion for sea bathing, Shanklin was being promoted as a spa whilst Ventnor had become an established resort.

Road transport within the Island was slow, uncomfortable and expensive. In 1820 a visitor wrote of the journey to Ventnor:

I found the Island was not easily reached, the sailing packets were formidable conveyances to bad sailors and invalids. A post-chaise from Ryde, with a boy to open the numerous gates, and a post-boy to drive, at 1s. 6d. a mile was expensive . . . unless very provident as to provisions we ran as much risk of dying from famine, by going to the back of the Island, as from consumption.

The increasing popularity of the Island with visitors soon prompted enterprising Islanders to begin running horse-drawn coaches - stage coaches or vehicles resembling end-door omnibuses - but high fares and tolls restricted their use to the wealthy. By 1840 much of the Island had some form of daily service, except on Sundays and during the winter months.

Early railways on the mainland not only carried passengers and goods more quickly than other forms of transport but were also profitable. A railway from London to Southampton opened in 1840 followed in 1842 by a branch to Gosport. In 1844 changes made by Parliament, linked with an easing of credit, led to a flurry of schemes for additional railways, including two in the Isle of Wight. They did not aim to provide a service for Islanders but were planned as links in a chain of communications between London and Ventnor. Depending on which muddy, potholed roads were used, Ventnor could be reached either from Cowes, where the Southampton steamers landed, or Ryde served by vessels from Gosport, Portsmouth and Southsea.

The first proposals for a railway in the Isle of Wight came to public notice in May 1845. Provisionally registered at Companies House as the Isle of Wight Railway Company, a group

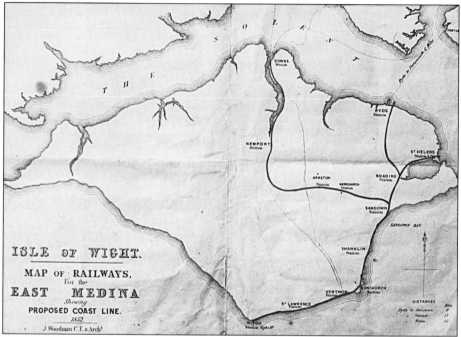

ISLE OF WIGHT.

MAP OF RAILWAYS,
For the
EAST MEDINA
Shewing
PROPOSED COAST LINE.
1852
J Woodman C.E. & Arch.

An outline map showing the route of the proposed 1853 east coast railway.

of promoters, mainly resident on the mainland, proposed to raise £300,000 for the construction of standard-gauge railways from West Cowes and Ryde to Newport and thence to Ventnor. The principal opponents were the Island's landed gentry. They wrote to the local newspapers objecting to the taking of their land for a railway which they claimed to be unnecessary. At several meetings there was support for the scheme, but the views of its opponents held sway.

Meanwhile a second scheme appeared. A London solicitor, Edwin Paul, provisionally registered the Direct Ryde and Ventnor Railway as a company on 20th October, 1845. The other promoters consisted of Thomas Paul, a London cabinet maker, and Thomas Hellyer, an architect and surveyor of Lind Street Ryde; he designed several Island churches built or rebuilt during the 1800s including Holy Trinity, Ryde and St John's, Oakfield. They issued a circular proposing to raise £120,000 by the issue of £10 shares for the construction of a railway from Ryde to Ventnor via Brading, Sandown and Shanklin. A preliminary survey established that the railway would be almost level with no cuttings or tunnels (a reference to the Isle of Wight Railway scheme which planned to run through a tunnel near Ventnor), it would neither destroy nor interfere with 'the Beauties of the Island' and was not likely to meet with opposition from any of 'the Landed Proprietors'. This proved a pious hope and the final utterance from the promoters referred to their inability to get a Bill placed before Parliament by the deadline of 30th November. With the 'consequent difficulty in strictly complying with the Standing Orders of Parliament it is not their intention to apply for an Act . . .'

The process of obtaining an Act of Parliament was a complicated and expensive matter; not something to be entered into lightly. However, it was rare for a railway to command total support from local residents and many landowners were reluctant to sell their property. An Act would provide the necessary compulsory purchase powers as well as authority to raise capital by the issue of shares and borrow money, usually in the form of debentures paying a guaranteed rate of interest.

The Railway Mania had to end. So many extravagant railways had been floated, many in competition with each other, that dividends from existing shares dropped sharply. Public confidence in railways received a severe shock and numerous schemes failed, including some that had secured Parliamentary approval. It was not until 1852 that the return of investors to the financial markets prompted fresh proposals for railways in the Isle of Wight. The most prominent scheme was for the Isle of Wight Railway, a network of 22 miles of lines that differed from the 1845 proposals only by having its southern terminus at Niton, then being promoted as a spa. A Bill applying for powers to build the railway went before Parliament, but when it came before the House of Commons in March 1853 its opponents gained sufficient support to have the Bill voted out.

The Direct Ryde & Ventnor Railway was resurrected in 1852 by Thomas Hellyer and J. Woodman who sought to build a railway from Ryde to the Undercliff passing near Brading, Sandown and Shanklin, through a short tunnel near Landslip to Bonchurch, Ventnor and St Lawrence before terminating near St Catherine's lighthouse at Niton. Branch lines were envisaged from Brading to a station and 'depôt' at St Helens, and from Sandown to East Cowes via Newchurch, Arreton and Newport. The scheme was abandoned before a Bill reached Parliament.

The Crimea War and its consequences for Britain's economy discouraged the promotion of railways for several years. Of course, some were quite content about their absence from the Island; in 1856 one writer remarked, 'Happily for the tourist, no *Railway* as yet profanes the quest of its vales'.

In 1858 details of five schemes appeared in local newspapers: three modest proposals for railways from Cowes to Newport, Yarmouth to Cowes and Ryde to Bonchurch, plus two ambitious undertakings each with lines from Newport to Cowes, Ryde and Ventnor.

A.F. Livesay and R.J.H. Saunders proposed the construction of a Ryde to Bonchurch railway. Beginning at a terminus near East Street Ryde, it would have proceeded in a southward direction past Smallbrook Farm, through deep cuttings near Beaper before looping east of Brading and west of Sandown and Shanklin. Beyond Shanklin there would have been a climb at 1 in 50 to cross a viaduct (one of two) at Cowlease Hill 700 yards long, 70 ft high, carried on 28 arches. A 100 ft deep cutting marked the approach to a terminus at Bonchurch Shute from where a road was proposed to the Nine Stones at Ventnor. At Ryde there would have been a horse tramway from the railway terminus through the streets and on an embankment along the seaward side of the Esplanade to a terminus close to the pier entrance. Of the other schemes, Messrs Birkenshaw and Conybeare put forward proposals for a network of lines based on Newport; their Ventnor line would have terminated in stone quarries high above the town.

A considerable rivalry developed between the Birkenshaw & Conybeare and the Livesay & Saunders schemes, especially at Ventnor. A public meeting was held in the town on 23rd December, 1858 chaired by John B. Martin, a great opponent of Livesay. Those attending the meeting adopted the Birkenshaw line because they regarded the cutting and viaducts in the Livesay scheme as impractical. Quite apart from the high cost, the railway would have had a detrimental effect on the view across Luccombe and a hopelessly inconvenient terminus on the outskirts of Upper Bonchurch. Despite this setback, Bills for three railways were presented to Parliament in the Autumn of 1858:

1. The Cowes & Newport Railway proposed to construct a railway from the north end of Cross Street, Cowes to near Towngate bridge, Newport and a tramway from the station at Cowes to Fountain Quay. The capital was £30,000 with borrowings of £10,000.
2. The Isle of Wight Railway. The Birkenshaw scheme for a railway from a wharf or pier at West Cowes to Newport and then to Ryde with branches to Sandown, Shanklin, Ventnor and to Ryde Pier. The proposed capital was £180,000 and £60,000 in loans.
3. The Isle of Wight Railway (Eastern Section) for:
   a. a railway commencing near East Street, Ryde and terminating 'near the High road from Shanklin to Bonchurch' at Upper Bonchurch;
   b. tramways from Ryde Pier to the terminus of the railway;
   c. a branch to a quay or landing place at Brading Harbour;
   d. a branch to a pier at Sandown;
   e. telegraphs in the Isle of Wight and to the mainland.

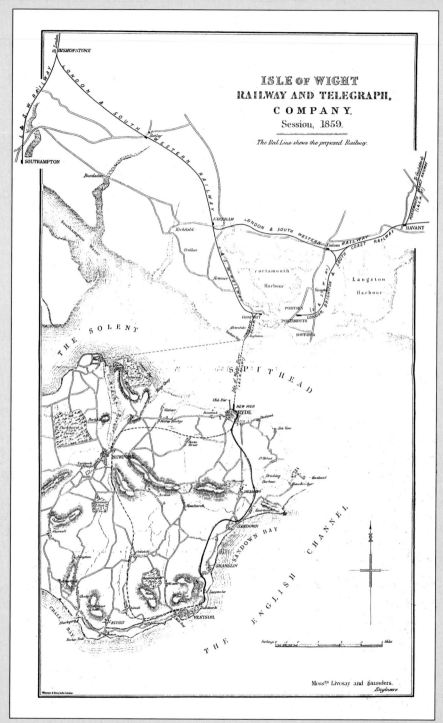

Map from Prospectus for the Isle of Wight Railway (Eastern Section) of 1859.

The route of the Eastern Section railway differed significantly from that proposed by Livesay and Saunders. In response to a petition from local residents it would have passed nearer to Brading, Sandown and Shanklin. But between Ryde and Brading there remained deep cuttings and the Shanklin to Bonchurch section contained a length with a gradient of 1 in 60 and two viaducts, one 396 yards and the other 264 yards long. The undertaking proposed to make agreements with the Ryde Pier Company and Isle of Wight Ferry Company for the exchange of passengers. The Eastern Section name distinguished it from the Isle of Wight Railway scheme and from other lines the promoters hoped to build. A Prospectus, issued in February 1859 under the name of the Isle of Wight Railway and Telegraph Company, claimed that it was an extension of existing schemes for a railway on the mainland to Stokes Bay and ferries and docks provided by the Isle of Wight Ferry Company at Ryde. A plan accompanying the Prospectus showed a continuation of the railway along the coast to Niton, before looping back across the Island to Newport and Ryde (although this extension was not in the Bill). The principal investors were James Simpson and Thomas Webster who subscribed for £1,000 and £500 of shares respectively. Messrs Livesay and Saunders could each afford to invest only £100 but, as events proved, this was a wise decision.

The Bill for the Isle of Wight Railway (Eastern Section), had to negotiate a series of hurdles in both Houses of Parliament, when there were opportunities to vote out a Bill in its entirety or amend its provisions. A committee of the House of Commons met in July 1859 to hear evidence from supporters and opponents. On this occasion, the opponents successfully convinced members of the committee that the railway would have a detrimental effect on the natural beauty of the Landslip. Powers to build the section beyond Shanklin were deleted from the Bill, the tramways at Ryde having already been sacrificed. A few weeks later, battle resumed before a Lords' committee. This time the committee reported on 8th August, 1859 that 'it was not expedient to proceed with the Bill'; as a result the whole Bill was lost. Of the three Isle of Wight Bills to go before Parliament, only that for the Cowes & Newport Railway became law.

Despite the failure of the Bill, the first recorded meeting of the Directors and promoters of the Isle of Wight Railway (Eastern Section) took place on 5th October, 1859 at the Pier Hotel in Ryde. Present were four people described as Directors: Messrs Simpson, Barrow, More and Webster. The promoters were listed as Messrs Fulton, Livesay, Saunders, Fisher, Beckinsale, and Porter.

The Directors and promoters were a disparate group of individuals with their own motives for taking part in what was a risky venture. Most of those named had been involved in earlier unsuccessful schemes. They might have owned land they hoped to see developed, or possessed skills that would be needed. Naturally all wanted a railway between Ryde and Ventnor, whilst some also desired links to the shore at Ryde and to other parts of the Island. In seeking to satisfy these aspirations the company spent considerable sums of money and almost went bankrupt in the process!

Only three of those attending that meeting became Directors of the Isle of Wight (Eastern Section) Railway Company: James Simpson, Alexander More and Thomas Webster. James Simpson became the first IWES Chairman; a well-to-do Civil Engineer with a business address at 26 Great George Street, Westminster, he was connected with the Chelsea Water Works and may not previously have had any experience of railway companies. It was through an acquaintance, Thomas Webster, that he first became aware of the possibilities for a railway in the Island. James Simpson had access to significant amounts of money as he made numerous loans to pay the bills and guaranteed borrowings from bankers. Less is known about Alexander More; he was described as a Gentlemen and although quoting an address at Bembridge had connections in Ventnor. On several occasions during the company's darkest days Mr More voiced the strong local support for the completion of the line. When the railway did eventually open to Ventnor he got up a committee to finance the celebrations.

Thomas Webster is perhaps the most interesting of the three. A Barrister at Law of 2 Great George Street, Westminster, he had a home address at Cliff House, Sandown and

ISLE OF WIGHT
RAILWAY AND TELEGRAPH
COMPANY.

ISLE OF WIGHT RAILWAY (EASTERN SECTION)
RYDE, ST. HELEN'S, BRADING, BEMBRIDGE, SANDOWN, SHANKLIN, BONCHURCH AND VENTNOR.

CAPITAL £75,000,
IN 7,500 SHARES OF £10 EACH—DEPOSIT £1 PER SHARE.

The liability of Shareholders limited to the amount of their Shares, and in the event of Act not being obtained, one moiety of the Deposit will be returned.

Provisional Directors.

*JAMES SIMPSON, 29, Great George Street, Westminster *(Chairman)*.
*The Hon. A. H. MORETON, Bembridge, Isle of Wight *(Vice-Chairman)*.
*BENJAMIN BARROW, Clifton House, Ryde, Isle of Wight.
PETER WILLIAM BARLOW, Blackheath, Kent.
SEPTIMUS BEARDMORE, 27, Albion Street, Hyde Park, W.
SIR CHARLES T. BRIGHT, 72, Old Broad Street.
THOMAS WILLIS FLEMING, South Stoneham, Southampton.
*WILLIAM RICHARD FISHER, The Lodge, Pinner, Middlesex.
*LEWIS D. B. GORDON, Abingdon Street, Westminster.
R. A. GLASS, 115, Leadenhall Street.
*ALEXANDER MORE, Bembridge, Isle of Wight.
*THOMAS NORTON, Abingdon Street, Westminster.
*THOMAS WEBSTER, Sandown, Isle of Wight.
THOMAS HALE, Sandown, Isle of Wight.
The Rev. D. I. HEATH, Brading, Isle of Wight.

The asterisk to the names of the Provisional Directors denotes such of them as are on the Committee of Management.

Bankers.
Messrs. WILLIAMS, DEACON & CO., Birchin Lane.

Engineers.
Messrs. LIVESAY & SAUNDERS, Portsmouth and Ventnor.

Solicitors.
CHARLES FRANCIS FISHER, Ventnor and Sandown, Isle of Wight.
GEORGE T. PORTER, 4, Victoria Street, Westminster.

Secretary.
JOHN THOMAS DARKE,

Offices.
28, Parliament Street.

The requirements of the Isle of Wight, in reference to improved communication, have on several occasions occupied the attention of persons, who, as owners of property, or residents, or visitors, were interested in removing or diminishing the annoyances, delays, and inconveniences attending the passage to and from the Island, and the disadvantages to which the Island is subject, from the absence of the facilities of transit long since afforded to other places.

The attempts of 1846 and 1852 for a Railway within the Island were wholly abortive, the defective communication of the Island rendering the success of such an attempt of little value until the obstructions of transit to the water side should be removed, and the access to the Island improved.

With this view, in the autumn of 1854 public attention was directed to the subject by the proposal to form the Stokes Bay and Isle of Wight Railway, Pier and Telegraph Company, for the following objects :—

First.—The constructing a Railway from the London and South Western Railway, near the Gosport Station, to Stokes Bay, with a Pier in the Bay suitable for the interchange of the traffic between the steam boat and the railway carriage directly, and without any break such as exists at Southampton, Gosport, and Portsmouth, and at which passengers might embark and disembark in all weather, and at all times of tide.

Secondly.—Communication by Steamers of improved construction between Stokes Bay and the Island, thus affording a sheltered sea passage of 3 miles between Stokes Bay and Ryde, in lieu of the exposed sea passage of 5 miles between Portsmouth and Ryde, with corresponding advantages between Stokes Bay and Cowes, thus in effect reducing the passage between London and the Island to three, instead of four and a half and five hours.

Thirdly.—The establishing Telegraphic Communication throughout the Island, and in connection with the main land, which having regard to the requirements of a large proportion of the residents and visitors, and the interrupted nature of the communication with the Metropolis, is of equal if not greater importance than either of the others.

This project, though brought out under the sanction of many influential persons, was threatened with so severe an opposition at the instance of persons interested in the existing monopolies, that it was found expedient to abandon the two latter, and to limit the application to Parliament in the session of 1855 to the first of the foregoing objects, for which powers were obtained by "The Stokes Bay Railway and Pier Act, 1855."

In the following Session, application was made to Parliament for the second object, and powers were obtained under "The Isle of Wight Ferry Act, 1856," for establishing a Ferry between Stokes Bay and Ryde, to be worked by vessels adapted for the embarking, conveying, and disembarking of passengers, carriages, goods, and other traffic, without incurring the annoyance and risk now experienced, and for the construction of Works at Ryde suitable for the accommodation of vessels, and of the passengers and cargoes to be conveyed thereby to and from the Island.

Considerable progress has been made with the works at Ryde, a sheltered basin for the loading and unloading of goods, and a landing place available at high-water and from half-flow to half-ebb for passengers, with ample quay space for goods has been provided, and is now open to and used by the public, and additional accommodation for vessels, goods, and passengers, will be provided during the ensuing summer.

The construction of the Stokes Bay Railway and Pier has been unavoidably delayed by the state of the arrangements with the London and South Western Railway Company; the Shareholders of that Company, at the half-yearly Meeting held in August last, passed unanimously the following Resolution:—"That the Directors be authorised and requested to conclude with the Stokes Bay Railway and Pier "Company, and the Isle of Wight Ferry Company, or either of these Companies, such agreements for "working the traffic or for leasing the Stokes Bay Railway, and for securing an efficient sea service to the "Isle of Wight, in connection with it and incidental thereto respectively, as the Directors may consider most "conducive to the interests of the Company;" and in pursuance of this resolution, arrangements have been concluded for ensuring the immediate completion of the works of the Stokes Bay Railway and Pier, with an efficient sea service to and from the Island.

The prospect of such improved communication at a very early period, by the arrangements made with the two Companies to which those undertakings were entrusted, aroused in the autumn of last year attention to the necessity of improved communication throughout the Island, and resulted in the announcement of a project, which in one of its most important features was in direct opposition to and rivalry with the interests of the Stokes Bay and Ferry Companies, and in other respects appeared ill adapted to the peculiar character and requirements of the Island.

The course of events gave importance to other considerations; a rivalry arose between the interests of Ryde, Brading, Bembridge, and Sandown on the east side, and Cowes and Newport on the west side of the East Medina. For the accommodation of the latter, two projects were announced.

The Isle of Wight Railway and Telegraph Company is projected for the purpose of securing Railway accommodation to the Eastern side of the Island, which embraces some of the most attractive spots, and possesses at Brading a large labouring, and at Bembridge an important residential population, in addition to the more populous districts of St. Helen's, Sandown, Lake, Shanklin, and Bonchurch, between the Termini at Ryde and Ventnor. This route contrasts favourably with any other between the same Termini, both as to engineering difficulties and the course followed between Ryde and Shanklin, with the additional recommendation of being a less expensive undertaking, and of forming as near an approach as practicable to the various centres of population.

The comprehensive system of Telegraphs, in connection with the Telegraphs at Southampton, Gosport, and Portsmouth, presents a distinctive feature of the undertaking, and is of the highest importance to the Island; while the connection with the works of the Ferry Company and of the Old Pier Company at Ryde, also a distinctive feature of the undertaking, will insure to the inhabitants at the back of the Island protection against any unnecessary delays at Ryde.

The identification of so many interests in connection with a scheme for the promotion of a Railway within the Island with the accession of contingent advantages so beneficially affecting every portion of the community is not likely soon, if ever, to recur. It appeals in the most direct and forcible manner to local interests and support; and for the purpose of enabling all classes of the Inhabitants to respond to the appeal and to co-operate for this object, the amount of the shares has been fixed at the small sum of £10 each.

The inconsiderable sum of £75,000 has, after careful computation, been found a sufficient amount of capital for the purposes of the above undertaking, if economically conducted, upon which amount, after a liberal allowance for working expenses, the existing traffic will yield a dividend considerably exceeding 5 per cent. per annum.

Applications for shares may be made in the accompanying form.

J. T. DARKE,

Secretary.

28, Parliament Street, S.W.,
February, 1859.

Prospectus for the Isle of Wight Railway (Eastern Section) of 1859.

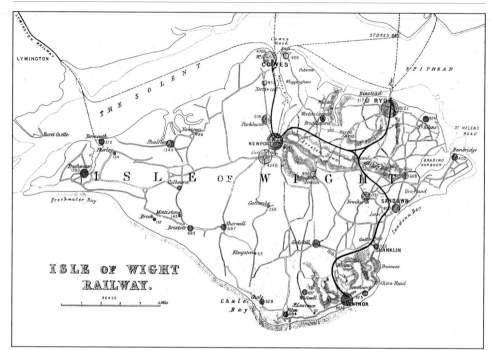

Map from Prospectus for the Isle of Wight Railway of 1858.

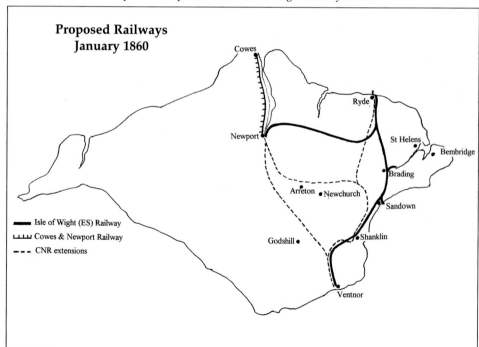

owned a sizeable estate in the neighbourhood. Thomas Webster became Chairman of the Isle of Wight Ferry Company, incorporated in 1856 to construct docks at Ryde and operate a ferry service between Ryde and Stokes Bay on the mainland. He knew Thomas James Willis Fleming of South Stoneham, Southampton, a magistrate and Deputy Lieutenant for Hampshire and Dorset, Grand Master for the Isle of Wight Masons, who briefly served as Member of Parliament for Winchester from February 1864 to 1865. Willis Fleming was Chairman of the Stokes Bay Railway, Tramway and Pier Company formed to build a railway on the mainland from a junction with the London & South Western Railway near Gosport to a pier at Stokes Bay. The Engineer of the Stokes Bay Company was Hamilton Henry Fulton, who seemed to make a living by generating interest in railway schemes and then charging the undertakings for his services! These three worthies saw the railway as a link in their undertakings from the London & South Western Railway via Stokes Bay and Ryde to the Undercliff near Ventnor.

Of the other promoters, mention must be made of A.F. Livesay and R.J.H. Saunders. Augustus Livesay is perhaps better known for his work in designing an elegant and imposing chapel, The Holy Spirit at Newtown. He became owner of Ventnor's gas and water works, the management of which he delegated to his son, J.G. Livesay. Richard Saunders worked as Engineer to the Ventnor Harbour Company (another company with Thomas Willis Fleming as its Chairman) formed in 1861 to build a pier at Ventnor. The firm of Livesay and Saunders of High St, Ventnor were architects - what better way could they have encouraged development in the town?

Finally two lawyers. Charles F. Fisher ran a law practice in Ventnor and Sandown; he acted as the local solicitor during the early years, usually in the issue of shares and negotiating the purchase of land. George Porter specialised in railway law and operated from offices at 4 Victoria Street, Westminster, an address that frequently appeared on company documents. Both he and Mr Fisher received shares in part payment and Mr Porter, especially, ended up with a sizeable holding.

Early entries in the minute books recorded the attempts to rally support in the Island in opposition to a resurrection of the Birkenshaw scheme promoted by Continental, i.e. mainland, interests. This revolved around the creation of local committees and had the desired effect; when it came to buying shares the members of those committees proved less helpful. Most meetings of the Board took place in London at 'Mr Simpson's' - 29 Great George Street, Westminster. The first half-yearly shareholders' meeting was at 'the Company's chief offices' at the Castle, Ryde, a rather grandiose building bordering the Esplanade. The company soon gave up the Castle but not until it had incurred a considerable cost in rent. The shareholders' meetings thereafter were generally held in London or Ryde; this reflected the two principal sources of capital with sizeable numbers of small Island shareholders outweighed by a handful of London investors.

At their meeting on 5th October, 1859 the Directors and promoters discussed the need to make a fresh application to Parliament for powers to construct their railway, and how the route could be changed to meet objections that had led to the rejection of the previous Bill. They resolved to divert the railway away from the coast via Wroxall, through a tunnel to terminate in the quarries overlooking Ventnor with the possibility of a tramway continuing to the town. This route had been proposed by other promoters, Ventnor residents favoured it and Wroxall was a better location from which to commence extensions. The diversion upset some residents of Luccombe and Bonchurch who pressed for a branch line, but without success. At Ryde the railway would end near Melville Street but continuing as a 'branch' to the Esplanade. A line from Sandown to Newport was envisaged and consultations were planned with the Cowes & Newport Railway concerning a joint station at Newport.

The Isle of Wight (Eastern Section) Railway Bill appeared before the 1860 session of Parliament. It proposed the formal creation of the company with powers to raise capital of £175,000 in shares and borrowings of £58,000 for the construction of:

1. A tramway (railway No. 1) at Ryde from the pier of the Ryde Pier Company to meet railway No. 2 at Melville Street
2. A main line (railways Nos. 2-4) from Ryde via Brading to Ventnor, a distance of 12 miles 3 chains
3. A railway (No. 5) from Smallbrook to Newport, a distance of 7 miles 64 chains
4. A connecting railway (No. 6) to the CNR at Newport, a length of 33 chains
5. A branch (No. 7) to a quay at Brading. It was 32 chains long and the quay 780 yards
6. A 67 chain branch (No. 8) to Sandown Bay and a 396 yards long pier

The Bill gave powers to the London, Brighton & South Coast Railway, London & South Western Railway, the Direct Portsmouth Railway, Cowes & Newport Railway, Stokes Bay Railway & Pier Company and the Isle of Wight Ferry Company to subscribe to the undertaking out of their own capital, guarantee interest and make working agreements. The Board of Trade, which reported on aspects of the Bill to Parliament, thought the subscription powers were rather too wide-ranging!

Also before Parliament was the Cowes & Newport Railway Extensions Bill. It applied for powers to change the name of the CNR to 'The Isle of Wight Railway'. From a junction with the CNR at Newport, one railway would have run to Ryde, another through Godshill and Wroxall to the quarries at Ventnor and a third branching from the Ryde line near Alverstone to run via Shanklin to Wroxall, where it rejoined the Newport to Ventnor line. The Bill was promoted by supporters of the erstwhile Birkenshaw scheme with the agreement of the CNR Board.

Immediate rivalry ensued as Island residents split into two camps. Newport advocated the CNR proposals whilst Ryde supported the IWES Bill but coolly, as the town opposed the tramway to the pier because it would cut off access to the sea front. Several landowners, including Sir Henry Oglander, Sir John Simeon and William George Ward, objected to the IWES proposals, although Simeon supported the CNR Extensions Bill. Fortunately much of the opposition of previous years had gone; the old antagonists had died and others were more favourably disposed to railways, on their own terms of course! Even the third Earl of Yarborough, whose predecessors had opposed all railways in the Island, supported the proposals - he was one of the first investors in the IWES.

The Bills were submitted to the Standing Orders committee of the House of Lords whose members took a cursory look at the competing schemes, threw out the CNR Extensions Bill and allowed the IWES Bill to continue to the next stage. On 22nd and 23rd March, 1860 a separate committee of the House considered the Bill in detail. Ryde Commissioners, the town's local authority, had been again placated by an agreement to abandon the tramway and build a road connecting Melville Street with the railway terminus. Of other objectors, counsel convinced the committee that most supported the CNR extensions and each had their own axe to grind. William George Ward's objections were considered spurious as a different route might have benefited his quay at Cowes. Sir John Simeon stated that railways radiating from Newport would better serve Island residents and considered the extra time needed for a journey between Ryde and Ventnor via Newport to be trifling. He objected to the IWES passing over part of his marshland at Ryde, but supported CNR Extensions that would have split it in half. The effects of the railway on Sir Henry Oglander's property near Brading was the subject of considerable discussion. Much was made of the way in which the IWES line would be in shallower cuttings than its predecessor and thus take less of his land. Francis Fuller, a surveyor who had gone over the route of the railway, maintained that Sir Henry's estate was poorly farmed and implied that its construction would have a positive effect on the badly-drained clay! Sir Henry was one of the few individuals to employ counsel to represent his interests.

Opponents dismissed Brading as a town that was not worthy of a railway. George Young opined: 'I do not think there is a Gentleman living at Brading except the Clergyman, his Curate and the Doctor - it is one of the most wretched villages imaginable'. Asked if the railway could expect many passengers from Brading he added 'I think not'. Henry Martin added 'It is a very miserable place - I know it well'. Of the 6,000 inhabitants, 'the principal persons there are labourers' and 'They do not travel so much by rail'. William Selby thought the line would be of no use to the Island. 'It will take the Cockneys* from Ryde to Ventnor and back to Ryde? . . . This is the only use I can see for it at present' - his comments were, however, put aside when it was ascertained he lived at Brook, miles away from the proposed route of the railway!

The Revd James White was one of several local residents to give evidence in favour of the Bill. Revd White had married well and resided at the manor in Bonchurch, a village in which he had lived for 52 years. A close friend of Tennyson, Thackeray and Dickens, he was precisely the class of individual that the company wanted to travel on its trains. He did not receive the aggressive cross-examination meted out to other witnesses.

Capt. Mark Huish told the committee that he had made 75 journeys backwards and forwards to London from Bonchurch since his retirement as General Manager of the London & North Western Railway, 18 months previously. As many as 20 private carriages would meet a boat at Ryde, besides coaches. Eight to ten coaches ran between Ryde and Bonchurch, but such was the crowding that he was obliged to write a day or so before intending to travel in order to secure a place. It took longer to travel from Bonchurch to Portsmouth than between Portsmouth and London.

The merits of Brading Harbour compared with the River Medina as a destination for coal barges was much argued over because the CNR line could have brought that precious commodity overland from Cowes. Residents of Bonchurch and Ventnor commented that coal would be cheaper if brought from Brading Quay than Cowes. Capt. Huish said he had been paying 38s. a ton for coals but sometimes the price was 45s. or even 50s. a ton. There was no proper landing place for goods at Bonchurch or Ventnor, and one collier had been wrecked on rocks below his house just three weeks earlier.

Counsel and witnesses voiced a real fear of invasion by the French. The route was considered most suitable for defensive purposes as it ran along the coast - one Lord remarked, 'it is to be hoped the railway will get there before the French'! Col (later General) Gordon,† deputy Quartermaster General, gave evidence in favour of the Bill and of the Sandown Bay branch in transporting troops and stores to nearby forts - the value of the branch was reduced after the Ryde to Newport line was abandoned and it was never built.

Whilst the main battle was won before the Lords' committee, the Bill still had to pass through the remaining stages in the House of Lords before undergoing a repeat of the process in the House of Commons, including a hearing before a Commons' committee.

Hamilton H. Fulton, the Engineer, had perhaps the most gruelling time. Counsel for the opponents sought to cast doubt on his estimate that the undertaking would cost £175,000, £50,000 less than the Livesay & Saunders scheme. As regards the railway at Ventnor, he was questioned as to the nature of the rock through which the tunnel would pass and whether the builders might expect to encounter water, all matters that would increase costs - he did not think much water would be encountered. Mr Fulton gave evidence that the platform would be about 100 ft long and close to the tunnel mouth. However, the deposited plans showed the railway ending in a gradient heading towards a 'precipice' - Sir Henry Oglander's counsel soon tied him in knots. This was compounded when he was unable to state either the length of proposed railway carriages or how many passengers they would contain; it seems he assumed the LSWR or LBSCR would work the line but he had failed to measure their rolling stock! Fortunately the next witness was John Fowler, another Engineer, who supported Mr Fulton's evidence. He confirmed that the line would terminate parallel with the Newport road and 'thus not disgorge its trains over the cliff edge'. Although he envisaged a frequent service of short trains, the 1,166 yds-long tunnel could be shortened by a furlong to enlarge the station and eliminate the gradient. The committee duly recommended these alterations at Ventnor and the Bill continued its progress through Parliament without further hindrance.

---

* A term in common use locally to denote anyone from the mainland.
† This was the same General Gordon who met his death at Khartoum in 1885.

Chapter Two

From Act to Action

The Isle of Wight Eastern Section Railway Act became law on 23rd July, 1860. It authorised the construction of:

1. A railway (No. 1) from Melville Street to Saint Johns Road, Ryde
2. A railway (No. 2) continuing from a junction with railway 1, passing near Brading and terminating near Lower Shanklin
3. A railway (No. 3) in continuation of railway 2 and terminating at Ventnor at or near the Stone Quarry adjoining the Newport Road
4. A branch railway (No. 4) to a quay at Brading
5. A branch railway (No. 5) to Sandown Bay and a 396 yds-long pier

The Act's 64 clauses contained sections that made the company subject to legislation in a number of public railway Acts. Dating mainly from the 1840s, they laid down rules for the management and operation of railway companies, including the issue of shares, audit and presentation of accounts, borrowing of money and the manner and timing of ordinary and extraordinary meetings of shareholders. Up to six Directors could be appointed, all of whom had to be shareholders holding a minimum of 50 £10 shares. A quorum at Board meetings was three. The Directors were listed as being James Simpson, Thomas Norton, Francis Atherley, Thomas Webster, Thomas Willis Fleming, and Alexander More. Hamilton Fulton became the Engineer. As not all the proposed lines had got through Parliament the Act restricted the amount of capital that could be raised to £125,000 in shares and loans to £41,600. The LSWR and LBSCR were given powers to raise capital of up to £20,000 each for the purpose of investing in the new railway.

The first Board meeting following the passing of the Act took place on 7th August, 1860 at 29 Great George Street, London when the Directors considered and approved designs for the common seal* and share certificates; each share certificate carried an impression of the company seal and bore the signatures of two Directors. That month, a Prospectus was published extolling the virtues of the company and inviting applications for shares.

At the next meeting in October James Simpson was elected Chairman and Francis Atherley his deputy. Major (later Colonel) Atherley lived at Landguard Manor, Shanklin. Like James Simpson, he loaned money on several occasions and guaranteed borrowings from bankers. The Board appointed Mr Morrison as Secretary at a salary of £100 per annum, subject to three months' notice, and Charles E. Reed the Treasurer and Accountant at a salary of £300 on the same terms. Half Mr Reed's salary was paid in shares and he had to employ staff needed to keep the accounts! Mr Reed took over the job of Secretary in April 1861. The Board suffered its first loss when Thomas Norton sent in his resignation; Frederick Twynam replaced him, one of a handful of mainland investors who held significant share holdings in the undertaking.

Within weeks another name became associated with the IWES - Capt. Mark Huish. Born in Nottingham, he entered the army of the East India Company, rising through the ranks. After leaving the army in 1837 he was appointed Secretary of the Glasgow, Paisley and Greenock Railway. Four years later he became Secretary and General Manager of the Grand Junction Railway and when it amalgamated with other companies in 1846 to form the London & North Western Railway, Capt. Huish became General Manager of the combined undertaking. He was described as a most able and forward-looking railway manager, although not a person to endear himself to those he dealt with. Capt. Huish remained General Manager of the London & North Western until November 1858 when he resigned following differences with 'certain other parties'. He retired to Bonchurch near Ventnor and appeared before the Parliament as a witness in favour of the IWES Bill.

---

* The locomotive depicted on the seal (reproduced on the title page) bore no relation to those eventually purchased by the company.

The passing of the Act brought a new air of realism to the Board. On 7th December Capt. Huish attended a meeting with the Chairman and his deputy to advise on problems they faced with finance and construction of the railway. He clearly made a good impression as James Simpson immediately offered him a seat on the Board. That meeting rejected a proposal to buy the Isle of Wight Ferry Company's works at Ryde over which the tramway would have run. Messrs Willis Fleming and Webster hoped to amalgamate the IWES, Isle of Wight Ferry and Stokes Bay companies into one and recoup some of their investments. Unfortunately their colleagues thought otherwise and, unable to accept this rebuff, the two men resigned from the Board.

At a meeting on 11th December, 1860 Capt. Huish expressed the opinion that Messrs Brassey, the well-known firm of railway contractors, would be willing to construct the railway and fund a 'considerable portion' of the capital. If the London & South Western and London, Brighton & South Coast railways could be persuaded to contribute £20,000 each, as the Act allowed, the line might open in 15 or 18 months. If these views were approved he would be willing to join the Board and work them out. This must have seemed like Manna from Heaven as the Board unanimously accepted Huish's proposals. Having pinned their faith on Capt. Huish the Board had to await the outcome of his negotiations, first with Thomas Brassey and then with the LSWR and LBSCR. The Board adjourned meetings repeatedly in the hope of some progress. In the meantime the first shares were issued, loans negotiated from the bankers and various outstanding bills paid.

Capt. Huish certainly made some progress in his negotiations with Thomas Brassey as the following letter from Brassey and his partner shows:

No. 4 Great George Street, Westminster
5th February 1861

My Dear Sir,
According to your request, I now put on paper what was said verbally respecting the Isle of Wight railway from Ryde to Ventnor including Brading Harbour branch of 32 chains - that if you could get the London and Brighton and London and South Western companies *each* to take £20,000 of the shares (£40,000) and one of these companies agreeing to work the lines, when made at 40 per cent of the gross receipts and also a bona fide subsequent contract by the public of at least £20,000 taken in shares (inclusive of any agent or officer of the Company's) - on these conditions we are willing to agree to do the earthwork, bridges, tunnel, fencing, ballasting and supply and lay Rails, Chairs, Sleepers and fastenings for a single line of railway for the sum of £123,000, taking payment £50,000 in shares and £73,000 in cash - the shares and cash to be paid in rateable proportions of each monthly certificate of the Engineer for the work done and materials supplied.

This amount (£123,000) does not include land, law, engineering, station buildings or station works, but only a single line of railway complete.

We are,
Yours truly
Thomas Brassey A. Ogilvie

To: Captain Huish
Bonchurch

Discussions with the LSWR predated the incorporation of the IWES. According to *Herapath's Railway Journal*, the LSWR had agreed to work one of the Isle of Wight railways at cost price in exchange for two seats on the Board for Capt. Mangles, the LSWR Chairman and a Director, Sergeant Gazelee. On 13th June, 1859 a committee of the LSWR Board met with a delegation consisting of Messrs Webster, Norton and Porter on behalf of the Isle of Wight Railway (Eastern Section). This time, the LSWR agreed to subscribe £10,000 and work the line if the Eastern Section company secured its Act of Incorporation and raised most of the capital. However, Parliament threw out the Bill and by the time the IWES came upon the scene circumstances had changed. The 1859 discussions coincided with a period when relations between the LSWR and LBSCR were very poor. Open warfare had broken out over the

London to Portsmouth traffic and there ensued a period of ruinous competition as each railway sought to outdo the other.* Although the quarrel was patched up in July 1859, LSW finances were overextended and no capital could be spared for non-essential matters. The LSWR Directors kept themselves informed of the progress of the IWES Bill through Parliament but letters from Mr Porter, the IWES solicitor, asking for assistance were studiously ignored. The LSWR Board went so far as to declare on 9th February, 1860, 'This Company decline any active support' in stark contrast to its attitude some six months earlier.

Capt. Huish clearly thought that he could improve upon Mr Porter's efforts and attended a meeting of the LSW Board on 21st March, 1861 when he stated the IWES case but to no effect. The LSWR Board had already met in July 1860 with a deputation from Ryde asking the LSWR to nominate two Directors to serve on a joint committee, apparently of the Stokes Bay and Isle of Wight Ferry companies, and to encourage traffic to pass via Stokes Bay to Ryde. The LSWR Board declined and with some foresight declared: 'it is the true interest of the Company to allow the Isle of Wight Traffic to find its own way', and that it duly did!

By May 1861 the IWES Board was desperate to gain support from the mainland companies and publicly offered seats on the Board to each one. The following month the Secretary read out a letter from Leo Schuster, the Chairman of the LBSCR. Not only did the mainland companies refuse to involve themselves in the undertaking but, more critically, no financial support could be expected:

> London Brighton and South Coast Railway
> London Terminus, SE
> 18th June 1861
>
> My Dear Sir,
> I saw Captain Mangles who takes the same view I do on the question of contributing a part of the capital towards the Isle of Wight Railway. The expenditure for Land, Stations, Law and Engineering not being ascertained, nor the entire capital subscribed, we are disinclined to go into the matter in the uncertainty of these important points involving our Company into a further outlay of money which we do not think it advisable to recommend to our respective Boards.
> Yours truly
> (Signed) Leo Schuster   Captain Huish, etc.

Although there were further exchanges of letters, the two mainland companies stuck to their decision and the only tangible result was a letter from Capt. Huish accepting a seat on the IWES Board.

Negotiations had begun for the purchase of land over which the railway would pass. Some landowners accepted shares in lieu of cash, but the company had to fund many purchases using money borrowed from the Hampshire Bank. A sizeable acreage was purchased from George Young for which he agreed to receive £1,350 paid-up ordinary shares. Mr Young had been involved in previous Island railway schemes but gave evidence against the IWES Bill because he believed there should be only one railway in the Island. An owner of shares in the Port of Portsmouth and Ryde Steam Packet Company and the Ryde Pier Company, he also served as Chairman of the latter for several years. George Young later maintained that the company was in financial difficulties and certain Directors had approached him for assistance. Before agreeing to join the Board he asked that 'one person should be removed from the direction, that was Mr Webster, because any influence I might have would be more than neutralized by his presence'. 'They did get rid of that Gentleman, and I joined them', for which purpose he purchased an additional £500 of shares. Thomas Webster's version of events was somewhat different; he had left the Board in George Young's favour, 'as I understand that he was popular in Ryde and I was unpopular'. Unfortunately for Mr Webster, 'the policy of the Company was entirely changed'.

In November 1861 the IWES Board decided to dispense with the services of the Engineer, Hamilton Fulton. Despite having received £1,000 in April 1861 he had not performed his work

---

* The story is covered in more detail by R.A. Williams in his book *The London & South Western Railway*. David & Charles, 1968.

with sufficient vigour (and was a companion of certain ex-Directors). The Board then discovered it did not possess details of the plans and specifications Fulton had sent out with the tender forms, and one contractor pointed out that they were at variance to those authorised in the Act. In the meantime Capt. Huish continued talking to Brassey whilst condemning Fulton's work as inappropriate and unnecessarily expensive; he considered that Brassey would be able to make savings in his tender of between £10,000 and £20,000. Fulton refused to accept the situation and when he sued the company the IWES lodged a cross-petition stating that it had been put to considerable expense by his unsatisfactory work. The matter was eventually resolved out of court, but there remained a dispute with Richard J.H. Saunders who asserted Fulton and the railway had employed him as assistant, or resident, Engineer. Mr Saunders also took the company to court and the whole process lasted until 1869 when he finally received some debentures.

Meanwhile negotiations began with a different contractor, a Mr Watson; possibly this was the same person who constructed the Isle of Man Railway and various Welsh lines. At one point the Directors resolved to award the contract to Watson, only to overturn the decision at the next meeting a week later; the Minutes for 2nd January, 1862 contained a list of tenders:

1. Thomas Brassey on 5th February, 1861 for £123,000 including £50,000 in shares. It excluded the stations and was conditional on a contribution of £40,000 from the LSW and LBSC, and their agreement to work the line together or singly after completion.
2. George Bolton on 1st August, 1861 for £140,000 including £40,000 in shares and £20,000 in debentures. The quotation included £7,000 for the stations.
3. F. R. Beeston on 6th August, 1861 for £126,936 of which £42,312 was in shares and £42,312 in debentures. It included £7,000 for the stations.
4. J. Watson on 14th October, 1861 for £127,000 including £35,000 in shares. The tender excluded stations.
5. J. Lucock on 5th December, 1861 for £127,000 including sidings and stations of which £42,333 6s. 8d. was in shares.
6. E. W. Morris on 19th December, 1861 for £52,000 included £32,200 in shares. The quotation was for Ryde to Sandown only. The shares were to be converted to debentures as soon as the company's borrowing powers could be used.

The list omitted a tender from James Taylor who had given evidence to Parliament that he was prepared to build the line for the amazingly cheap figure of £96,155 - he clearly got fed up with waiting!

After several meetings with Watson or his Engineer, Watson demanded a part payment in cash secured by Promissory Notes of Directors; they refused to make themselves personally liable so he faded from the scene. Hamilton Fulton attended a Board meeting on 19th January, 1862 when he produced a tender from Henry Bond - with Watson's tender dismissed correspondence began with him. Henry Bond was not well known and this approach to the IWES seems to have been one of his first acts as an independent railway contractor. Hamilton Fulton may have met him through dealings with the contractors Brassey and Ogilvie when they were building the Stokes Bay railway of which Fulton was Engineer. It is reasonable to suppose therefore that Henry Bond had been working for Brassey in some capacity. By 1864 Henry Bond was operating from offices at 19 Great George St, Westminster as a 'contractor for Public Works'.

Eighteen months after the passing of the Act of Parliament the shareholders and public were still waiting for some signs of progress. The Directors had little news to give and for a shareholders' meeting on 13th February, 1862 wrote:

> Negotiations are in progress with an influential contractor for the construction of the whole undertaking from Ryde to Ventnor, and for the opening of the first section from Ryde to Shanklin in the spring of 1863, and upon the conclusion of these negotiations the works will be immediately commenced.
> Much of the delay has been caused by the negotiations with the South Western and Brighton Railway Companies, but these negotiations have not yet resulted in such an arrangement as the Directors can recommend the Shareholders to confirm.

On 20th March, 1862, after considering letters from a number of engineers, the Board appointed John (later Sir) Fowler as Engineer at a fee of £1,000 in cash, £2,000 in debentures and £3,000 in shares. He operated from an address at Queen Square Place, Westminster and as Engineer to the Metropolitan and Metropolitan District Railway companies was responsible for the Inner Circle of lines in London. By 1869 he was Engineer for at least 12 railway companies in addition to the Isle of Wight Railway; later work included the design of Victoria station and the Tay and Forth bridges. The IWES Board asked John Fowler to examine the Parliamentary Plans and sections to see what savings could be made. Fowler informed the Board on 3rd April that he was preparing a fresh estimate of costs, a proper specification and tender upon which the contract might be let. He expected no difficulties in letting the contract in contrast to the Board's past attempts!

Thomas Brassey was clearly the contractor whom the Board wished to build the line. He had an excellent reputation and took shares in payment. But Brassey knew all about poverty-stricken companies and to ensure that the shares did not become worthless wanted the LSWR and/or LBSCR to make a financial contribution to the undertaking. Despite lengthy discussions, John Fowler had to report on 22nd October that his negotiations had broken down.

Fowler had also been in touch with Henry Bond and produced another letter from him. A fortnight later on 4th November a signed specification and tender was put to the Directors, who resolved to instruct the solicitor to draw up an agreement. On 2nd December, 1862 Henry Bond met with the Board to sign and seal a contract for the construction of a railway from Ryde to Ventnor and a branch to a quay near Brading at a cost of £126,000 excluding the stations - work started within the month.

Chapter Three

Construction and Opening

The construction of the railway from Ryde to Ventnor was one of the largest engineering projects in the Island at that time. Fortunately, the company employed an able Engineer in the shape of John Fowler, and the IWES Board could call on the services of Capt. Huish, whose experience as a railway manager was of great value, especially as the other Directors apparently had no experience in building or running a railway.

Traditionally the commencement of work on a railway began with a ceremony at which a local or national dignitary turned the first sod. Surprisingly the anxiety to get started seems to have overcome desires for such frivolity; this was in direct contrast to other less successful railway schemes in the Isle of Wight. The local press were left to report the arrival of the first of the contractor's men on 24th December, 1862, and by 1st January work had begun on the more difficult parts of the contract at the Ventnor end of the line. The Directors claimed that the clay soil in the north of the Island could not be worked until the dry weather. In reality the company did not possess all the necessary land.

The plant and materials, possibly just for the construction of the tunnel, were shipped from the River Severn to Brading Quay and then hauled to the work sites by horse power. (The quay was probably that owned by Sir Henry Oglander - the IWES Board rejected a proposal to buy it and the railway built its own structure.) Elsewhere construction work began with the help of horse-drawn carts hired from local farmers. Although the contractor brought some workmen with him, he hired casual labour locally; there was no shortage of applicants as wages were appreciably higher than those to be earned on the land. It is suspected that some equipment, including at least one locomotive (see Chapter 15) and skilled workmen, came from the Stokes Bay railway contract on the mainland which was nearing completion.

In February 1863 John Fowler, the Engineer, reported to shareholders that most of the land between Shanklin and Ventnor had been placed in the contractor's hands and was being fenced. On the site of the tunnel, workmen had sunk two shafts to the intended depth and had started digging the tunnel itself; work on the remainder of the line was about to begin. Two months later water inundated the north shaft of the tunnel; a 25 hp steam pumping engine proved unable to cope with the influx of water and a more powerful engine had been sent for. In the meantime the contractor switched work to the line north of Shanklin.

In June 1863 the Board appointed Robert Hicks of 4 Victoria Street, Westminster as Secretary and Accountant in place of Charles Reed who resigned. His salary of £150 per annum included the cost of employing any clerks to keep the accounts and any additional office accommodation - the burden of managing the railway's finances would fall on his shoulders. Robert Hicks was already Secretary of the Severn Valley Railway, another company of which John Fowler was Engineer. On 3rd July the Board considered Mr Fowler's estimate of £17,500 for the construction of the stations, signals and telegraphs and later that year let a contract to Henry Bond for the stations. John Fowler's office produced two sets of plans for station buildings. There was a two-storey design for Sandown and Shanklin with accommodation for the station master and a single-storey version for Brading and Ventnor; although the latter was never used for Ventnor, similar buildings in timber were erected at Ryde and later at Wroxall.

By July 1863 about five miles of line had been fenced, eight bridges were under construction and others finished. Some small cuttings had been completed with temporary track laid to carry spoil to embankments. The Engineer confidently reported: 'A large quantity of permanent way materials is on the ground, and I see no difficulty in opening the line between Ryde and Shanklin on the 1st March next.' But Capt. Huish was not so easily satisfied and on 8th September, 1863 he wrote:

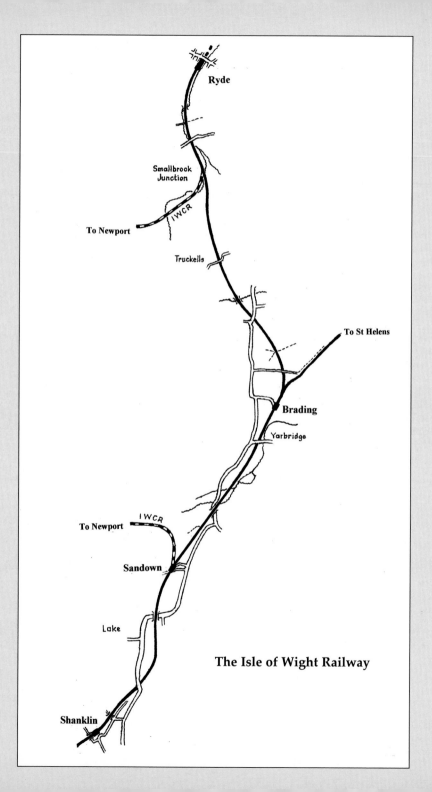

Ryde

Smallbrook
Junction

To Newport

IWCR

Truckells

To St Helens

Brading

Yarbridge

To Newport

IWCR

Sandown

Lake

The Isle of Wight Railway

Shanklin

I rode over the Works yesterday, and was greatly disappointed at the progress made. I am sure if greater energy is not exhibited Mr Fowler's promise of the line to Shanklin being ready by March cannot be realized. Our unusually fine summer has not been utilized as it should have been, and, now that we may expect broken weather, the difficulties will increase. Mr Bond has certainly not gone the way to make the Work a profitable one to himself. I have written fully on the subject to Mr Airey, and now that the harvest is concluded, and men are plentiful a push should be made.

I hope the Board will be careful in signing the Contractor's Certificate, for unless the Work has been carefully measured up I should hesitate to say that much if anything more is due to him.

On 7th October, 1863 the Board resolved 'That the permanent Engine Sheds &c. be erected at St Johns Road, but that no expenditure be made beyond what is absolutely necessary for the temporary accommodation at St Johns Road of the passenger traffic'. Another resolution reflected their concerns: '. . . the Board beg to express to Mr Fowler their great anxiety that no delay should occur in completing the works to Sandown, so as to admit of the opening in the early Spring of next year, and that he will impress this strongly upon the contractor'.

In December the elements contrived to interrupt progress in levelling the site of the station at Sandown and opening out nearby cuttings. The *Isle of Wight Times* reported the collapse of a bridge at Lake on 18th January when it fell into the roadway. This was not an isolated occurrence as on 9th April Hyde bridge collapsed whilst being tested by driving a heavy wagon across it. Wet weather caused havoc with the earthworks and in March 1864 a number of slips took place in the clay cuttings near Brading. Two hundred extra men were taken on and work even continued on Sundays - something that was frowned upon by certain local residents, including Capt. Huish, who was described as 'a gentleman . . . whose character stands high for Christian principle'. At his suggestion the IWR contributed £25 towards the salary of a scripture reader to minister to the workmen.

For the shareholders' meeting on 18th February, 1864, the Directors reported that, with the exception of one property between Shanklin and Ventnor, all the necessary land was in the possession of the contractor and the stations at Ryde, Brading, Sandown and Shanklin were under construction. The Engineer added:

The efforts of the Contractor have been chiefly applied, during the last half-year, to the Works between Ryde and Shanklin, and I have his assurance that this part of the Line shall be opened for public traffic, in accordance with his contract, in the month of May next.

At a meeting on 19th January, 1864 the Board asked Capt. Huish to prepare suggestions for staffing and operating the line. On 2nd March, 1864 he reported the receipt of applications for the post of Manager from a Mr Page and a Mr Tomlin, both of whom were considered equally suitable. John Fowler also produced an application from a Mr Rouse. Capt. Huish was asked to interview them and at the next meeting on 5th April a list of five names was put before the Board. After careful deliberation the board appointed Mr Rouse 'Manager of Traffic, Locomotive Superintendent and Superintendent of Permanent Way' at a salary of £250 per year from 1st May and subject to six months notice on either side. But on 20th April the Directors were told of a letter of rejection from Mr Rouse so they selected W.R. Page. He evidently did not like what he saw, for in the Minutes for 23rd May there was a sharply worded report; he had been absent from the Island for the previous 13 days and failed to keep any appointments. The Board duly cancelled Page's employment.

Left without a Manager at this critical time, the Board asked John Fowler and Capt. Huish to make arrangements to get the line opened as far as Shanklin. Myles Fenton, Manager of the Metropolitan Railway and a Mr Burnett (probably Robert H. Burnett, resident Engineer and locomotive superintendent of the Metropolitan Railway) did some work for the IWR at this difficult time for which they each received 50 guineas (John Fowler was Engineer of that company so the connections are obvious). Mr Fenton also received £43 13s. for materials purchased from the Metropolitan Railway.

On 4th May Mr Fowler gave a progress report to the Board; he was asked to arrange for the provision of mile and gradient posts. On 22nd June Capt. Huish reported that the telegraph had been installed by the Electric and International Telegraph Company, of which he was Chairman! He also ordered furniture, uniforms, tickets, lamps, hand flags and barrows; Edmundson ticket cases for each station alone cost £17 8s. The Board had already approved a list of proposed fares, tolls for goods and the railway's bye-laws. 'Messrs Smith & Co. the Booksellers' tendered for the rental of bookstalls at the company's stations (W.H. Smith was a friend of Capt. Huish). The sparcity of the platform coverings sparked off an enquiry to the Engineer asking where the bookstalls could be accommodated.

The same meeting approved the appointment of Joseph Bourne to the post of Manager on the same terms as previously, but taking effect from 24th June. Joseph Bourne remained Manager and Engineer of the IWR during its early and rather shaky years. He was not an Islander for he later asked the Board to defray some of the costs of moving his family and furniture to the Isle of Wight. The matter was referred to Capt. Huish who must have mellowed in his old age as Mr Bourne received a cheque for almost £500 the following February!

The arrival of locomotives and rolling stock heralded the approaching completion of the railway to Shanklin. George Pritchard of Southsea successfully tendered for their shipment to the Island at a cost of £260 - neither Beyer, Peacock nor the Railway Carriage Company would deliver them further than the nearest convenient point on the mainland. The local newspapers failed to record when deliveries commenced but, according to the *Isle of Wight Observer*, all the carriages and wagons were on the line by 23rd July, 1864.

On 1st June, 1864 the Secretary, Robert Hicks, wrote to the Board of Trade giving notice that the railway would open in one month. However, the locomotives and rolling stock had not arrived, and Joseph Bourne had to wait until 11th August before he could send a telegram confirming that the railway was ready for inspection. Col. Yolland visited the Island on behalf of the Board of Trade on 19th August and rode over the line in a special train drawn by two locomotives. His report is worth reproducing:

Railway Department
Board of Trade, Whitehall
20 August 1864

Sir

I have the honor to state for the information of the Lords of the Committee of Privy Council for Trade in obedience to your minute of the 29th Ult. that I yesterday inspected a portion of the Isle of Wight Ry. commencing at a temporary station at Ryde and ending at Shanklin Station, a length of 7 miles and 13.5 chains.

This line is single throughout with double portions or sidings at the Stations at Ryde, Brading, Sandown a passing place and Shanklin, but the land has been constructed and the overbridges have been erected for a double line, if hereafter required.

1. The width of the single line at formation level is 18 feet on embankments and 16 feet in cuttings: the gauge is 4 ft 8½ in., and the space between the lines where there are two is 6 feet. There are 6 over and 6 under bridges in addition to one under river bridge. These are all constructed of rubble masonry with brick facings, and arched or cast or wrought Iron Girders. There are slight appearances of movement in some of the Wing Walls and Abutments, but nothing of any importance. The greatest span for under bridges is 30 feet at the Square and 34 ft 8 in. at the Skew. In one of the under bridges with cast iron girders, of small span, the strength of the girders is not sufficient without taking into consideration the strength of the longitudinal sleeper on which the rail is laid.

2. The permanent way consists of a flat-bottom rail in lengths of 24, 21 and 18 feet laid upon transverse sleepers of bolted timber 9 x 4½ in. and 8 ft 11 in. long. 9 for the 24 feet, 8 for the 21 and 7 for the 18 feet rail, and the rails are fixed down to the sleepers by a fang bolt and a wood screw on the sleepers adjacent to the joints and at every alternate sleeper, while the remainder are secured by wood screws alone. The joints are fished.

3. The ballast is of chalk and is stated to be 1 foot deep under the undersides of the sleepers. The steepest gradient is 1 in 70 and the sharpest curve had a radius of 29 chains. The line is in fair order, but has been finished off during the dry weather. Some of the cuttings and banks are composed of blue clay and when the wet weather sets in, these may be expected to give trouble and will require to be carefully watched. And when the line is first opened for Traffic the packing will require to be thoroughly attended to from the nature of the ballast.

The line is to be worked with Tank Engines. Turntables large enough to turn these Engines have been put-up at Ryde and Shanklin.

In making my inspection I noticed that the following items required to be attended to.

1. a short portion of fencing alongside the River Yar was required.
2. some damaged copings required to be taken out and most of the other copings wanted careful packing.
3. facing points leading to sidings at Brading and Sandown stations were to be taken out and instructions were given that these matters should be attended to at once - as well as setting back the fencing at the end of the platforms.
4. there is a ballast pit near Brading Station, not now connected with the main line - if it is hereafter to be used - proper stations and distant Signals to protect it will be required to be put up.
5. an additional fang or through bolt is required at the sleepers adjacent to the Joints - and one is to be added for each rail on these sleepers, where wood screws alone have been used to fasten down the rails to the sleepers I recommend that it be fixed inside the rails. Six months may be allowed for this to be attended to.
6. I have not received the undertaking as regards the working of the line but I understand the Train Staff System is to be adopted. The company are also to undertake to insert the fang bolts in the course of six months.

I here now therefore recommend that their Lordships may sanction the opening of the portion of the Isle of Wight Railway between Ryde and Shanklin.

I Have the honor to be Sir
Your most obedient servant
W. Yolland

The railway from Ryde to Shanklin opened for passenger traffic on Tuesday 23rd August. Unfortunately the drought that probably assisted completion of the work ended on the opening day with pouring rain and a bitter north wind. The first passenger train left Ryde at 6.00 am with a dozen passengers but those later in the day were better patronised, 'a great number of the inhabitants met to see the first train off and gave a round of lusty cheers, Mr More, one of the Directors, with his happy face, being present'. The local press reported that there would be no 'demonstration of the scene' but the event was nevertheless celebrated at Sandown where guns were fired, flags hung out and many of the trains cheered on their way. This contrasted with Brading where no-one turned out to see the first train. Staff at Shanklin waited until the rain stopped in the afternoon before hanging out the flags! The following day the weather returned to normal and many Ryde people travelled to Sandown to avail themselves of the bathing facilities. Takings during the first four days were £260 and about 4,000 people had been carried, a most satisfactory amount given that income came solely from passengers - goods traffic did not begin for several weeks.

At a meeting on 27th August, 1864, Joseph Bourne reminded the Board of the need to insure the company's assets. The Secretary was instructed to obtain rates from the North British Insurance Company and if satisfactory to arrange the taking out of a policy; George Young just happened to be a Director of the insurance company! The Board also had to cope with a flurry of requests for free passes over the line. The contractor Henry Bond and his two assistants were granted one first and two second class passes whilst more first class passes were issued to Messrs Webster and Fuller. Mr Wayland of the *Isle of Wight Times* had his application refused.

At a shareholders' meeting on the same day as the Board meeting, Capt. Huish somewhat incautiously let slip that the Engineer 'was shooting grouse in Scotland after the labours of his parliamentary campaign'*. Mr Fowler's written report is worth reproducing in its entirety:

> The Wharfage Works required for the completion of the shipping accommodation at Brading are in hand, and will still further facilitate and cheapen the supply of coals to the line.
>
> From Shanklin to Wroxall the works of construction are nearly completed, and the Contractor will proceed with the ballasting and laying the permanent way so soon as he has properly trimmed and drained the formation, and provided the necessary ballast for the purpose.
>
> The excavation of Ventnor tunnel has an opening throughout its length and a large portion ready for the necessary brickwork; but the Contractor's arrangements for providing bricks and proceeding with the brickwork has been dilatory, and much time has been lost, but even now there is no difficulty in completing the works from Shanklin to Ventnor, so as to be open for public traffic during the ensuing summer season.

The Engineer failed to mention the date when the two ends of the tunnel met - the rival gangs of navvies had celebrated the event with a fight. In January 1865, after the tunnel had been opened out, the contractor set up a brick works nearby to supply bricks for lining the walls. Alexander More, one of the Directors, laid the first brick in the tunnel on 20th February and then presided over a celebration dinner in Ventnor for the workmen.

At the beginning of May it came to the notice of the IWR Board that the contractor was in financial difficulties and had begun negotiations with a finance company. On 23rd May work at the Ventnor end of the tunnel stopped and about 60 workmen were dismissed without notice. The following month it became clear that the contractor would be unable to complete the contract. He had arranged to be paid off by the Warrant Finance Company, which took over his obligation to complete the line.

Construction eventually recommenced under the management of Mr Dorrell, an associate of Thomas Brassey. More in hope than expectation, in August 1865 the IWR Board asked Joseph Bourne to make arrangements to open the line as far as Wroxall with a coach service thence to Ventnor. The Engineer mentioned the proposal that month in his report to shareholders: '. . . I do not think the line can be opened throughout to Ventnor before the end of the year, but it may be opened to Wroxall much sooner, if thought desirable'. Trains continued to terminate at Shanklin for another 12 months. The reason for the delays became clear in a letter that appeared in the railway press:

> Mr Editor, - Although I possess no shares in this undertaking, I take an interest in it in many ways. I must confess my feeling on reading the Directors report, is one of commiseration with the Shareholders. The line was promised to be opened for the spring traffic, then for the summer, and now for the Christmas. I question very much the possibility of its being finished by that time, and I doubt whether the Directors sincerely believe so either. The other day I walked by it, and found the Ventnor side deserted, and has been so for weeks, and about a score of navvies at Wroxall. If they are the only hands to complete it, these men will perform wonders. Why even the ground for the stations is not marked out, leaving alone the work in the long tunnel . . .
> Yours Truly
>   Francis Player
>   Ariosto Villa, Ventnor, Isle of Wight   8 August 1865

The *Isle of Wight Observer* for 14th October, 1865 was more positive when it carried a detailed account of the state of the line:

> It being reported that a number of men were working at the station yard at Ventnor, and feeling anxious to have the line completed, we started to see what was doing, and here found a number of men engaged in cutting and blowing away the rock on the side of the hill where the station is intended to be. (We could have wished it would be in some other part of the town; however, better

---

* *Who's Who* recorded that Mr Fowler owned over 70,000 acres of moor in Scotland and listed deer stalking as a pastime; he never did become an MP.

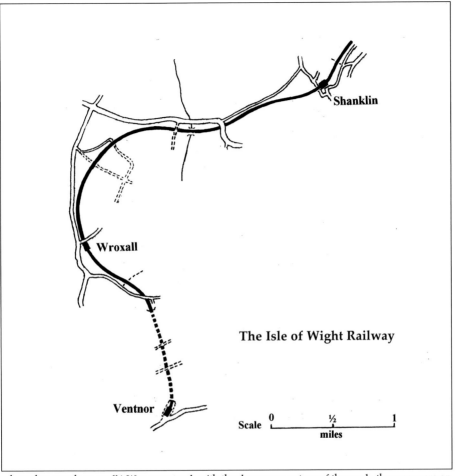

Shanklin

Wroxall

The Isle of Wight Railway

Ventnor

Scale 0   ½   1
miles

here than nowhere at all.) We were struck with the dangerous nature of the work, the men were on the side of the cutting which is almost perpendicular and 60 to 70 feet deep, drilling holes for blasts of gunpowder, whilst others were engaged picking off loose lumps . . . As one of the employees was going through, we asked to walk with him, and he being civil enough to hand us a tin with a candle in it we entered the tunnel, but it was some time before we could distinguish any object. The first thing was a number of candles appearing like stars on a dark night, and on coming closer we could observe the tunnel for some length bricked to full size, and at the end of the brickwork were a lot of bricklayers, on side walls about 10 yards in length, working in a style we never witnessed - all as busy as bees. The length of the walls up here is about 400 yards. Beyond this for a distance of 150 yards is a row of candles on either side of the tunnel, looking like one of the streets in London by gaslight, with a string of miners busy - some with drills, others wielding large hammers driving wedges, others with picks getting loose pieces, which the labourers are loading into wagons. This is really a sight worth seeing. On nearing the Wroxall end we found another long length of tunnel completed, and we were informed it is being done at the rate of 10 yards per day. From the rapidity with which the bricks are being laid, we had doubts as to its character, but on examination we found it to be straight, true and neat; more so than is generally the case than with buildings in the neighbourhood. On remarking as to the quality of the work, we found that Mr J. Fowler, the Engineer-in-chief, had been through the work and given Mr J. Dorrell, the contractor, and Mr Sharp, the inspector, credit for

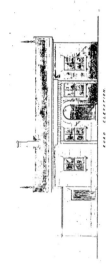

Isle of Wight Railway   Eastern Section

BOOKING OFFICE FOR BRADING & VENTNOR

Scale 8 Feet to one Inch

END ELEVATION

SIDE ELEVATION

RAILWAY ELEVATION

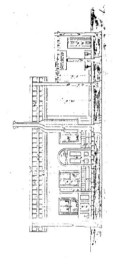

The plans on these facing pages show two designs for the proposed stations at Brading and Ventnor.

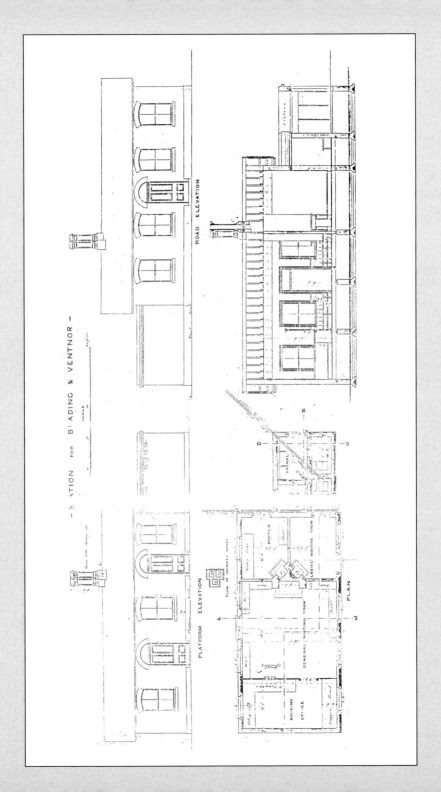

— STATION FOR BLADING & VENTNOR —

ROAD ELEVATION

PLATFORM ELEVATION

PLAN

BOOKING OFFICE

GENERAL WAITING ROOM

LADIES WAITING ROOM

W.C.

URINAL

PLAN OF CHIMNEY SHAFT

Proposed station for Sandown and Shanklin

PLATFORM ELEVATION

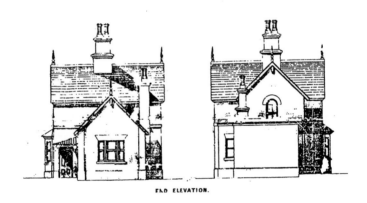

END ELEVATION.

FRONT ELEVATION.

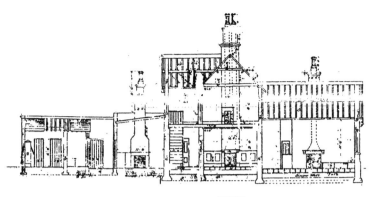

SECTION.

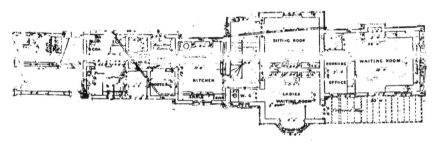

GROUND PLAN.

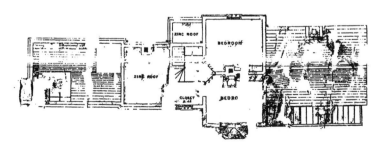

CHAMFER PLAN

A posed view of the locomotive *Ryde* at Ryde station in 1864 with a line up of staff on the platform. One of the top hatted gentlemen is probably Joseph Bourne.   *IWSR Collection*

'The first train to officially enter Shanklin station, 1864' read the caption with this print. Like that of Ryde the absence of passengers implies that it was taken just prior to the opening of the line. The station building has a bay window fronting the platform and the booking office to the right has been provided with a short covering - Sandown was similarly provided. In the background can be seen the short-lived carriage shed. The connection in the foreground probably leads to the incomplete extension to Ventnor.   *R. Brinton Collection*

the way the work was constructed. Arriving at Wroxall, we examined the mortar machines, and brickmaking by steam. The clay here is pressed into moulds and passed through the machine, passing in and out as regularly as a clock ticks, and the bricks are knocked out onto a strap that carries them along to the men, who put them on barrows, and run them into the kilns to be burnt. We were informed that one machine makes 15,000 bricks per day. There were a number of men at work here - no irregularity in working - very different to when we saw the work six months ago. Mr Dorrell, who was just going to Shanklin with his locomotive and a train of ballast trucks was present a few yards along the line from the tunnel. Having asked to be allowed to go to Shanklin, we were kindly welcomed, and on getting up we were struck with the neat and compact appearance of the engine, and so beautifully clean we could almost fancy it was introduced to the drawing room after its day's work was done. There was not much time to examine the work from Wroxall to Shanklin, but we found the line permanently laid and nearly complete in ballast, and we could not help noticing the neat appearance of the cuttings and embankments and substantial look of the bridges, several being completed, and two or three in hand. We have no doubt we shall see the opening of the line to Ventnor in the coming year.

In October 1865 the IWR Board discussed how to raise money to pay for the construction of stations at Wroxall and Ventnor. The original estimates of £12,000 for Ventnor and £1,500 for Wroxall were pared down to £7,000 - £8,000 for the two and in November the Board authorised John Fowler to spend £7,000 at Ventnor. When Warrant Finance Company refused to do the work a contract was let to Messrs Smith & Taylor.

During the winter of 1865-1866 several slips took place in the clay embankments and cuttings following a period of heavy rain. Despite working shifts seven days a week, the contractor's men had not made much progress with the tunnel. The *Isle of Wight Times* reported, 'A train of trucks loaded with sand came through the tunnel on 28th January, and was unloaded within 10 yards of the road'. However, a later entry in the same newspaper confusingly reported that the first train ran through the tunnel on 23rd March. Meanwhile, Smith & Taylor were using two steam excavators to enlarge the site of the station at Ventnor. The firm also constructed some wooden buildings in their workshops at Portsmouth, but when they attempted to transport the materials over the line the finance company refused to permit them to pass over 'their' part of the railway (i.e. from Shanklin to Ventnor)! The Engineer in his report to shareholders in February 1866 pointedly omitted to forecast when the line would open - he had been wrong so many times previously.

In June 1866 the finance company wrote to the IWR Board claiming the work they were required to carry out had been completed. But by then the IWR Board could neither pay the finance company nor Smith & Taylor. John Fowler offered to find £1,000 to get the stations finished and Joseph Bourne was authorised to spend £500 to help get the line ready for opening. After a further delay the IWR wrote to the Board of Trade on 7th August, 1866 stating that the railway was ready for inspection, and announced publicly that it would begin carrying passengers on 1st September. Col Yolland made an inspection but identified a catalogue of deficiencies in his report dated 29th August:

The Tunnel is lined throughout with brickwork with blue Lias Lime Mortar. It is mostly through the greensand rock, which is represented as standing well, but the lining has been put in, as an additional security, as the rock sometimes flakes off. A good deal of water has been met with and a considerable quantity continues constantly running through the Tunnel. As the lining is only a thin one, this Tunnel will require to be carefully looked after.

An Engine (Tank) Turntable has been put in at Ventnor Station, but those at Shanklin and Ryde Stations have either been discontinued or cannot be used at present.

The ballast is of broken stone, and is stated in the details to be laid to a depth of 1 foot below the under surface of the sleepers, but there is evidently a deficiency of ballast on portions of the line, which must be supplied.

A station is named in the details as having been constructed at Wroxall, with a portion of double line at it, but neither have been constructed as yet - and the Terminal Station at Ventnor, has no shelter, no conveniences, or waiting rooms, and it is altogether at the present time, a wretched

One of a series of photographs taken of Ventnor station soon after the opening of the railway to the town in 1866. A train stands in the main platform with an assortment of carriage stock and the birdcage-roofed brake carriages at both ends. Compare the different lettering styles of wagons Nos. 15, 21 and 40, the latter has dumb buffers.   *R. Brinton Collection*

The train waits to leave from the main platform at Ventnor, unusually showing a locomotive facing north. In the background can be seen the steep-sided cutting leading to the tunnel mouth. Note the signal to the right.   *R. Brinton Collection*

Terminal Station. The siding is placed too near to the main line - and the check rails at some of the crossings are not placed at the proper distance from the rails. The platform is incomplete. The fencing is deficient at Shanklin Station and at places along the line - and in some cases the lower rail is buried so as to leave the fencing insufficient against cattle.

There are some damaged rails and a good many damaged sleepers that must be taken out and replaced with sound ones, and there are a good many short bolts in the fished plates, that require to be taken out and replaced by larger ones. The entrance to a culvert and the sides of some of the cuttings require to be cleaned out and this culvert (at 9 mls. 75 chs.) appears to have sunk considerably in the centre and will require to be looked at.

The line requires lifting, straightening and packing, the cutting especially at Ventnor Station.

A cutting at Wroxall is through bad material, and will in all probability give trouble, and require the slopes to be eased off on the eastern side.

The Board of Trade promptly instructed the IWR to defer opening for one month. To add to the problems a landowner, Joseph Diggle, wrote to Col Yolland to complain about the state of an occupation crossing near Wroxall. The letter referred to a recent accident involving the death of one of the company's servants, one of his tenant's horses and the destruction of a wagon, etc. Apparently the surface had not been properly metalled and the contractor's locomotive ran into a horse-drawn wagon stuck on the crossing. The IWR had to find £14 11s. 2d. to pay the surgeon and more money to finish off the crossing properly.

Frustrated by the delay the IWR took matters into its own hands. Capt. Huish vividly recounted at a shareholders' meeting how Joseph Bourne, with 100 workmen, had laid 3,000 yards of ballast in 11 days and put right the deficiencies so obvious to Col Yolland. Apparently the fencing was missing because the Warrant Finance Company had run off with it! On 4th September the IWR asked the Board of Trade to arrange for a second inspection; Col Yolland reported on 8th September, 1866 and this time it was favourable.

On Monday 10th September, 1866 the extension to Ventnor opened for passenger traffic - goods traffic over the extension had begun some weeks before. Again the local press reported the day's events. The first train arrived at Ventnor at 8.00 am having taken 25 minutes for the journey from Ryde. Its arrival was marked by the explosion of a number of fog signals witnessed by excited crowds. The first departure was well filled and over 900 persons travelled to and from Ryde on the first day. It was said that Ventnor could now be reached in four hours and seven minutes by rail, road and ferry from London. Staff decorated Ryde station with flags and the engines with flower designs and flags. No attempt was made to decorate the station at Ventnor as it was far from complete.

Because of the poor financial position the festivities at Ventnor were organised by a committee. At a banquet held at the Marine Hotel 15 toasts were drunk to the success of the railway! Speakers commented about the company's financial problems and difficulties in boring the tunnel through St Boniface Down. J.B. Martin, a local shopkeeper and one of the oldest inhabitants, referred to the town's growth but added that its expansion had been at a standstill for several years. Capt. Huish, with a characteristic lack of tact, referred to Ventnor's apathy towards the railway company. In one of his London clubs it had been stated that 'Brighton was one of the most fashionable watering places, Bournemouth a nice place to live in, but Ventnor, of all places in the world, the one to be buried in'. For Capt. Huish this statement proved somewhat prophetic - within a year he had died and been buried in nearby Bonchurch.

A number of events were held for locals and visitors. In the afternoon athletic sports were held at Steephill, courtesy of Mr Judd. The band of the Royal Marines played in Dr Leeson's grounds at St. Boniface House where 1,000 people had tea and attended a concert. An illumination of Bonchurch cliffs by fireworks between 9 pm and 9.30 pm rounded off an enjoyable day. The *Isle of Wight Times* reported the running of 'an especial train' advertised to leave Ventnor at 11.00 pm. Although a long train, several passengers had the dubious pleasure of standing during the journey - possibly the first such occasion on the Isle of Wight Railway, but certainly not the last!

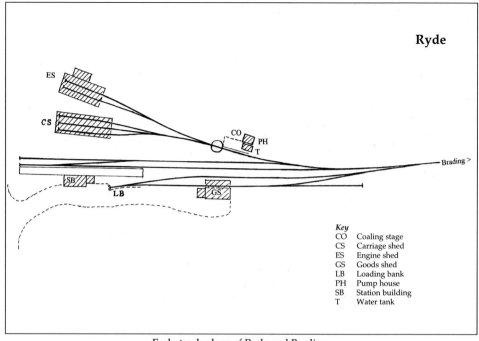

Ryde

Key
CO　Coaling stage
CS　Carriage shed
ES　Engine shed
GS　Goods shed
LB　Loading bank
PH　Pump house
SB　Station building
T　Water tank

Early track plans of Ryde and Brading.

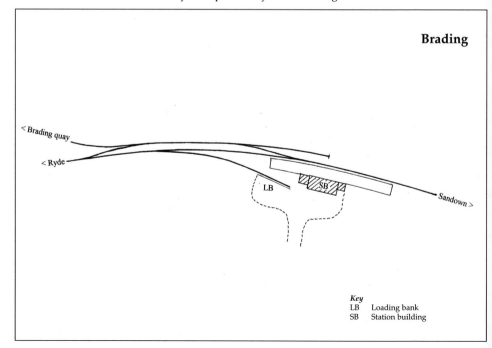

Brading

Key
LB　Loading bank
SB　Station building

Chapter Four

The Railway Described

The railway engineered by John Fowler was not an easy one. Parts of the line had substantial cuttings or embankments and there were a number of steep gradients in places, particularly on the section beyond Shanklin. There was some criticism of the condition of the railway handed over by the contractor and the company spent significant amounts in bringing it up to a reasonable standard. The state of the bridges and culverts came in for particular comment because of the unstable nature of the clay cuttings and embankments. Almost certainly the stations were incomplete when the line opened in August 1864, particularly sidings, and during the following Autumn sizeable bills were paid for 'pavements for Stations' and additional building and carpentry work. Although there is no evidence of a formal programme of work, local builders contracted to carry out numerous improvements to goods and passenger accommodation during the late 1860s and 1870s, whether it be lengthened crossing loops, platform and more sidings.

The distances given in this chapter were measured from the terminus at St Johns Road, Ryde and have been taken from a report by Joseph Bourne to the Board in 1866. He listed the condition of every culvert and bridge between Ryde and Shanklin. That section alone had 24 culverts, eight underbridges and six overbridges, the greatest span was 30 ft in the square and 34 ft 8 in. in the skew. All the bridges were constructed in red brick, except for four that used iron; road bridges were generally 25 ft on the square whilst culverts were mainly barrel shape of 4 ft diameter. With the exception of the tunnel, land was purchased and overbridges constructed with provision for double track should that be required at a later date.

The terminus at Ryde was situated immediately to the south of, and at right-angles to, St Johns Road. The 200 ft platform on the up side of the line had a 'temporary' wooden single-storey building containing the booking office, a small office for staff and toilets; a covering along the length of the building gave passengers some protection from the elements. Within months a second wooden building was constructed between the station building and the road for use as a refreshment room. Behind the platform, sidings led to a wooden goods shed and a loop to an end dock. Opposite the platform a run-round loop gave off a connection to two buildings - one for carriages and the other an 'Engine House'. The wooden carriage shed measured about 156 ft long by 35 ft wide and contained three tracks. The brick engine shed could accommodate four engines in two roads and measured about 72 ft by 33 ft; a small smithy and workshop were located halfway along its east side. The site was hemmed in by Monkton Mead brook; it flooded the station and workshops on numerous occasions over the years. A plan prepared by John Fowler's office and now in the care of the National Railway Museum shows a spur to the engine and carriage sheds passing a coke platform, a water tank and pump house and across a small turntable before splitting into separate tracks to the sheds. The turntable was a legacy from the days when tender engines were the norm - railways such as the IWR worked solely by tank engines were still rarities. Although mentioned in the Inspecting Officer's report in August 1864, by the date of his next visit in 1866 the turntable was out of use and may have already been removed; the connections to the sheds were then rearranged and a siding added between the loop and carriage shed. A wooden stores' building was also built behind the locomotive shed.

Passenger accommodation proved inadequate and, within two years, a wooden platform had been built alongside the run-round loop, to permit the dispatch of trains immediately following each other or after an up train had arrived. In October 1868 the station building was enlarged to provide additional booking office accommodation, ladies' and general waiting rooms; further small sums were spent in 1869-1870 on extensions to the station and goods yard.

On a parcel of land bought from Sir John Simeon for the line to Melville Street was the company's office in an existing building called 'Uncle Tom's Cabin'. In July 1870 Mr Rayner (a land agent) offered £600 for the office and land, but the IWR deferred a decision until the Ryde Pier Company indicated how much it would need for its horse tramway from the station to the pier. The pier company asked for a small plot valued at £50, but after some correspondence the IWR insisted on selling the whole for £650.

The completion of a horse tramway to the pier in 1871 prompted an enlargement of the station across St Johns Road. Each of the three platform tracks was taken across the road on the level where they merged to form an end-on junction with the tramway; just beyond, a short siding led to a two-road shed for tramcars. This allowed the IWR to extend the platforms, but gates had to be closed across the road each time an engine ran round a train. The main platform was also extended at its south end following the removal of the loop to the goods shed.

Although there was covered accommodation for the locomotives and passenger rolling stock, the railway possessed virtually no tools or machinery with which to maintain them. Two years later the General Manager reported an increase in running costs and the Board asked him to bring forward proposals for improvements. The following year the accounts contained an entry for workshops and machinery amounting to £3,814 'not yet commenced and in abeyance'. In June 1868 £99 was spent on the construction of a wagon repair shop measuring about 80 ft by 15 ft, a temporary smithy, presumably to permit an enlargement of the workshop, and the purchase of a screw-cutting lathe. Another season passed before the Board authorised an extension to the erecting shop (actually the locomotive shed). In September 1869 Mr Griffiths, a local builder, submitted a quote of £240 for the construction of an iron structure described as a paint shop. One of the Directors visited the Island and at the next Board meeting on 13th October recommended a permanent building costing no more than £500. Soon afterwards work began on a workshop using Ventnor stone; it measured about 88 ft long and 36 ft wide and was equipped as a locomotive erecting shop and smithy. During 1870 the company purchased a traverser at a cost of £90 5s. A contemporary plan of doubtful accuracy showed that there was no separate siding to the workshop and the traverser was used to transport locomotives sideways from an adjacent siding.

On 9th June, 1870 Joseph Bourne attended a Board meeting and produced drawings for a locomotive hoist, water tank and associated works. Anxious to see the new water supply in use the Board accepted a tender of £256. 11s. from Messrs Lloyd and Foster. Unfortunately they wanted full payment one month after delivery so Mr Bradley, an ironmaker of Kidderminster, was prevailed upon to accept payment in two halves. Mr Bradley received £100 in August but, concerned that he would not receive the rest, insisted on a written agreement that the water tank, etc. remain his property until the whole amount was paid - he received a cheque in October 1870 as promised. A water tank was placed on the roof of the workshop alongside a windmill installed to pump the water from a well. The tank bore the inscription 'IWR 1870' and had a working capacity of 4,800 gallons. In February 1871 Mr Bradley tendered for the supply of five 5 ton cranes for use at Ryde, Brading Quay, Sandown, Shanklin and Ventnor. His price of £69 10s. each including delivery to Ryde was the cheapest and, moreover, he accepted £200 on delivery and the remainder six months later. In December 1871 the company spent £700 on a furnace 'for resetting and adjusting springs and retyring wheels'. The Board agreed in the following February to purchase a badly needed wheel lathe from Messrs J. Buckton & Co. for £470, terms being £50 upon delivery and the balance in monthly instalments of £35; it cost £1 to insure and between £10 and £15 to fix in place.

To accommodate the additional machinery the Board approved a recommendation by Joseph Bourne to build a replacement locomotive running shed and convert the existing building to a machine shop. The original buildings had been built on land bought from Sir John Simeon in 1861 but the surplus was sold in December 1866 to an estates company linked to the Ryde Station Company, an abortive scheme for a railway from St Johns Road to the shore. In October 1870 the railway exchanged some land with the estates company so that Monkton Mead Brook could be diverted to create space for the workshop. The land later passed into the ownership of the Webster family who let it out to a Mr Meader; he proved somewhat less accommodating when the railway attempted to buy more land on which to build the running shed. He demanded so much compensation that in June 1872 the Board ordered that the shed be built on the opposite side of the station. The following year Francis Morton & Co. of Liverpool, well-known suppliers of corrugated iron buildings, charged £600 for the supply and erection of a corrugated iron building measuring roughly 90 ft by 30 ft on foundations built by the IWR. The shed had accommodation for six engines on two tracks, all with inspection pits, there were double doors at each end and a row of glass toplights along each side. However, it lacked proper accommodation for the fitters, mess rooms and lighting or ventilation. Close to the shed was a covered coal stage served by a separate siding and a small brick building to house the sand furnace. To gain access to the shed track had to pass over land owned by Dr Lind, Chairman of the Ryde Pier Company; his executors held out for the best possible price and prevented the railway from using the running shed until March 1874. That year the IWR spent over £200 in converting the old running shed to a machine shop; this included the installation of shafting to machines powered by a stationary boiler bought specially for the purpose. Two years later a 70 ft by 20 ft corrugated iron carriage and wagon shop was constructed in the yard south of the workshop buildings, accessed from the workshop's traverser. At the same time additional tools, a crane and machinery were purchased. This was the last expense of any size on the workshops but there was a rearrangement of the track layout once the coal stage had been moved, principally by the provision of additional sidings to the workshop buildings. It seems the traverser was then placed into the carriage shed and the number of sidings to the shed reduced - how long it remained there is unknown.

On 3rd June, 1875 the IWR Board accepted a tender from E. Pritchard for the construction of a second track as far as Smallbrook for the exclusive use of the Ryde and Newport Railway. Col Hutchinson, the Board of Trade Inspector, insisted on the construction of waiting rooms and 'water closets' on the island platform at Ryde because it would be used exclusively by IWR trains; the original platform was for RNR trains. In October 1879 the island platform was rebuilt, again in wood, and a footbridge provided between the platforms in connection with the construction of the railway to the pier. At some date the refreshment room was incorporated into the station building and rebuilt in more durable materials - the building was roughcast in later years.

Leaving the station, the railway headed south away from the town of Ryde. The line began to climb as it bore to the left to follow Monkton Mead Brook. About half a mile from the terminus it crossed the brook before encountering a short siding that faced down trains. The siding existed by 1866 but the site was obliterated by the track for the RNR added in 1875. A short distance on, the line passed under Smallbrook Lane (0 mile 60½ chains), a public road. It entered a right-hand curve before approaching the site of Smallbrook Junction where the line to Newport parted company; it is the location of the present interchange station with the Isle of Wight Steam Railway.

Beyond Smallbrook the line crossed the brook for a final time before the climb stiffened for about half a mile through Whitefield Woods. Near Truckell's cottages the railway passed below a public road (1 mile 74½ chains) as it surmounted the watershed between Monkton Mead Brook and the streams that fed into Brading Harbour. The line fell steeply and curved to the left through a series of clay cuttings towards Brading. Crossing a stream it passed under the Ryde to Brading road at Rowboro (2 miles 42½ chains), today called Rowborough, followed shortly after by a cattle creep (2 miles 60 chains). Then began a long curve to the right as it passed below Wall Lane, a road leading to Brading Quay (3 miles 15½ chains). Brading station was entered on a falling gradient on a sharp right-hand curve.

Brading station (3 miles 36 chains) was situated away from the centre of the village at the end of an access road. The attractive single storey building in red brick with yellow brick lintels over the doors and windows was on a 200 ft platform to the up side of the line. Unlike Sandown and Shanklin, the building contained no accommodation for the station master. At the north end of the platform a short siding led to a loading dock. The branch to Brading Quay

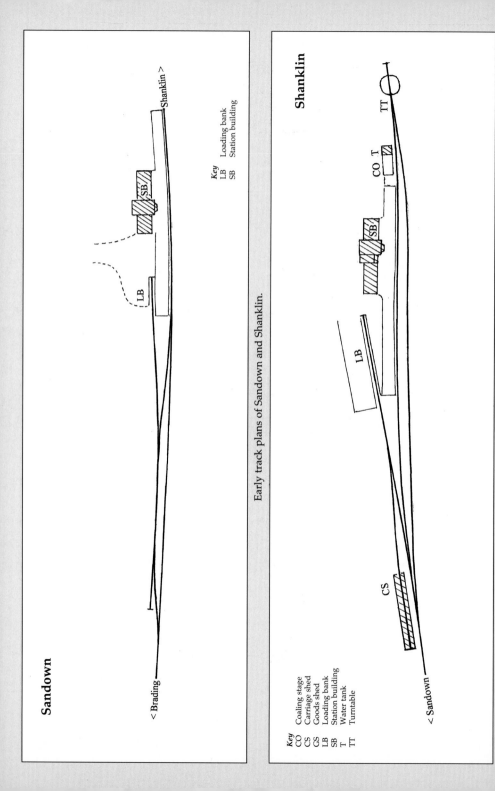

Early track plans of Sandown and Shanklin.

Sandown

Shanklin >

< Brading

SB

LB

Key
LB Loading bank
SB Station building

Shanklin

< Sandown

CO T

TT

SB

LB

CS

Key
CO Coaling stage
CS Carriage shed
GS Goods shed
LB Loading bank
SB Station building
T   Water tank
TT Turntable

joined the main line on the down side by means of a trailing crossover; a second connection formed a crossing loop. It could be used by goods trains but passenger trains were not officially permitted to pass there. At a later date the company extended the loop towards Sandown and constructed a down platform, possibly in the latter half of 1870 when £166 3s. 5d. was spent on works at Brading and Brading Quay. The theft of some clothing during a break-in led to the suggestion that a house be provided for the station master, but this was not acted on until 1877 when alterations and extensions were made to the station yard.

Col Yolland did not mention the branch to Brading Quay presumably as it carried goods traffic only; companies were obliged to submit for inspection only lines that would carry passengers. Brading Quay was planned to have a simple run-round loop and a headshunt leading to a wooden jetty. How long it remained in this state is unknown, but when the jetty and tipping facilities were finished in August 1865 three 150 ton vessels could discharge at the same time. Additional sidings provided in 1870 proved to be the first of several alterations; the most expensive were in 1876 when the IWR spent almost £500 on extending the jetty. In 1879 minimal repairs were put in hand, but soon afterwards the Brading Harbour Improvement and Railway Company line to St Helens opened for goods traffic and the jetty fell into disuse.

Leaving the station at Brading the line crossed a footpath, then described as a cattle creep (3 miles 40½ chains). On the up side was a ballast pit used by the contractor and described in the Minutes as Brading Quarry; Col Yolland commented that the rail connections had been removed by the date of his inspection. Years later the IWR put in a siding when the quarry came back into use for the supply of chalk to cement works on the Bembridge branch. The railway curved gently to the left as it followed the west bank of the nearby River Yar; the track was barely a foot above river level and prone to flooding. The line then passed under Yarbridge bridge, also known as Marshcombe Shute road bridge (3 miles 70 chains). It and the adjoining river bridge were the responsibility of the railway; the latter had to be rebuilt in 1869. After Yarbridge the line left the river as it climbed gradually across water meadows on a low embankment to pass over a cattle creep (4 miles 38 chains), the river (4 miles 48½ chains), the Brading to Sandown road on a girder bridge at Morton Common (4 miles 53 chains) and Sandown Farm bridge (4 miles 60 chains). Then followed a stiffer climb through a deep cutting passing under Gills bridge, a wooden structure carrying a footpath (4 miles 78 chains), before entering Sandown station (5 miles 30 chains).

Sandown station was situated well away from the main centre of population and many years passed before the town expanded to fill the intervening land. Despite being the only crossing place for passenger trains, an early plan prepared by John Fowler's staff showed a single 200 ft platform on the down side of the line. The simple two-storey station building built by Henry Bond in yellow brick lacked all adornments. On the first floor there were two bedrooms and a 'closet' for the station master and his family. The ground floor had a sitting room, kitchen and other facilities. A single-storey extension contained a tiny booking office and waiting room; a door to a separate ladies' waiting room led off the platform, part of which was covered. A note on the original drawings commented on the absence of accommodation for the telegraph and porters: 'this is much needed'. It was not long before the ladies' waiting room became the station master's office; the telegraph and first lever frame was located there.

Plans showed that trains were to cross in a loop to the north of the platform, and the only other siding was a facing connection to a dock at the up end of the platform. This antiquated arrangement avoided the provision of two platforms but must have been a considerable inconvenience. Within a short time, possibly by the time the extension to Ventnor opened in 1866, a crossing loop opposite the platform and a primitive second platform had been provided. In September 1869 the Board decided to rent Simeon Lodge from Mr Pritchard as a residence for the station master. The following year several hundred pounds were spent on the station yard and in the creation of offices for the General Manager. This would seem to date the construction of a two-storey extension at the south end of the building for offices; the work had been completed by August 1871 when Joseph Bourne was known to be based there.

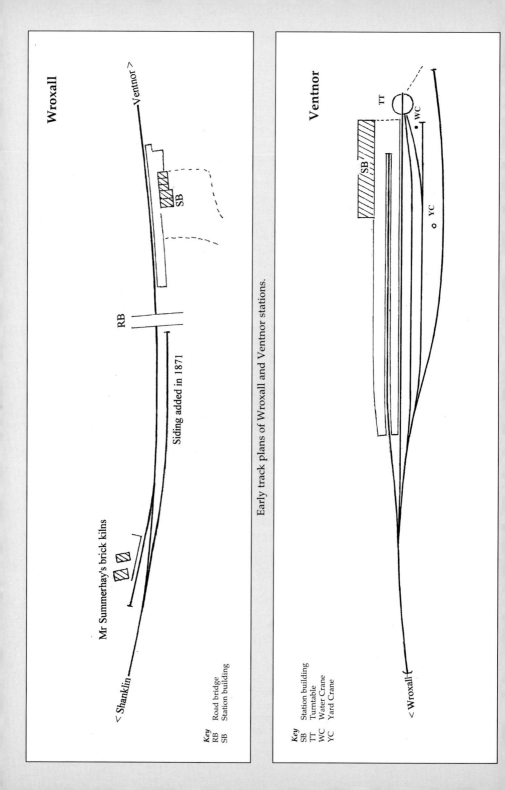

Wroxall

Ventnor >

SB

RB

Siding added in 1871

Mr Summerhay's brick kilns

< Shanklin

Key
RB   Road bridge
SB   Station building

Early track plans of Wroxall and Ventnor stations.

Ventnor

TT

WC

SB

YC

< Wroxall

Key
SB   Station building
TT   Turntable
WC   Water Crane
YC   Yard Crane

In the six months ending December 1870 more alterations were carried out for the Isle of Wight (Newport Junction) Railway to Newport, on which construction was about to start. The Newport line left from the station on the up side in a northerly direction but immediately curved sharply to the west as it descended steeply to the valley of the Eastern Yar. The IWR provided a second face to the up platform and a canopy (the frontage to the station building on the down platform received no covering until many years later), a run-round loop for IWNJ trains and a crossover between the two companies' tracks - it was not signalled and service trains did not normally use it. Permanent way materials for the IWNJ were landed at Brading Quay and transported by rail to Sandown; locomotives and rolling stock came by the same route. In 1874, at the request of the IWNJ, the IWR extended the up platform and canopy by 50 ft and (in late 1874 to early 1875) provided a wooden footbridge between the platforms. A small signal box immediately north of the up platform worked the new signalling and point work. The work cost £438 10s., half paid by the IWNJ.

Leaving the station, the railway to Ventnor bore to the left on a curve that sharpened further as the line climbed before crossing the turnpike road at Lake (5 miles 63 chains) on a cast-iron girder bridge. A few yards beyond there was a small underbridge that had been added as part of an agreement with a local landowner after the railway opened. After a brief fall, the line began to climb as it passed below the turnpike at Lake Skew bridge (6 miles 37 chains) near the cliff gardens. There used to be two large fields between the railway and the cliff edge but now there are just a few yards of park land - an indication of the amount of cliff erosion at this point. Just beyond the road bridge on the up side was a halt built in 1889 to serve the nearby cricket ground. The railway then headed inland to Shanklin station (7 miles 9 chains), again situated at the back of the town. The varying gradients on this section reflected the undulating heath land that has long since disappeared under housing.

The original site of Shanklin station was intended to be somewhat closer to the Old Village but was relocated in April 1862 following a request from Admiral Carter, a local landowner; he agreed to sell sufficient land for an approach road through the fields to the station. Station Road later passed into the care of the local authority, was renamed Regent Street in 1896 and eventually became the main shopping street. The town grew to fill the land between the cliff top and the railway line.

Of the station itself, the building and 200 ft asphalted platform were located on the down side of the line. A rather stark two-storey station master's house faced the road flanked by single-storey wings, one each side. On the platform side a small canopy over one wing of the building gave some protection from the elements - the ornamental ridge tiles were a later addition. A mirror image of that at Sandown, the station master's house had a bow-fronted window on the platform side; unfortunately the frontage was rather close to the track and the bay window was soon removed. The sidings were at the north end of the station; a facing connection led to a loading dock and platform for carriages and horses despite the lack of suitable rolling stock for the conveyance of either! An additional kickback siding led to a wooden carriage shed that by 1866 was already shored up and had to be demolished shortly afterwards. There was also a weighbridge and weighhouse. At the south end of the station the tracks ended at a turntable next to a coal stage and water tank. It was not long before the line opened to Ventnor so these facilities can have been in use for only a short time; the turntable was out of use by the time Col Yolland went over the line in 1866. The construction of a refreshment room was deferred when the prospective tenant refused to pay enough rent to justify the cost of its provision.

In June 1872 the *Isle of Wight Chronicle* reported on alterations to improve waiting accommodation, build a second platform and extend the main platform at the Ventnor end - the loop having been relaid and lengthened the previous year. This may also date the provision of a lever frame in the station master's office, similar to that at Sandown, and proper home signals. Even so, the system of single line working was unchanged and passenger trains were not officially permitted to cross there. The goods sidings were extended in 1874-1875 and again in 1878.

Col Yolland reported that the 4 mile 12¾ chain Shanklin to Ventnor section, apart from the ¾ mile tunnel, had five overbridges and seven underbridges 'all well constructed and substantial'. Leaving Shanklin the line to Ventnor crossed Landguard Manor Road on a single-arch brick bridge and then turned sharply to the west as it began a gruelling climb at a gradient of 1 in 70 up Apse Bank. Almost half the 1¼ mile climb was in a deep cutting (called Sand cutting) passing under Hyde Lane, Hyde and Sand Cutting road bridges in the process. On 23rd April, 1868 the IWR Board authorised the addition of a siding near Sand cutting for George Young as part of a package deal for the purchase of land; some of the £162 1s. 7d. cost was defrayed by using old permanent way materials. Emerging from the cutting, the line passed over a cattle creep bridge and Apse Reach bridge; nearing the top of the bank the gradient eased as the railway below Three Arch bridge (8 miles 51 chains), a considerable brick-faced structure that seemed far too lavish for the footpath it carried; two arches measured 25 ft and the third 27 ft on the square. Emerging from the cutting, passengers were presented with a magnificent view across the Arreton valley towards Blackwater. To the west could be seen the tower of Godshill Church nestling amongst the trees. Having negotiated a gentle 90 degree curve to the left around St Martins Down, the line headed in the direction of Wroxall across Winstone bridge (8 miles 71 chains). Near here, a private siding opened on 3rd July, 1867 to serve a brick pit owned by Mr Pritchard. This may have been the site of sidings and sheds erected by the contractor during construction of the line. The Board identified land on which they stood as surplus once the contractor's plant and sheds had been removed; during 1869 the locomotive *Ryde* disgraced itself by derailing on a temporary turnout at this point. The gradient stiffened as the line rose above the surrounding land on an embankment for the remaining distance to the outskirts of Wroxall crossing a cattle creep and Yard Farm bridge on the way.

According to Col Yolland, the intended station and crossing loop at Wroxall (9 miles 64 chains) had not been built when he inspected the line in September 1866. However, although the Minute book is silent on the matter, a platform must have existed by November as passenger receipts began that month. The railway ran along the back of the village on a shelf cut into the hillside. The station was located a few yards south of Wroxall bridge, a three-arch road overbridge leading to Cook's Castle (an 18th century romantic ruin). There was a single platform on the up side faced in stone, a feature exclusive to Wroxall and Ventnor - other stations on the line had red brick walls and coping. The small single-storey building had a similarity to that at Brading but was in wood; the station master lived in a nearby cottage. To the north of the road bridge, a strip of land gave access to a goods siding; during its construction in 1871 a train ran into the siding, collided with some wagons and injured a labourer working nearby. Unlike the other stations, there was no loading bank and thus no provision for loading and unloading horses, carriages, furniture vans, etc. On the opposite side of the line a spur served Mr Summerhays' brick kilns. This may have been the siding referred to in March 1866 when a Mr Cropper asked for a siding to his brickyard - the IWR agreed to lay in a turnout and track to its boundary if he continued the siding onto his land. Facing Shanklin-bound trains, it later formed a headshunt to a siding leading to Messrs Flux's bacon factory. Despite the existence of plans to provide a crossing loop during IWR days the only change seems to have been the rebuilding of the station building in more durable materials - it was roughcast in later years. Home and distant signals were provided in each direction in accordance with Board of Trade regulations.

Wroxall benefited from a decision to sell off surplus land adjoining the line that had been earmarked for the Central Lines' extension from Newport. That line would have climbed from the valley floor alongside the railway from Shanklin for a considerable distance, before joining it several hundred yards beyond Wroxall station. In 1870 a small plot of land, valued at £100, adjoining the station platform passed into the ownership of a Mr Grant in lieu of money owed to him. He developed the site by constructing a two-storey hotel including on the ground floor a refreshment room opening directly onto the platform. The remaining land on each side of the station approach and north of the Castle Road bridge was divided into 15 plots and put up for auction by Mr Raynes on Monday 29th August, 1870. One plot consisted of the cottage occupied by the station master who was forced to find his own accommodation. The auctioneer proved unable to sell them all, and Joseph Bourne had to act as intermediary in negotiations between the IWR Board and prospective buyers. The company laid down some conditions to the sales: railway embankments could be used only for planting 'without injury to the Railway' and covenanted to claim no compensation if there were land slips. After lengthy haggling, the land eventually was sold for a total of £1,050. One of the buyers was the Reverend Pound of Appuldurcombe who purchased several plots; Yarborough and Appuldurcombe Terraces were built on some of the land.

Leaving the station, the railway curved to the left before passing over an occupation crossing. There followed a curve to the right as the gradient eased shortly before Wroxall tunnel road bridge (10 miles 31½ chains); it had three arches measuring 26 ft 7 in., 25 ft and 22 ft on the square. The summit of the line at about 300 ft above sea level was reached just before the tunnel entrance. At 1,312 yards long, the tunnel was somewhat longer than the 1,166 yards authorised by Parliament; it was straight except for curves to the right near each entrance, falling for most of the way at 1 in 173. The tunnel mainly passed through greensand rock that had a tendency to flake, and as a precaution the contractor lined it with a thin layer of brick. Col Yolland remarked on the considerable amount of water that ran through the tunnel. Ventnor station (11 miles 25 chains from Ryde) was 276 ft above sea level in a deep cutting made light by the reflection from the brilliant white chalk hillside that took many years to mellow.

The site of Ventnor station was said to have been favoured by the local population as it would not spoil the amenities. Having said that, its location high above the town was inconvenient, to say the least. Stone quarries are known to have existed on the site since at least 1841 and many years before that, if local folklore is to be believed. The story goes that French prisoners of war, who were housed at Bonchurch during the Napoleonic War, worked in the quarries and cut out caves that were later used by local coal merchants for their stores; certainly some of the stonework is particularly fine and it is said that some caves contain graffiti carved into the walls by prisoners. The quarries were considerably smaller than the area we can see today and early photographs show the existence of a steep narrow cutting in the approaches; in later years the whole site was opened out to permit an enlargement of the station.

Despite Col Yolland's satisfaction with the works, passengers had to contend with an incomplete station for some time. A proposed track plan differed significantly from that actually laid out. At the far end of the platform a traverser would have served the main platform and run-round loop, whilst behind the platform a dock road and a short kickback siding sufficed for goods traffic. Opposite the platform the plan showed a siding leading to a carriage shed 'to be removed from Shanklin' and an engine house complete with a coke wharf, well and pumping engine.

For the opening of the station in 1866 a narrow and quite short platform had been built. The platform and run-round tracks were connected at the far end of the station to a turntable large enough to accommodate a Beyer, Peacock 2-4-0T; Col Yolland mentioned that turntables at Ryde and Shanklin had either not been installed, or could not be used, so one was evidently moved to Ventnor. A track ran along the back of the platform. Adjacent to the station yard were some small wooden sheds, one being used as a ticket office and another for passengers - it seems the wooden station building promised by Smith & Taylor never did get built, nor did a proposed goods shed utilising materials recovered from the demolition of Shanklin carriage shed.

In May 1869 the IWR Board authorised the construction of a water tank and a crane near the turntable. In August Joseph Bourne proposed alterations estimated to cost £448 11s. 5d. that the Board resolved 'be proceeded with forthwith'. This involved the completion of a permanent booking hall and waiting rooms - they came into use the following December.

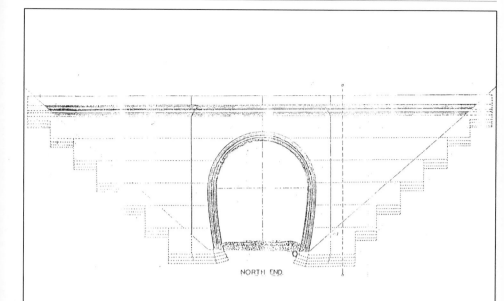

NORTH END.

An Engineer's diagram of Ventnor tunnel.

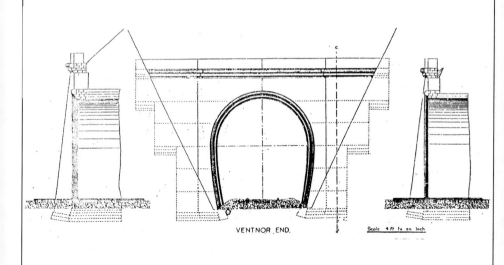

VENTNOR END.

Scale 4 ft to an inch

One matter about the supply of water for locomotives demonstrates how the IWR Board was thinking at the time. In August 1869 John Livesay, Secretary of the Ventnor Gas and Water Company wrote offering to provide 5,000 gallons for £40 per annum. The Board refused to accept the offer and during the following 12 months the two parties haggled over the amount of water to be supplied; the IWR first demanded 6,000 gallons a day for that price, then 5,500 gallons. Eventually they accepted the original offer, with an additional 1,000 gallons charged for a princely 1s. 6d. extra!

In a plan dated 1872 we see that trains then arrived in the original platform; the locomotive ran round its train and shunted to the bay platform that had been provided with a second face. Additional sidings had been laid in the goods yard for coal merchants, and a spur led to quarry workings near the tunnel mouth. An extension of the original goods siding connected also with the turntable. During the early 1870s the platforms were extended towards the tunnel mouth forcing locomotives and stock to enter the tunnel when shunting. In 1876 the company spent £549 6s. 7d. on more alterations that included the construction of a large goods shed in local stone.

Whilst passengers appreciated the convenience of separate arrival and departure roads, someone realised it was downright dangerous to draw every train into the tunnel whilst shunting from one platform to the other. The obvious solution was to connect the bay road with the turntable and this was done during alterations in 1877. The bay platform became the 'arrival and No. 1 departure road' whilst the other platform became 'No. 2 departure road' - a reverse of previous arrangements. The station was inspected by Major F.A. Marindin in September 1877 on behalf of the Board of Trade who sanctioned the alterations subject to a few minor adjustments.

The Inspecting Officer made only a passing reference to signalling. When the line to Shanklin opened there were two train staffs controlling the single line sections: Ryde to Sandown and Sandown onwards. Later the staff and ticket system was adopted, supplemented by a telegraph wired to the booking office at each station. Although Ryde and Sandown were each provided with a signal and points man, the station master had responsibility for safe working of trackwork, signals and telegraph. The signalling was rudimentary but quite typical of branch lines before the onset of block signalling. A relatively unknown firm, Messrs Hart and Son of Brigg near Scunthorpe, supplied the signalling at stations along the line. No clear photographs have been located of these, the first generation of the company's signals, but an extract from an advertisement is reproduced on page 53. Placed adjacent to the station building, each signal post carried one or two arms worked by levers near the base of the post. Turnouts leading to the crossing loops at Brading and Sandown were described as self-acting, but staff were still exhorted to check them prior to the arrival of a train. They could be held over by weighted levers but interlocking of turnouts and signals was notable by its complete absence. The 1864 edition of the rules and regulations described the meaning of the various flags, lamps and signals:

Flag or lamp	Signal arm	Instruction
red is a signal of danger	horizontal	stop
green is a signal of caution	at 45 degrees	proceed slowly
white is a signal of all right	vertical (in post)	go on

Hand signals (by either signal or flag) were to be used by day and lights at night.

The limitations of the signalling would have made itself apparent during a busy summer season. Sandown, Shanklin and possibly Wroxall had signal and point connections brought together in a small lever frame installed in the station master's offices. The passing of the 1874 Regulation of Railways Act obliged the company to provide interlocking of points and signals whenever significant alterations were carried out. The first occasion this happened was for the opening of the RNR to Ryde in 1875. Stevens & Co. supplied a signal box (located at the south end of the main platform) and a 35-lever frame interlocked with signalling and turnouts at a cost of over £1,000. At the insistence of the Board of Trade Inspector, they also provided ground frames controlling connections to sidings at the south end of the station, Appendix Three contains a drawing of Ryde station showing essentially the same arrangement as that installed nearly 20 years later. Two years later the company spent over £2,600 at Ventnor, including the cost of signalling and interlocking supplied by Stevens & Co. A signal box containing 15 levers, of which three were spare, was constructed adjacent to the tunnel mouth; the brick base seems to have been constructed by a local contractor but the timber upper works had the appearance of a Stevens' box. Unlike the original signals, those supplied by Stevens had arms that could not be lowered below 45 degrees; distant signals had arms identical to those on stop signals; it was much later before the arms were differentiated by a fishtail cut in the end. As late as 1878 distant signals were not being lit at night and enginemen were warned to approach 'every station with great caution'! Shunting Ventnor yard was particularly dangerous and justified special instruction in an 1878 Rule Book. In the tunnel there were two gongs, one 60 yards and the other 100 yards from the tunnel mouth. The signalman would use the following codes:

> 1 strike of the gong, *to stop*
> 2 strikes of the gong, *to put back*
> 3 strikes of the gong, *to go ahead*

The permanent way detailed by Col Yolland in his 1864 report was typical of railways built in the 1860s. Perhaps the weakest components were the sleepers that had been made from local timber felled during construction. The contractor made no attempt to treat or season the wood so their condition deteriorated quickly. Many were condemned within months of the opening and the rest replaced in the years to 1872. Ballast came from deposits unearthed during construction; sandstone quarried at Ventnor was later used but it still demanded careful maintenance. The fencing also required constant attention and in October 1868 Joseph Bourne wrote:

> The fencing in many places between Ryde and Shanklin is becoming very bad, which I have to renew. On this part of the line only part of the ditching has been cut and none of the quick planted. November to March being the most favourable months for these operations it would be advisable that I should have the authority say to put on two men during this time and by this means we should get the work completed in from two to three seasons. The costs would be from £35 to £40 per mile, and there are about 17 miles to do.

For several years thereafter the accounts recorded sums expended on 'ditching and quicking' i.e. hedging. More significantly, a wholesale replacement of the rails and fittings took place in the 1870s. As an example, 441 yards of permanent way was renewed in the six months ending December 1870 at a cost of £306; next year the company had begun selling old rails, etc. to Mr Bradley; other redundant materials were used to add or extend sidings. Even so, flat bottom wrought-iron rails were still being purchased in 1875 when a second track was laid between Ryde and Smallbrook; they were 24 ft. long and weighed 57 lb. per linear yard. In March 1876 the IWR Board decided to buy steel rails for use in Ventnor tunnel and yard. Three months later 150 tons of bullhead rails were ordered and two years later, in July 1878, it was decided that all future rails would be steel.

Contemporary writers described the appearance of newly built railways as akin to the Wild West, and it was many years before the earthworks blended into the countryside. More seriously the railway suffered from numerous earth slips. During construction the gault, a blue or bluish grey clay known locally as Blue Slipper became exposed in several places and the actions of heavy rain quickly turned it to a slippery state with predictable consequences. In March 1866 Joseph Bourne wrote a long epistle about the condition of the line, which the Secretary faithfully copied into the Minute book. During the winter of 1865-1866 there had been slips in cuttings at Truckells, at Rowborough and Wall Lane, Brading. Small slips also took place in 'Chalk Cutting Brading', 'Sandown Cutting' and in 'the embankment at

Sandown'. Additional side ditching was required and several bridges and culverts needed attention. A bridge at Rowborough and Morton Common girder bridge had been rebuilt; in March 1866 repairs were being made to a cast-iron girder bridge at Lake and another bridge at Yarbridge was waiting to be begun. Three years later a major slip took place at Rowborough bridge where the pier and part of the wing wall on the south-east side moved; it cost £150 to put right problems caused by bad weather during the winter of 1868-1869.

In 1871 two heavy slips occurred in Sandown cutting and at Rowborough. A Mr Wendt wrote to the Board of Trade complaining that he had been delayed by about six hours on 20th April due to a slip on the site of an earlier slip the previous Friday. Col Yolland happened to be in the Island, and on 17th May wrote that the company was doing its best to deal with slips that were only to be expected given the nature of the clay at various points along the line. He concluded by commenting on the need to replace large numbers of decayed sleepers of which many were in a bad state. Their replacement 'cannot be completed too quickly.'

An advertisement for signalling by Hart & Co.

ISLE OF WIGHT RAILWAY.

RULES

FOR

WORKING THE LINE.

1. A **Train Staff** or **Train Ticket** is to be carried on the Engine of each Train to and fro, without which no Engine is to be allowed to start.

2. Two Train Staffs will be employed, viz.:

One between Ryde and Sandown - **Square, RED.**
One between Sandown and Shanklin - **Circular, GREEN.**

3. No Engine or Train is to be permitted to leave either Ryde, Sandown, or Shanklin unless the Staff for the portion of the Line over which it is to travel is then at the Station.

4. If no second Engine or Train is intended to follow, the Staff is to be given to the Driver, who will fix it in the place made for it on his Engine.

5. If another Engine or Train is intended to follow before the Staff can be returned, a Train Ticket, stating "**Staff following,**" will be given to the Driver in charge of the leading Train, who will fix it in its place on the Engine, the Staff itself being given to the Driver of the last Train; after which, no other Engine or Train can leave the Station, under any circumstances whatever, until the return of the Staff.

6. The Train Tickets are to be kept in a Box fastened by an inside spring; the Key to open the Box is the Train Staff, so that a Ticket cannot be obtained without the Train Staff.

7. The Train Staffs, Ticket Boxes, and Tickets are painted or printed in two different colours: **Red** between Ryde and Sandown, and **Green** between Sandown and Shanklin: the inside Springs and the Keys on the Staffs being so arranged that the Red Staff cannot open the Green Box, nor the Green Staff the Red Box.

8. The Ticket Boxes are fixed by two brackets in the Office, the brackets being turned up at the end to receive the Train Staff when at the Station.

9. The Clerk in charge, Inspector, or person in charge for the time, is the **sole** person authorised to receive and deliver the Staff.

10. An Engineman taking the Staff, or Ticket, beyond the Station to which it belongs, or leaving a Station without the Staff, or Ticket, as hereinbefore explained, will subject himself to dismissal, although no accident may arise.

11. **Enginemen are not to start from Ryde, Sandown, or Shanklin until the Guard has given the usual signal, and the Train Staff or Train Ticket has been fixed in the proper place on the Engine.**

12. A Guard is not to give his Driver a signal to start until he is satisfied that the Driver has got the Train Staff, or Ticket; and he will be held equally responsible with the Driver in the event of a Train starting without the Staff, or Ticket.

13. The usual Special Train Tail Signal, "**Engine following,**" is to be used for the guidance of the Platelayers and Gatekeepers upon the Line.

14. Ballast Trains are to be treated in every respect like Traffic Trains, as regards the Staff and Ticket arrangements.

15. In the event of an Engine or Train breaking down between two Telegraph Stations, the Fireman is to take the Train Staff to the Telegraph Station in the direction whence assistance is expected, that the Staff may be at that Station on the arrival of an Engine. Should the Engine that fails be in the possession of a Train Ticket instead of the Staff, **assistance can only come from the Station at which the Train Staff has been left.** The Fireman is to accompany the Assistant Engine to the place where he left his own Engine.

JOSEPH BOURNE,
General Manager.

GENERAL MANAGER'S OFFICE, RYDE, August, 1864.

G. BUTLER, PRINTER, "ISLE OF WIGHT OBSERVER" OFFICE, COLONNADE, RYDE.

Rules for working the railway, 1864.

Chapter Five

Services in the Early Days

We have seen how the railway altered the landscape in the eastern part of the Island but what of its effect on the population? It had, of course, a novelty value for those who had not seen railways on the mainland (and there were many of those) or the first railway from Cowes to Newport. On the other hand, the railway swept tenants and their owners from its path whilst the consequential growth of towns along the route caused more upheavals. For those who could adapt there would be jobs as first the railway recruited labour and then others rushed to satisfy the demand for accommodation from visitors attracted from the mainland. Such changes could never be reversed - for better or worse, the need to serve the tourist would dictate the future.

A lack of co-ordination in the steamer, tramway and railway services to and from the Isle of Wight was a feature of the company's early years, and it is a wonder that so many visitors made the hideously inconvenient journey. Ferries to the Island departed from Southampton, Stokes Bay or Portsmouth and landed at either Cowes or Ryde. Of the three, the most convenient was Stokes Bay where the railway ran straight to the pier but the location could be rather exposed in bad weather. The LSWR, having invested so much money elsewhere, did little to advertise the route and forced most passengers to change trains at Bishopstoke (now called Eastleigh). At Portsmouth the railway terminated well away from the steamer piers. Southsea Pier (later renamed Clarence Pier) opened on 1st June, 1861, followed by a horse tramway to the railway terminus on 15th May, 1865. Arrangements at Ryde were equally unsatisfactory: a tramway along the pier began operating a week after the IWR opened to Shanklin, but there remained a gap of over half a mile between the pier and railway station. The unfortunate traveller with wife, children, luggage, etc. had to make his own way across Ryde, and it was hardly surprising that many avoided the railway and made the whole journey to their destination by road. The *Isle of Wight Observer* was moved to report:

> The main feature of the line was, clearly, connection with Ventnor and the beautiful Undercliff; and until the intervening four miles, and very heavy ones they are by road, are overcome, the traffic with that district can scarcely be said to be more than touched. The coach still occupies an hour from Shanklin station to Ventnor and the inconvenience of the change is so great that parties still employ carriages throughout (from Ryde) to escape it.

The stations at Ryde, Brading, Sandown and Shanklin were situated well away from the locations they needed to serve. At Ryde the station was at the back of the town and a considerable distance from the principal source of passenger traffic at Ryde Pier. Brading, Sandown and Shanklin were at the end of approach roads, that at Sandown involved a weary uphill walk from the town centre! Wroxall station had a convenient location close to the village but the terminus at Ventnor was high above the town. Perhaps the best that can be said was that the railway did not destroy the beauty spots that other schemes would have done. In an attempt to ameliorate the situation the provision of 'fly and omnibus' services at Ryde, Sandown, Shanklin and Ventnor cropped up in the Minute book on several occasions. In 1864 the company made agreements with the proprietors of local livery stables, Messrs Mew & Co., a Mr Hillier and with Messrs Bush and Judd for the carriage of passengers between Shanklin and Ventnor. The agreements stipulated that two horse-drawn omnibuses had to meet every train to and from Shanklin, the IWR paid 1s. per passenger and through tickets were sold for the whole distance to Ventnor. The local press reported the withdrawal of the Ryde to Ventnor coach *Felicity* when the railway opened and its operation between Shanklin and Ventnor. The railway may have owned some horses as Bush and Judd charged £21 18s. 2d. in January 1865 for 'keep of horses'. In addition, the Board on 27th August, 1864 had authorised the construction of a stable for four horses at Shanklin and the purchase of a horse for

ISLE OF WIGHT RAILWAY.

TIME TABLE FOR AUGUST, 1864.

		7 5	10 0	11 30	3 50		
Waterloo to Portsmouth	dep.						
London Bridge to Portsmouth	dep.	10 40	1 25	3 10	6 55		
Ryde from Portsmouth, by Boat	arr.	8 0		11 0	3 0		
Waterloo to Stokes Bay	dep.						
Ryde from Stokes Bay, by Boat	arr.	11 29		2 25	6 25		

DOWN TRAINS from RYDE.

WEEK DAYS.

		1 & 3 cl.	1 & 2 cl.	1 & 2 cl.	1 & 2 cl.	1 & 2 cl.	1 & 2 cl.	1 & 2 cl.	1 & 2 cl.	12 0	1 & 2 cl.	3 50
RYDE	dep.	6 0	8 30	10 0	11 0	12 0	1 0	3 0	4 0	5 0	6 0	7 30
BRADING	dep.	6 10		10 10	11 10	12 12	1 12	3 17	4 12	5 10	6 10	
SANDOWN	dep.	6 17	8 42	10 17	11 17	12 20	1 20	3 17	4 20	5 17	6 17	7 42
SHANKLIN	arr.	6 25	8 50	10 25	11 25	1 25		3 25	4 20	5 25	6 25	7 50
VENTNOR (by Coach)	arr.			11 30					5 25			8 25

SUNDAYS.

		1 & 2 cl.	1 & 2 cl.
RYDE	dep.	8 30	7 0
BRADING	dep.	8 40	7 10
SANDOWN	dep.	8 47	7 17
SHANKLIN	arr.	8 55	7 25

UP TRAINS from SHANKLIN.

WEEK DAYS.

		1 & 3 cl.	1 & 2 cl.	1 & 2 cl.	1 & 2 cl.	1 & 2 cl.	1 & 2 cl.	1 & 2 cl.	1 & 2 cl.	1 & 2 cl.	1 & 2 cl.
VENTNOR (by Coach)	dep.	6 40	8 0	10 0	12 0	3 20	4 0	5 5	6 10	7 35	8 10
SHANKLIN	dep.	6 47	9 10	10 10	12 5	7 35	5 10	9 5	9 35	7 42	8 17
SANDOWN	dep.	6 55	9 17	10 17	12 12		4 12	9 50			8 25
BRADING	dep.	7 5		10 25	1 20	3 40	4 20	5 40			8 35
RYDE	arr.		9 30	11 35	1 30	7 35	4 30	10 5		8 0	8 35

SUNDAYS.

		1 & 2 cl.	1 & 2 cl.
VENTNOR (by Coach)	dep.	9 15	7 45
SHANKLIN	dep.	9 22	7 52
SANDOWN	dep.	9 30	8 0
BRADING	dep.	9 40	8 10

		1 & 2 cl.	1 & 2 cl.	12 0	1 & 2 cl.
Ryde to Portsmouth (by Boat)	dep.	7 50	10 0	12 0	
Waterloo from Portsmouth	arr.		1 15	5 50	
London Bridge from Portsmouth	arr.	11 15	2 40	5 20	
Ryde to Stokes Bay (by Boat)	dep.	7 30	10 25		4 55
Waterloo from Stokes Bay	arr.	11 0	2 30		

Greenwich Time will be observed at all the Stations.

FARES.

RYDE to		1 cls.	2 cls.	3 cls.	1 cls.	2 cls.	3 cls.
Brading	4 Miles	1 0	0 9	0 6	1 6	1 1	0 9
Sandown	6 Miles	1 3	1 0	0 8	2 0	1 6	1 0
Shanklin	8 Miles	1 8	1 2	0 10	2 6	1 9	1 3
Ventnor (by Coach)	12¼ Miles	2 8	2 0	—	3 6	2 6	—

Single — Double

VENTNOR to Shanklin (by Coach)	4¼ Miles	1 0	1 6
Sandown	6½ Miles	1 3	2 0
Brading	8¾ Miles	1 6	2 6
Ryde	12¼ Miles	2 8	3 6

Single — Double

Monthly and Season Tickets issued on advantageous Terms on application to the General Manager, Ryde.

LUGGAGE.—First Class Passengers are allowed 112lbs., Second Class Passengers 100lbs., and Third Class Passengers 56lbs. of personal Luggage only—all excess will be charged for according to distance. All Luggage must be properly addressed. All Packages and Parcels left in the Carriages and Luggage not being claimed by the owner will be charged for the fare from the most distant station from which the Train started at the convenience of the owner; but Passengers desiring such accommodation, may leave their Luggage at the Booking Office until the arrival of a subsequent Train. Parcels cannot re-book at an intermediate station by the same Train.

Every person attempting to defraud the Company by travelling without having previously paid his fare, or by riding in, or upon a Carriage of a superior class to that for which he has booked his place, or by continuing in or upon a Carriage after having been requested to leave the same by an officer, and in any other manner whatever to evade the payment of his fare, is liable under the Company's By-Laws to a penalty not exceeding Forty Shillings.

Tickets issued at intermediate Stations can only be given conditionally on the chance of there being room in the same class of Carriage on the arrival of the Train; and if there be no room, the money will be returned for any Ticket produced at the Booking Office immediately after the departure of the Train for which it has been purchased. Tickets are not transferable.

Children under three years of age travel free; and those above that, and under twelve, half-price. Tickets must be shown to the Company's servants when required, or delivered up on leaving the Station; Passengers not producing their Tickets are liable to be charged the fare from the most distant station from which the Train starts. Passengers are requested to obtain their Tickets before entering the Carriages.

The arrival and departure of the Trains at the hours fixed for the departure of the Trains is not guaranteed, nor will the Company hold themselves responsible for any delay. The doors of the Booking Office will be closed punctually at the hours fixed for the departure of the Trains; and the office and station will remain closed till 15 minutes before the next Train is due. The Company do not guarantee any correspondence between the trains mentioned in this Time Table and other trains stated; neither will they be accountable for any loss, inconvenience, or injury arising from delays.

INCIVILITY.—The Directors request that any instance of Incivility or Misconduct on the part of persons in the service of the Company may be reported to the General Manager. No Gratuity, under any circumstances, is permitted to be taken by a servant of the Company. Any servant accepting a Gratuity is liable to immediate dismissal.

JOSEPH BOURNE, General Manager.

General Manager's Office, Ryde, August, 1864.

G. BUTLER, PRINTER, "OBSERVER" OFFICE, COLONNADE, RYDE.

'Brading Yard'. In November 1864 Capt. Huish wrote that it was desirable to seek arrangements with the two pier companies at Ryde, so that 'omnibuses and flys' might be run to the ends of the piers to enable passengers and their luggage to transfer directly to and from steamers without a change of conveyance. A few coach services survived but their patronage declined sharply once the railway opened to Ventnor; it is not hard to see why: speed, comfort and fares all compared unfavourably with the railway. Those same coaches found employment between station and town or on excursions to places not reached by the railway.

The timetable for August 1864 showed that the company provided a relatively frequent service with two trains crossing at Sandown. Two months later some timings had been adjusted and by November there were only seven trains per day worked by one locomotive. Most stations reported that passenger figures exceeded expectations, the exception being Brading which was not heavily used - not all trains stopped there. In the first full summer of operations (1865) there was an advertised service of 12 trains daily between Ryde and Shanklin, taking approximately 20 minutes for the journey. The frequency was clearly in accordance with John Fowler's opinion that 'The way to work the Isle of Wight Railway is to develop the traffic by giving numerous trains'. Following the opening of the line to Ventnor the same number of trains took 30 minutes. This was a creditable performance considering the state of the track and earthworks. On Queen Victoria's Coronation Day anniversary in 1865 (28th June)* trains were filled to capacity. The 1 pm working from Ryde loaded up to 16 carriages, two-thirds of the passenger fleet! Since the platforms were only 200 feet long, it is more likely the train ran in two parts - the first carrying a 'train follows' board to warn of the second portion. During the off-season a greatly reduced service operated, and this led to complaints during the winter of 1865-1866 about the meagre service; no trains left Ryde between the hours of 12.0-3.0 pm and 5.0-8.0 pm, despite an engine standing there in steam.

Joseph Bourne supplied the Board with weekly summaries of takings and a comparison with income a year previously. Whilst most weeks showed a satisfactory increase, there appeared the occasional explanation why a particular week had performed poorly. The figures emphasised the seasonal nature of passenger and parcels traffic and how income could be affected by the weather - a wet autumn or spring was not calculated to do much for finances. On the other hand a busy summer would tax the resources of the railway to the limit.

No sooner had the railway opened than a writer in the *Isle of Wight Times* for 8th September, 1864 wrote that many visitors brought to Shanklin by the railway had 'great difficulty in finding the beauty spots' and the area urgently needed improved sign posting, better roads and gas lighting. Two months later on 3rd November the paper reported the formation of a gas company, 'the prospects of success being so very encouraging'. There was much comment that all rooms in Ventnor, Shanklin and nearby were full. Much of Ventnor's growth occurred before the coming of the railway, but the greater accessibility of the town stimulated the construction of a number of hotels. At Shanklin, the village grew into a sizeable holiday resort: half a dozen hotels in 1851 had become 43 in 1871. This was repeated at Sandown, 'a village by a sandy shore', where bathing huts jostled with crowds on the resort's beaches. Proprietors of the beach huts received commission from the IWR on sales of combined railway and bathing tickets - a trip by train from Ryde to Sandown's beaches for the bathing became quite popular. George Young commented that the size of Sandown 'is not as great as at Ventnor. It is a different class altogether - there is a higher class at Sandown - it is a place more for health'.

With much of its custom coming from or going to the mainland, the IWR was anxious to conclude agreements to co-ordinate train and ferry services. In October 1864 Capt. Huish reported that the LSWR would run fast trains during November, leaving at about 9.45 am from London to Portsmouth and at 5.00 pm from Portsmouth to London. There were agreements to carry H.M. mails, newspapers and with Messrs Chaplin and Horne, carriers to the LSWR, for the carriage of goods to and from the Island. Newspapers benefited from the railways which delivered them to the remotest parts of Britain, including the Isle of Wight.

* The anniversary of Queen Victoria's Coronation on 28th June, 1838 was celebrated as a public holiday in the Isle of Wight until 1939.

Isle of Wight Railway Staff in the nine days ending 3rd September, 1864

Traffic Department

Ryde		Brading		Sandown		Shanklin	
Station Master	30s.	Station Master	20s.	Station Master	25s.	Station Master	25s.
Booking Clerk	18s.			Booking Clerk	8s.	Porters (2)	15s.
Policeman	15s.			Signalman	15s.		
Porters (2)	15s.			Porter	15s.		
Asst. porter and							
Lamplighter	15s.						
Nightwatchman	15s.						
Signalman and							
pointsman	18s.						
Storekeeper	8s.						
Clerk	25s.						
Two guards	21s.						

Locomotive Department

Two enginemen	7s. each *
Two firemen	3s. 6d. *
Fitter	7s.*
Engine cleaner	3s.*
Engine cleaner	2s.*
Engine cleaner	1s.*
Driver of water engine	3s.*
Carriage cleaner	1s. 6d.*

Permanent Way Department

Two inspectors	30s. each
Engineman	7s.*
Fireman	3s. 6d.*
Rope runner	3s. 4d.*
Sixgangers	4s.*
25 platelayers	3s.*
19 'on ballasting'	3s.*

* The daily rate of pay, other rates were weekly.
The above excludes the General Manager, Secretary and his staff.

Maximum passenger and goods rates

Passengers -	first class	3d. per mile,	4d. for distances of up to one mile.
	second class	2d. per mile,	3d. for distances of up to one mile.
	third class	1d. per mile,	2d. for distances of up to one mile.
Carriages -	up to one ton weight	4d. each per mile.	
	per extra ¼ ton	1d. per mile.	
Freight -	horses	4d. each per mile.	
	cattle	3d. each per mile.	
	calves	2d. each per mile.	
	pigs	2d. each per mile.	
	sheep	1½d. each per mile.	
	Coal, coke etc.	3d. per ton per mile.	
	Sugar, grain, cotton, wools	3d. per ton per mile.	
	Fish, drugs, iron etc.	3d. per ton per mile.	
	Boilers, cylinders, timbers etc.	1s. per mile.	
Parcels -	up to 7 lb.	4d. per mile.	
	7-14 lb.	5d. per mile.	
	14-28 lb.	8d. per mile.	
	28-56 lb.	1s. per mile.	
	56-100 lb.	no restriction.	

The Company may make a minimum charge for passengers and goods equivalent to the charge for 3 miles.

Even so Messrs Knight & Son of Ventnor complained about high charges for the carriage of London newspapers. W.H. Smith negotiated a contract for the exclusive privilege of establishing bookstalls, selling newspapers and placing advertising boards at stations; this led to a profusion of enamel signs extolling the virtues of a variety of products, so much a feature of IWR stations. In the first agreement reached in 1864, Smith's agreed to pay £60 for a rental of 12 months, but with a reduction until the line to Ventnor opened. When the contract came up for renewal on 1st January, 1869 Alexander Beattie gained an improvement to £100 per annum for seven years.

Not everyone approved of the opening of a railway. The American writer Henry James visited the Island in 1870 and wrote:

The Isle of Wight is at first disappointing. I wondered why it should be, and then I found the reason in the influence of the detestable little railway. There can be no doubt that a railway in the Isle of Wight is a gross impertinence, is in evident contradiction to the natural style of the place. The place is pure picture or is nothing at all. It is ornamental only - it exists for exclamation and the water-colour brush. It is separated by nature from the dense railway-system of the less diminutive Island, and is the corner of the world where a good carriage-road is most in keeping. Never was a clearer opportunity for sacrificing to prettiness; never was a better chance for not making a railway. But now there are twenty trains a day, so that the prettiness is twenty times less. The Island is so small that the hideous embankments and tunnels are obtrusive; the sight of them is as painful as it would be to see a pedlar's pack on the shoulders of a lovely woman. This is your first impression as you travel (naturally by the objectionable conveyance) from Ryde to Ventnor; and the fact that the train rumbles along very smoothly and stops at half a dozen little stations, where the groups on the platform enable you to perceive that the population consists almost exclusively of gentlemen in costumes suggestive of unlimited leisure for attention to cravats and trousers (an immensely large class in England), of old ladies of the species denominated in France *rentières*, of young ladies of the highly educated and sketching variety, this circumstance fails to reconcile you to the chartered cicatrix which forms your course.

James's description of his fellow travellers gave an excellent picture of the railway's early patrons. The reason for this was quite simple - the cost of fares. The 1860 Act laid down the maximum rates the company could charge for passengers and goods. Railway fares were less than the coach fares to Ventnor (2s. single and 3s. return) but were still higher than most people could afford. Most Island residents, if they travelled at all, walked or used the carriers' carts. Even so, the IWR, in common with other railways, had an obligation under the 'Cheap Trains Act' of 1844 to run Parliamentary trains with accommodation for passengers at a fare of 1d. a mile, usually the first down and up trains of the day. In January 1869 the Board received a 'memorial from the working men of Ryde' asking for trains and fares at 1d. per mile. In response the Board authorised the issue of tickets at reduced rates:

To or from:	Brading, Sandown and Shanklin	Wroxall & Ventnor
monthly tickets	10s.	13s. 4d.
fortnightly tickets	6s.	7s. 9d.

Despite numerous requests for third class trains, the Board instructed Joseph Bourne in October 1868 to run no more 'than is really necessary'. The railway possessed no third class carriages so second class compartments had to be used, much to the anger of second class ticket holders. A few months earlier the Board had agreed to the conversion of three composite carriages into 'Smoking Carriages', a response to the passing of the 1868 Regulation of Railways Act that required railways to provide accommodation for smokers.

Arguments for and against the running of trains on Sundays had existed since the very beginning of railways when the Lord's Day Observance Society and clergymen opposed the operation of *any* Sunday trains. Later some opponents accepted the provision of a limited service except at church times. One of the members of the IWR Board, Capt. Huish, was very much against Sunday trains and initially persuaded the Board not to run any. Representations

From VENTNOR to PORTSMOUTH and LONDON.

UP.

	WEEK DAYS													SUNDAYS		
	1 2 3	1 & 2	1 & 2	1 & 2	1 & 2	1 & 2	1 & 2	1 & 2	1 & 2	1 & 2	1 & 2	1 & 2	1 & 2	1 & 2	1 & 21 & 2	1 & 2
Ventnor ...... by Coach dep.	7 45	9 30		12 0		2 45	3 45	4 0		6 0	7 30	8 30		10 30	4 25	8 30
Shanklin ...... by Train dep.	8 45	10 40	11 40	1		2 51	3 51	5 5	5 6	6 6	7 36	8 36		10 36	4 31	8 36
Sandown	8 51	10 46	11 46	1 6		2 57	3 57	5 6	5 12	6 12	7 42	8 42		10 42	4 37	8 42
Brading	8 57	10 52	11 52	1 12		3 5		5 4	5 20	6 20	7 50	8 50		10 50	4 45	8 50
Ryde ...... arr.	9 5	11 0	12 0	1 20		3 4		5 20								
Ryde to Stokes Bay ... by Boat dep.	10 30			1 45	4 5		5 45									
Waterloo ...... by Train arr.	2 34			5 40	7 45		10 10									
Ryde to Portsmouth ... by Boat dep	9 40	11 30		3 15		4 50	6 15									
London Bridge ...... by Train arr.	1 15	4 25		7 45		9 45	9 40			9 15						
Victoria ...... ,, ,,	1 22	4 35		7 50		9 50										
Ryde to Portsmouth ... by Boat dep.	9 40	11 30		1 50		4 50				4 30						
Waterloo ...... by Train arr.	1 18	3 15		5 31		10 10										

From LONDON to PORTSMOUTH and VENTNOR.

DOWN.

	WEEK DAYS									SUNDAYS		
	1 2 3	1 & 2	1 & 2	1 & 2	1 & 2	1 & 2	1 & 2	1 & 2	1 & 2	1 & 2	1 & 21 & 2	1 & 2
Waterloo to Stokes Bay ...... dep.		9 30		8 0	11 0			3 10				
Ryde ...... by Boat arr.			11 20		2 20			6 25				
Waterloo to Portsmouth ...... dep.			7 5			11 30			3 50			
Ryde ...... by Boat arr.			11 5			3 10			7 30			
Victoria to Portsmouth ...... dep.				6 35	9 55	11 40			4 0			
London Bridge to Portsmouth ... dep.				6 40	10 0	11 45			4 5			
Ryde ...... by Boat arr.				11 5	1 40	3 10			7 30			
Ryde ...... dep.	8 0	10 0	12 10	2 0	3 15	4 15	5 30	7 0	8 0	10 0	2 0	8 0
Brading	8 10	10 11	12 18	2 8	3 23	4 23	5 36	7 8	8 8	10 8	2 8	8 8
Sandown	8 14	10 24	12 24	2 14	3 29	4 29	5 42	7 14	8 14	10 14	2 14	8 14
Shanklin	8 20	10 30	12 30	2 20	3 35	4 35	5 50	7 20	8 20	10 20	2 20	8 20
Ventnor ...... by Coach arr.		11 30	1 30		5 35				9 30			

An 1866 timetable.

from some travellers resulted in a change of mind and the Board authorised Joseph Bourne to operate a morning and evening train to and from Ventnor, whilst keeping an account of the revenue generated. In deference to Capt. Huish the Board decreed that trains must not run at church times. Pressure for an additional train during the summer season, however, prompted the decision in June 1865 to run a midday train leading to complaints received from the local clergy and prominent residents. A shareholder, Mr Barrow, sought to put a stop to the trains at a meeting on 6th October, 1866 when he proposed a resolution 'that no trains should run on the Isle of Wight Railway during the hours of Divine Service on Sundays'. Capt. Huish, Chairman of the meeting, hinted that the Directors had strongly disagreed on the subject. He made his thoughts plain: 'To encourage a large Sunday traffic would prove a great scandal to the Isle of Wight, it is not desirable that people should be rushing backwards and forwards . . .' In his view one morning and evening train were ample and added 'I will always lift up my hand and voice to prevent the desecration of the Sabbath'. Thomas Webster spoke of the nuisance caused by an influx of excursionists from the other side of the water to the residents of Sandown, Shanklin and Ventnor, and advocated doing away with the midday trains. Capt. Huish, however, remarked that the midday train would probably be taken off 'as usual' on 1st November and the question was whether it should be put on again in May. After further words from James Simpson and Alexander Beattie, shareholders agreed to leave the matter in the hands of the Directors. When the argument about Sunday trains surfaced again in 1867 the following letter was copied into the Minute book as a record of the company's policy:

Isle of Wight Railway
General Manager's Office
Ryde
April 10th 1867
R. Hicks Esq.

Dear Sir,

Easter Traffic

I am running the trains on Good Friday as on Week days, with a Midday train on Easter Sunday - this is the only addition I am providing for the above occasion, and is precisely what we did last year and which was found to answer every purpose.

The late Captn Huish and myself went thoroughly into the matter of running Excursion trains at reduced fares, and we came to the conclusion that it would not be to the Company's advantage to do so, in fact we were of opinion that it would reduce the receipts and increase the working expenses. It must be remembered that we have only a line of 12 miles, the fares being low, and we have no manufacturing towns from which to draw Excursionists, and I think the Board will agree with me that our only course is to confine ourselves to affording a good local Service of trains, and at the same time one that shall work in well with the Steamers leaving the mainland for the Island and vice versa.

We may occasionally advertise an Excursion at reduced fares if the Steam Packet and Pier Companies will join us, and so bring people from Portsmouth Southampton Cowes &c. to our Stations at single fares for the double journey, the Excursionists travelling by our Ordinary trains which would entail no extra working cost, but both the Companies named are not disposed to come to any such arrangement this Easter.

Yours truly
(Signed) J. Bourne

During the summer of 1867 Sandown Bay was host to military manoeuvres, and the resulting traffic led to the provision of a temporary halt said to have been at Yarbridge; more likely it was near Morton Common. Reduced fares for groups and additional trains in connection with special events became a frequent occurrence. The increased summer traffic was already obvious when Joseph Bourne wrote:

Rocket waits for passengers in the station yard at Ventnor. Behind can be seen the temporary booking office and accommodation for passengers. A carriage stands at the buffers of the bay platform. The building in the background appeared in several photographs but seems never to have been completed.   *R. Brinton Collection*

A slightly later view of Ventnor station showing the addition of lighting and temporary coverings at the end of the platform and to the front of the booking office. The short siding on the left was soon extended to connect with the turntable, just visible in the foreground.   *R. Brinton Collection*

Isle of Wight Railway
General Manager's Office
Ryde
June 24th 1867
R. Hicks Esq.

My dear Sir,
    I am adding three trains to the time table for July, this will give 14 trains each way per day which is two trains each way per day in addition to our last July's table, and which Mr Fowler agrees with me will afford an ample service. It will necessitate our keeping three Engines in Steam, but I will so arrange that should one of them be crippled the service can be worked by two.
        Yours truly,
        (Signed) Jos. Bourne

Clearly the locomotive situation left little margin for failure and, despite the financial position, a fourth locomotive was purchased in time for the 1868 summer season. Additional platforms were constructed at Ryde and Ventnor so that a train could depart after another had arrived, or to permit the dispatch of two trains consecutively. Timetables continued to publicise a service that could be maintained by two trains working from Ryde - additional trains ran unadvertised. The majority of income came from passenger traffic and this naturally took priority. It soon became regular practice to work goods trains through the night in order to free the day for passenger services. Goods traffic was never sufficient to make much difference between profit and loss in a year but it was very important to the economy of the Island. Coal came from Brading Quay to station yards where local merchants rented small stores. To satisfy the demands of the rapidly growing resorts building materials were carried, particularly timber and Welsh slate imported at Brading or ballast, stone, brick and cement from several small quarries, brick and cement works situated near the railway (George Young said his business manufactured 1½ million bricks in 1868). The provision of water, sewerage and gas supply systems demanded more supplies. Other traffic passed to and from a timber yard on land adjacent to Sandown station leased from the IWR and following the construction of a gas works at Shanklin. The Gas Company built a works in Landguard Manor Road, west of the railway on land provided, after some hesitation, by Major Atherley; the IWR refused to lay a siding when the gas company declined to pay for its installation, so coal supplies had to be carted from the station. There were also the thousand and one items that any self-respecting Victorian house or business might need - the railway carried them all.

    Mention should be made of the staff employed by the company to work its trains. We have already seen that the appointment of a General Manager did not go smoothly, but these difficulties were soon overcome. Capt. Huish had the task of recruiting other employees for the opening of the railway to Shanklin in 1864. A summary of the numbers and wages of those in post when passenger services began is on page 58. Each station master had responsibility for his staff and for the safety of arriving and departing trains. Naturally a good number were based at Ryde, but the existence of only a station master at Brading was surprising; the railway soon took on a boy assistant. The two enginemen and firemen reflected the requirement for two trains, whilst the differing pay of cleaners indicated the pecking order when cover was needed for absences and emergencies. The large number of permanent way men emphasised the amount of work necessary to keep track and earthworks in good condition. The solitary fitter must have had his work cut out! By way of comparison it should be noted that an agricultural labourer then earned between 7s. and 12s. a week and the rent of a cottage might be two guineas a year. There was no mention of working hours but it is fair to say that an employee would be expected to work whenever required - long hours, seven days a week and no holidays were the norm. Messrs Bourne and Hicks each received two or three weeks' leave of absence annually at the company's convenience - they were the exception.

    Employees generally received small increments in their pay at regular intervals. Within a short time the station master at Ryde gained an increase in lieu of rent, whilst his booking clerk was awarded 2s. per week on account, presumably, of an increased workload - soon afterwards Ryde's station master was dismissed for 'intemperance'. The chief officers received the greatest pay increases. In December 1866, during the midst of a financial crisis, Joseph Bourne persuaded the IWR Board to increase his salary from £250 per year to £400 backdated to the previous October. In an agreement that could be terminated at six months notice on either side he received a further £50 per annum for every ½ per cent of ordinary dividend over 3 per cent (he had to wait a few years to benefit from this). Within a month the Board awarded Robert Hicks, the Secretary and Accountant, an increase of £50 per annum backdated to 1st October. He had already received an increase when the railway opened to £200 per annum, plus £100 in shares for past services. Both these individuals were paid in quarterly instalments but other employees received their pay fortnightly. Other wage rates discussed by the Board included those of Mr Topham, the General Manager's assistant and audit clerk. His requests for a pay rise were repeatedly deferred throughout 1867; he finally gained an increase from £120 to £150 a year commencing 1st January, 1868 but died later that year - the Secretary took on the audit work and presumably Joseph Bourne then had to do without an assistant.

Naturally the railway was not blessed with infallible employees and in the early years had its share of insubordinate porters, careless signalmen and accident-prone enginemen. Here are a few details from staff records:

S.B. was probably the gentleman known to locals as 'Hellfire Jack'! He joined the railway on 14th August, 1864 as an engine driver at 7s. per day and inevitably incurred a number of fines during his short career. On 24th June, 1865 he was fined 2s. 6d. for running into Ryde station too fast and damaging the stop block. On 30th June 6d. was deducted for using a daily return for a memo. On 19th August he neglected to wash out his engine and received a fine of 2s. 6d. On 23rd August the Manager imposed a fine of 10s. for being absent from the stations thus delaying the departure of his train. On 3rd March, 1866 he again damaged the stop block at Ryde station and received a fine of 20s., later reduced to 10s. There were further fines of 2s. 6d. and 5s. on 19th August and 1st September respectively; this must have been the last straw as he left the company's service the following month.

W.W. joined the IWR on 1st April, 1865 as a cleaner on a wage of 3s. per day, but was promoted on 2nd September, 1865 to fireman at 3s. 3d. per day and within months to engineman at 4s. 6d. per day. On 28th April, 1866 he received a fine of 2s. 6d. for leaving his engine at Sandown to get beer. More seriously, the Manager demoted him to labourer on 20th January, 1870 for tying down the safety valve of his engine! The following December he reverted to the position of engineman and maintained an unblemished record in the company's service until his death in October 1880.

Neglect was not the exclusive preserve of locomotive men; W.P. joined the IWR on 14th August, 1864 as a signalman on a wage of 12s. rising to 15s. per week. On 2nd September, 1865 he received a fine of 2s. for failing to put a special train board on a train and for not cleaning the carriage windows - obviously the signalling duties were not onerous. A further fine of 1s. 6d. followed for not attending to his signals at Ryde station and during 1866 there were five more fines varying from 1s. to 5s. on each occasion. He left the IWR in June 1869.

Finally a bad start to a career: A.S. joined the railway on 1st May, 1865 as a greaser on a wage of 3s. a day. That month he was fined 30s. 6d., being half the cost of a carriage door broken during shunting.

The Manager had day-to-day responsibility for the railway and reported regularly to the Chairman and Capt. Huish - a traffic committee also existed for a time. Returns to the Board of Trade indicated that the number of passengers increased steadily during the 1860s. However, the working expenses were somewhat inflated as certain payments should strictly have been classed as capital expenditure. The Minute book for 10th July, 1866 contained a typical explanation of the position for the previous half year (note the lack of punctuation in the text!):

Actual Balance Sheet of the Half year - shewing a gross receipt of £4,338 against £3,856 in the corresponding half year and an Expenditure of £2,712, against £2,037 in the corresponding period was submitted by the Manager and examined.

From this Statement it appears that the net profit on the half year is £1388.11.10 against £1614.1.1 in 1865 . . . while the net profit is £225 only less than in the corresponding half year the Expenditure on Permanent Way and removal of Slips the whole of which has been charged against Revenue is £534 more and there is also an additional charge included against Revenue for replacing axle box covers of over £100. Under these circumstances, and looking to the extraordinary bad weather with which the Company had to contend in the earlier part of the year, the Committee cannot but regard the Accounts as satisfactory and creditable to the Manager.

| Year ending 31st Dec. | Passenger traffic Numbers carried | | | Season tickets | Goods traffic | | Gross receipts | | Working expenses | % of receipts |
	First	Second	Third		Minerals tons	General tons	Passengers £	Goods £	£	
1864	15,203	74,011	2,410	10	1,324	172	3,365	212	1,828	n/k
1865	40,378	200,208	12,232	37	13,695	2,463	9,159	1,146	4,802	47
1866	47,188	220,575	13,719	51	8,477	5,867	11,108	1,231	6,823	55
1867	57,147	309,560	18,407	87	19,145	n/k	16,226	1,665	18,551	103
1868	no return made									
1869	58,311	309,015	26,667	-	13,983	17,774	16,607	3,406	13,097	65
1870	72,200	302,715	26,920	-	16,254	13,177	17,477	3,349	13,076	63

The figure for working expenses in 1867 was inflated by legal costs of £1,098 and 'Miscellaneous' expenses of £9,274.

Captain Mark Huish died at the age of 58 on 18th January, 1867. He was buried near his home at Bonchurch, away from the railway that had become such a part of his life. The Minutes for 29th January contained the following tribute:

> The Board cannot proceed to business at this Meeting without recording their deep sense of the irreparable loss which the Company has sustained in the lamented and premature death of Captn Huish whose experience in Railway matters, and habits of business, rendered his services invaluable to this Company.

> **Resolved**

> That the Secretary be directed to forward a copy of this resolution to Mrs Huish and to express the condolence and sympathy of the Board for the irreparable loss which she in common with this Company and the Public has sustained.

The local newspapers faithfully recorded his death and printed detailed obituaries about a man who had done so much to get the railway built. For all his disagreements with others he was much respected in the Island for his charitable good works.* Major Atherley, who had been caught up in the railway's financial problems (see Chapter Seven), resigned. To fill the vacancies Alexander Beattie MD and Thomas Norton, both Directors of the South Eastern Railway, were invited onto the Board. In 1869 James Simpson, already a sick man, retired as Chairman and died the following year. His place as Chairman was taken by Alexander Beattie, and Joseph Bravo eventually became his deputy. Later that year Albert Ricardo, Chairman of Warrant Finance Company, joined the IWR Board.

In this chapter we saw something of the manner in which the railway served its public during its early years. In the next chapters we see how aspirations to be the Island's premier railway and accumulating financial problems affected the company.

---

* Margaret Huish's memorial to her husband can still be seen close to their home in Bonchurch. Near the station in Mitchell Avenue is Huish Terrace commenced by the Captain in 1867. His previous career as a railway manager was largely unknown to most Islanders prior to his death.

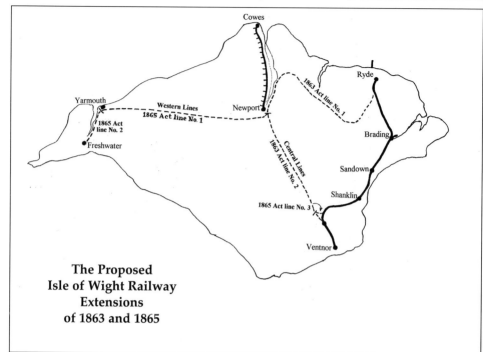

The Proposed
Isle of Wight Railway
Extensions
of 1863 and 1865

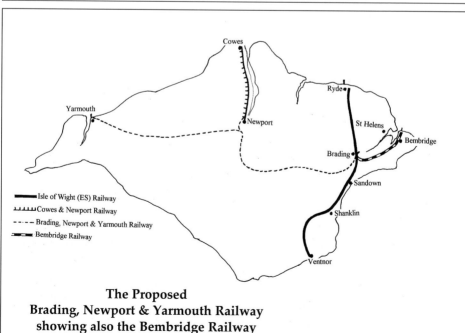

The Proposed
Brading, Newport & Yarmouth Railway
showing also the Bembridge Railway

Chapter Six

Grand Ideas - Extending the Railway

It was clearly in the minds of some of the promoters and Directors that the Isle of Wight (Eastern Section) Railway would be the first in a network of railways throughout the Island. Four separate Acts of Parliament were eventually obtained:

1. The 1860 Act - the Eastern Section from Melville Street Ryde to Ventnor with branches to Brading Quay and a pier at Sandown Bay
2. The 1863 Act - a Central Lines scheme from the IWES at Smallbrook to Newport and thence south to join the IWES near Wroxall
3. An 1865 Act - the Western Lines from Newport to Yarmouth and Freshwater
4. A second 1865 Act - powers to operate steam vessels to and from the Isle of Wight

Only the Eastern Section came to be built albeit excluding part of the line at Ryde and the branch to Sandown Bay. Even before the IWR secured its Act of Incorporation it was obvious that the Cowes & Newport and Isle of Wight (Eastern Section) railways would need to be connected. Unfortunately, the attitude of the two companies to each other resulted in a gulf that proved to be somewhat greater than the seven to twelve miles that such a railway might run. Several witnesses for and against the 1860 IWES and CNR Bills gave evidence to Parliament that the promoters should jointly promote lines in the Isle of Wight. A committee with representatives from both companies met on several occasions during 1860 but without any positive result. When later asked if the committee came to any conclusions Mr Pring, a Newport coal merchant, bluntly responded: 'Yes but it went off for I believe the Lawyers tried hard to work one against the other and the Engineers to work one against the other and it went to the dogs'.

The Eastern Section Bills of 1859 and 1860 included proposals for a branch railway from Ryde to Newport but on each occasion objections from the CNR and local authorities led to their rejection. For the 1861 Parliamentary session, there were two Bills - an IWES proposal for a branch from Sandown to Newport and a repeat of the CNR Extensions Bill for railways to Ventnor and Ryde. Faced with more expense, the IWES Board decided on 1st January, 1861 not to proceed with their Bill; the same fate awaited the CNR Bill. Later that year James Simpson succeeded in negotiating a deferment of the Isle of Wight Valley Junction Railway; it would have run from a point between Brading and Sandown to Newport. He was not so successful with the Bill for the Newport & Ryde Direct Railway that was placed before the 1862 session of Parliament. When it went before a committee of the House of Commons, counsel for the IWES gained an admission that the Newport & Ryde was a 'contractors line', a railway to be built and then offered for sale at a profit. The committee rejected the Bill but warned the two Island companies that: '. . . Railway communication between Newport and Ryde is desirable and that if the existing Companies do not come to some arrangement for effecting that purpose they will lose all right to oppose future schemes . . .'

On 4th November, 1862, the IWES Board decided to proceed with a Bill in the next Parliamentary session. It proposed a change of name to 'The Isle of Wight Railway Company' (the title had some kudos with the public) and the following:

1. A tramway from the authorised terminus of the railway at Melville Street, Ryde to the south end of Ryde Pier, a length of 35 chains - this time it ran down the centre of the Esplanade and curved to connect with the pier tramway
2. Railway No. 1, from a junction with the IWES at Smallbrook to near High Street, Newport (actually near the road from Newport to Barton's village about 100 yards east of the bridge across the River Medina), a distance of 7 miles 71 chains
3. Railway No. 2, continuing from an end-on junction with railway 1 to join the IWES near Wroxall, 7 miles 12 chains

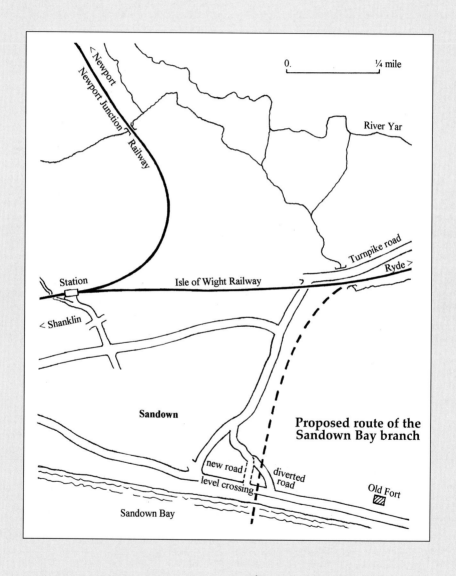

Proposed route of the Sandown Bay branch

4. Railway No. 3, leaving railway 1 near Newport Gas Works to join the CNR close to its Newport terminus. Just 23 chains long, it crossed the river some 440 ft below the existing river bridge and quay on a bridge with a 15 ft headway and an opening span 30 ft. wide

Called the Central Lines, the railways were financed by capital that would earn profits only from those lines. The Bill proposed working agreements with the CNR to build, maintain and use its railways, and with the Ryde Commissioners, Ryde Pier Company, Isle of Wight Ferry Company, and Stokes Bay Railway.

The inclusion in the Central Lines Bill of a tramway at Ryde followed discussions between the Ryde Commissioners and Capt. Huish, George Young and John Fowler. On 23rd December, 1862, in the hope of gaining the acquiescence of the Commissioners, the IWES Board resolved to proceed with the purchase of land at Ryde for the road and carry out their obligations set out in the 1860 Act. The Ryde Commissioners had been stung by criticisms that they failed to prevent construction of objectionable quays by the Isle of Wight Ferry Company and were determined not to further despoil the town; they petitioned Parliament in opposition to the tramway. There followed more negotiations, and a hearing in front of a committee of the House of Lords' before the company gave way and presented a revised Bill, minus the tramway. Suitably chastised, the Board decided on 12th March, 1863 to terminate the railway at St Johns Road. After receiving correspondence from the Ryde Commissioners, Robert Hicks, the Secretary, wrote in October to explain that the railway had no legal powers to compel others to sell it land to form a road approach to the railway station at Melville Street. Additionally, the Board had since decided not to build the station and did not consider the road necessary either! This decision did nothing to endear the IWR to the Ryde Commissioners and it was just as well that further attempts to build a rail link could be left to others.

Initially the IWES wished to promote the Central lines (then called the Isle of Wight Central Railway) jointly with the CNR and share costs. But in December 1862 the CNR refused and insisted that the Ryde to Newport line must not be opened before the others; it also reserved the right to withdraw support whenever it wished! Later the CNR petitioned Parliament in opposition to the Bill, as did the local authority at Newport. In deference to their objections the IWES deleted the branch to the CNR, and the remainder of the Bill became law on 28th July, 1863.

The Act authorised the appointment of two additional Directors and separate capital of £180,000 in £10 ordinary shares and £60,000 in debentures for the Central Lines; three years were allowed for compulsory purchase of land and five years for completion. The change of name took effect from 1st January, 1864. A further £25,000 in preference shares and £8,300 in loans could be raised for the Eastern Section line, but £3,000 had to be found to fund preliminary expenses for the extensions. A clause in the Act committed the company to open the Newport to Wroxall line within one year of that from Ryde to Newport, or pay the CNR a penalty of £50 per week. The IWES Board gained some solace from the knowledge that the CNR would have to obtain its own Act for a branch line between the two railways. This they achieved in the following Parliamentary session.

In 1864 another Bill became law. The Bembridge Railway, Tramway & Pier Act created a company with powers to build a railway from Brading along the south bank of Brading Haven to a pier at Bembridge. At an IWR shareholders' meeting a few days later Capt. Huish linked the Bembridge Railway with the problems at Ryde by claiming that passengers could be landed at Bembridge and transferred direct to the train - the IWR had been given running powers. He claimed '. . . the little line in question would be of essential service to the IWR'. The whole scheme was later abandoned.

At Ryde the stalemate reached in 1863 lingered on. In September 1864 the IWR Board repeated its desire for a railway north of St Johns Road, but negotiations with the Ryde Commissioners fell on stony ground. Despite this the Ryde Pier Company and the Isle of Wight Ferry Company each promoted Bills for tramways between their respective piers and the intended railway terminus at Melville Street. In response to a letter from the RPC, the IWR Board held a special meeting on 12th January, 1865 to consider the competing schemes.

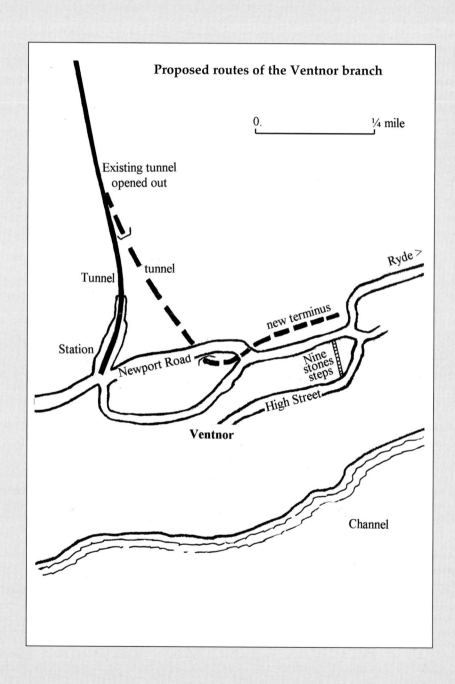

Proposed routes of the Ventnor branch

Letters from John Fowler and Capt. Huish expressed the opinion that tramways would be a waste of money and preferred a railway connecting the IWR with the steamers; John Fowler actually suggested fares that might be charged for each passenger. All this assumed that the RPC and IWFC would amalgamate their undertakings and build a railway along an extended and adapted pier in partnership with the IWR. Events did not go quite as Capt. Huish desired as the RPC, with George Young in the Chairman's seat, gained approval for its tramway. Meanwhile the IWFC became insolvent and its liquidators sold out to the pier company. There matters rested for the remainder of 1865.

For the next session of Parliament, a number of individuals promoted a Bill to create the Ryde Station Company. It would have run from the IWR at St Johns Road to a central station near the Castle before crossing the Esplanade to run alongside, and as an extension of, Victoria Pier. The IWR could ill afford to oppose the Bill and negotiated with Thomas Webster, who acted on behalf of the promoters, the insertion of clauses protecting the IWR's interests and granting running powers over the railway. However, the station company proved incapable of raising the necessary capital, and after more delays the RPC obtained an Act for an extension of its horse tramway the whole distance to St Johns Road; it opened in 1871. The IWR contributed half the Parliamentary costs and had an option to become a joint owner of the tramway; although the IWR Board called a meeting to sanction the purchase just two shareholders turned up!

Powers for construction of the Central Lines had been obtained in anticipation of the early completion of the Eastern Section. When this proved impossible the Board wisely deferred any work. This did not prevent the IWR from promoting more Bills in the Autumn of 1864. Following a failure to reach working agreements with the ferry companies, a Bill appeared proposing to raise an additional £20,000 in shares and £6,600 in loans as separate capital to finance the provision and working of steam vessels on routes connecting Cowes, Ryde, Bembridge and the mainland as far east as Brighton. The Board of Trade managed to stop attempts to build such quays, jetties, etc. as 'the Company may think', but otherwise the Bill encountered virtually no opposition and became law. Despite having spent sizeable sums in obtaining the Act there was no evidence that the matter was taken any further; the ferry companies were more willing to co-operate and by then the IWR had financial problems. Even so the powers remained in force until the company ceased to exist in 1923.

The Isle of Wight Railway No. 1 Bill applied for powers to raise the following capital:

1. £65,000 in shares and £25,000 in loans for the purchase of the CNR. The Board of Trade lodged an objection as the proposed capital exceeded that held by the CNR.
2. £75,000 in shares and £25,000 in loans for the Eastern Section line from Ryde to Ventnor
3. £20,000 in shares and £6,300 in loans for the Central Lines extensions
4. £160,000 in shares and £53,000 in loans for the 'Western Lines' that this Bill was also to authorise

Railways proposed in the Bill were as follows:

1. The Western Lines. From a junction with the Central Lines extension south of Newport, a line ran west to Yarmouth before continuing across the River Yar to a terminus in Pound Green Road west of Freshwater Bay, a total length of 11 miles 78 chains.
2. A Ventnor extension from a junction in a cutting north of Ventnor tunnel, through a separate 450 yds-long tunnel to St Boniface Terrace. Just 48 chains long, it was intended to be part of the Eastern Section.
3. The third part of a triangle of lines linking the Eastern Section with the Central Lines at Wroxall. Financially, it was part of the Central Lines.

The IWR Minutes failed to indicate who were the principal advocates of the Western lines. Whilst nominally an IWR scheme, an entry implied that the IWR Board would pay preliminary expenses but expected others to put up capital for the remainder of the works. Sir

Charles Fox surveyed the route but when payment was not forthcoming he issued a writ against the IWR; in January 1867 he received a mortgage on the Eastern Section's surplus land as security. The company paid off the debt in 1871.

The Ventnor extension had been in the minds of the Directors for several years. They had decided as long ago as 1860 to extend the railway to a point known locally as the Nine Stones but nothing was done at the time. In January 1865, following the appearance of proposals for tramways within the town, the IWR called a public meeting to gauge support for an extension to St Boniface Terrace. One of the Directors, Alexander More, maintained that there were already heavy financial commitments and this line would cost another £25,000. He produced a petition from landowners who opposed the line, but it was joined by two others signed by residents who supported it! Capt. Huish maintained that the proposed extension would not destroy more than two cottages and would greatly increase the value of property in the district, giving very great facilities to residents. The great difficulty was to get enterprising builders to erect suitable houses in Ventnor and the neighbourhood to make it a second Brighton! In May 1865 the IWR Board announced their intention to give up the extension in deference to the wishes of the townspeople. More likely, it had no hope of raising the necessary money. If built, the line would have emerged from a separate tunnel roughly where Huish Terrace is today, passed under Newport Road (now Mitchell Avenue) and turned 90 degrees to the east, before crossing the road a second time to reach a terminus behind St Boniface Road.

In opposition to the Central and Western Lines was a Bill promoted by Sir Charles Fox for the Brading, Newport & Yarmouth Railway; he believed that a railway could be built more cheaply that the IWR scheme. The Bill proposed to raise £170,000 in shares and £56,000 in loans for a railway from the 'Bembridge Railway Junction' (70 yards south of the Brading station) to Newport and Yarmouth, where a terminus was planned adjacent to a pier. There would also have been a tramway at Yarmouth, a branch around the north-west edge of Newport to join the CNR near its station and another from a junction near Adgestone to Sandown Pier. This was not the pier proposed by the IWES in 1860 but a structure to be built by the Sandown Pier Company; the pier company's Chairman was Thomas Willis Fleming and Directors included Francis Atherley and Alexander More.

A Lords' committee considered the Bills on 8th and 9th May, 1865. Witnesses in support of the IWR Bill claimed that the IWR offered the best chance for the creation of a network of railways in the Island managed by one company. The Brading Bill generated much opposition from Yarmouth residents who objected to the effects of the railway and tramway on the town - a Lords' committee rejected the Brading Bill in favour of the IWR proposals.

The Isle of Wight Railway (Extensions) Act authorised the construction of the third leg of the triangle at Wroxall and the lines from Newport to Yarmouth and Freshwater. Additional capital consisted of £39,000 in ordinary or preference shares and loans of £13,000 for the Eastern Section, and the desired capital for the Central and Western Lines. The Board could be increased by the addition of two Directors to oversee Western Lines matters - there were no powers to purchase the CNR.

Although there had been a brief mention of the Central Lines in December 1864, the Minutes recorded nothing positive until August 1865 when the Board decided to appoint four additional Directors for the Central and Western Lines, as authorised in the Acts of 1863 and 1865. John Fowler was asked to state his terms for becoming the Central Lines' Engineer and various expenses, mainly on Parliamentary matters, were paid from the IWR capital account but attributed to Central or Western Lines costs. The Board instructed solicitors to begin negotiations with landowners but not to serve any notices of compulsory purchase. In October two proposed land purchases were referred to arbitration and George Young agreed to sell a plot at Wroxall. Directors later denied a formal arrangement had been made with Henry Pinnock for land near Whippingham; this would have prevented the abandonment of the line. On 2nd January, 1866 Capt. Huish recommended the purchase of land and construction of bridges and culverts for a single track, except at stations; several thousand pounds would be saved and he believed a single line would have sufficient capacity for the traffic. The Board approved the issue of a Prospectus for the Central Lines later that month (it seems not to have been issued), but this decision may have been to counter the efforts of other promoters who placed a Bill before Parliament for a railway between Sandown and Newport; the IWR petitioned in opposition and the House of Lords threw out the Bill.

In their next report to shareholders the Directors reported negotiations for the construction of the line from Ryde to Newport and predicted that 'this valuable route for passengers and general traffic may be completed in twelve months after it is commenced'. Shareholders passed resolutions at a meeting in February 1866 appointing William McAndrew and Joseph Bravo as the Directors for the Central Lines. In the following July, with some dissent from George Young, Thomas Webster and John Bailey Denton joined the Board as Directors of the Western Lines. Even so the Minutes remained silent as regards any progress on the extensions throughout the spring and summer of 1866 - given the problems in funding the line to Ventnor this was hardly surprising.

Compulsory purchase powers granted for the purchase of land in the 1863 Act expired at the end of 1866. On 23rd October, the Board authorised the Chairman, George Young and Capt. Huish to discuss the matter with the CNR as the extensions were 'of deep interest' to them. George Young approached local landowners for support and, sufficiently encouraged, persuaded the IWR Board to seek to revive powers for the Central Lines. James Simpson emphasised that landowners and others with an interest in the Ryde to Newport line had to guarantee £25,000 in land and shares. Despite Mr Young's efforts, he raised only £5,000 to £6,000 from Newport residents and the powers were struck out by a committee of the House of Lords. This served only to make matters worse as the IWR had no compulsory purchase powers, nor could it abandon the lines and recover money that the Chairman and deputy Chairman (James Simpson and Major Francis Atherley) had pledged as a Bond (guarantee) to the Treasury:

> Railways in the 1860 Act, date of Bond 18th January, 1860 - £20,000
> Railways in the 1863 Act, date of Bond 22nd December, 1863 - £28,000
> Railways in the 1865 Act, date of Bond 25th January, 1866 - £27,840

In addition the IWR had been required to place 8 per cent of the proposed capital in the custody of the Court of Chancery. The Treasury would cancel a Bond when the lines opened or after 50 per cent of capital had been spent, but was forfeit if there was no satisfactory progress within five years. The Treasury cancelled the first Bond following the completion of the line from Ryde to Ventnor in 1866; an attempt to recover the remainder began in May 1867 when George Porter inserted clauses abandoning the Central and Western Lines in the company's Bill, then before Parliament. The CNR were appraised of the position and told the IWR would not oppose a Ryde to Newport line if they chose to promote it! Later that month it became clear that changes to the Bill at that stage would jeopardise its progress, and, fearing the loss of the money-raising powers, the company had to stand aside and let it become law. Fortunately the Abandonment of Railways Act 1850 empowered the Board of Trade to authorise abandonment without the need for a special Act. In a letter to the Board of Trade, George Porter wrote:

> ... no part of the Capital of £200,000 and £160,000 authorised in the Acts of 1863 and 1865 for the construction of the 'Central' and 'Western' Lines have been subscribed, but the Chairman and Deputy Chairman of the Company have given Bonds to the Treasury for payment of the deposits for both these lines and from which Bonds they are desirous of being released.

On 28th April, 1868 the Board of Trade sanctioned an application to abandon the Central and Western Lines. That ended the dream of building a rail system throughout the Isle of Wight. As we shall see later, the Directors had opportunities to operate other lines but never again would the IWR attempt to extend its own railway.

Isle of Wight (Eastern Section) Railway Company

Deposit of £1 0s. 0d. per Share

First Call of £2 0s. 0d. per share

NOTICE IS HEREBY GIVEN that in pursuance of a resolution of the Board of Directors, the proprietors of shares in the Company are hereby required to pay a call of two pounds per share on their respective shares, on or before the 17th day of November next, either to the Company's Bankers, Messrs Williams, Deacon and Co., Birchin Lane, London, or to the Treasurer of the Company, Mr Chas E. Reed, 4 Victoria Street, Westminster. Shareholders who have not paid the Deposit of £1 per share on their shares, are also required to pay such deposit with the above call.

Dated this eleventh day of October, 1860.
By order,

CHARLES MORRISON,
Secretary

The Castle, Ryde, Isle of Wight.

Extract from the Balance Sheet to 30th June 1864

Receipts	£	s.	d.	Payments	£	s.	d.
To Amount received on Shares	80,387	10	0	By Preliminary, Parliamentary and Legal Expenses	10,518	17	8
To Debentures	40,750	0	0	By Surveying & Engineering	6,524	18	5
To Temporary Loans	10,000	0	0	By Land and Compensation	29,956	11	11
				By Works	74,095	0	0
				By Directors'& Auditors Remuneration	1,400	0	0
				By Interest	4,294	18	10
				By Debenture interest	463	0	7
				By Brokerage, Commission, Printing, Stationery, Rent, Advertising etc.	2,029	6	6
				Balance - viz. cash at bank	868	6	11

Chapter Seven

Mainly Financial

By the 1860s people had become reluctant to invest in railway schemes for the Isle of Wight after losing money when undertakings failed. The IWES was seen as having no better prospects for success than those that had gone before. However, the promoters tempted sufficient investors to subscribe to the undertaking and this satisfied Parliament that the company had sufficient financial support. Against all the odds, the IWES gained its Act of Incorporation and became an established railway company.

The original investors consisted principally of the Directors and their friends in London. The company's Ventnor solicitor, Charles Fisher, persuaded a few Island residents to buy shares but most held only a single £10 share and none subscribed more than £100. As the promoters were quite unable to raise all the necessary £125,000 capital themselves, the search began for more investors.

The costs associated with gaining Parliamentary sanction were huge and significant debts had built up by the time the Bill became law. A Prospectus was issued in August 1860 inviting subscriptions for shares, and on 10th November, 1860 the *Isle of Wight Observer* carried a notice announcing the first call of £2 per share from shareholders in order to pay initial expenses; the first shares were issued in the following January. Entries in the Minute book recorded a breakdown of income and expenditure for the six months ending 30th June, 1861. To balance expenditure of over £8,000, £4,057 had been received from investors and a 'temporary loan' included £3,000 borrowed from Hampshire Bank.

In an editorial on 21st June, 1862 the *Isle of Wight Observer* commented that the IWES offered the best prospect of paying a dividend, but the Islanders as a whole had been indifferent to invitations to take shares in the undertaking. In November a shortage of capital forced the Board to seek a further loan to pay immediate debts. Prompted by George Young, money was borrowed from City Bank, of which he was a Director; this was in addition to the loan from Hampshire Bank.

The Board's report to a shareholders' meeting on 24th February gave an optimistic forecast of the railway's potential earnings. During the summer months there were eight journeys per day by horse-drawn coaches, plus three vans of luggage to and from Ryde and Ventnor. Between Ryde and Sandown there were a further six coaches or omnibuses - these figures did not include wagons carrying heavier goods and coal. The Board confidently predicted that annual earnings of the line would be £28,920, which after deduction of 50 per cent for working expenses, left a profit of £14,460 per annum; they did not expect the cost of land to exceed £35,000. This information was given wide publicity so that potential investors living on the mainland would be tempted to buy shares. The IWES raised nearly £100,000 in the next 18 months, much to the credit of Capt. Huish who knew how to present a company in the best possible light.

With most of the ordinary share capital issued, the IWR could borrow a further £41,600 by the issue of interest bearing debentures for fixed periods of, say, three years. The shareholders gave assent to their issue at the next meeting on 7th August, 1863. Powers were obtained in the Central Lines Act to raise an additional £25,000 Eastern Section capital by issuing preference shares paying interest at 5 per cent per annum and to borrow an additional £8,300; the preference shares counted before ordinary shares if and when a dividend could be paid. By then some Directors were making loans to pay the contractor. The Chairman, James Simpson, personally provided sizeable sums for which he received an allotment of shares; in June 1864 he found £4,000. Others did work for which they received shares in lieu of cash: in October 1864 the Board gave Capt. Huish £250 in 25 paid up shares and A. F. Livesay and R. J. H. Saunders each received 25 shares for surveying. Another regular recipient was one of the company's solicitors, George Porter, because of his unending legal expenses. On 20th April the Board gave orders that a further call of £2 per share be made - £9 a share had then been called up. A balance sheet for the six months ending 30th June, 1864 showed the position shortly before the opening of the line to Shanklin. Almost £30,000 had been expended on land and over £74,000 paid to the contractor in a mixture of cash and shares; temporary loans stood at £10,000. The Board later authorised the issue of a circular to shareholders inviting their subscription for preference shares - their necessity was attributed to inheritance of considerable Parliamentary and other expenses, including additional station accommodation.

For public consumption, details of income conveniently appeared in the press. Although 'the summer traffic was altogether lost through the delay in opening', the railway carried 33,552 passengers in the period ending 19th September and parcels alone brought in £1,243 17s. 8d. It was not mentioned that this made little impression on the debts and, of course, staff and other running costs had to be paid. In October visitors to the Island 'nearly evaporated' whilst November was one of the 'flattest months' - this did not prevent optimistic talk of the next year's profits. In December 1864, James Simpson and Francis Atherley loaned £6,000 to pay the contractor. The revenue account generated a profit, albeit a small one, but the debenture interest could only be paid by securing a six-month loan of £2,000 from City Bank.

Despite the Board's efforts, the IWR owed the contractor a considerable amount. Henry Bond took the company to court in January 1865 for additional work incurred in constructing the stations at Ryde, Brading, Sandown and Shanklin. He also objected to being charged freightage over the line at the same rate as others. On the other hand the Engineer, John Fowler, and Capt. Huish were vocal in criticising the progress of the works at Wroxall. This merely soured relations between the contractor and the company.

As 1865 dragged on Henry Bond found himself in financial difficulties. He had problems in selling on the shares received in payment, and an approach to the IWR Board for help in placing shares on the Stock Exchange List met with little success. Matters were no better for the company as it had borrowed substantial sums from bankers, and the position concerning the remaining capital was somewhat complicated. Under a Deed of Covenant with City Bank, the Directors each undertook to find subscribers for 300 ordinary shares, but by March 1865 only Capt. Huish had disposed of his allotment. Some preference shares were held as security for promissory notes given for loans from the bank, whilst the bank held other shares as security for more borrowings. At one point the Board attempted to consolidate the finances by negotiating a larger loan with City Bank to pay off that with Hampshire Bank!

With all its capital issued or pledged for loans, the IWR applied to Parliament for powers to raise additional capital. The Isle of Wight Railway (Extensions) Act, promoted for the Western Lines, authorised the issue of £39,000 in second preference shares and more debenture stock for the Eastern Section. At a sitting of the Lords' committee hearing evidence on the Extensions Bill, Henry Bond tried to register an objection because he considered the value of his shares would be reduced by the increase in capital - the IWR objected to his *locus standi* and the committee refused to hear him.

But it was too late for the contractor. On 16th May, 1865 two Directors of Warrant Finance Company attended an IWR Board meeting when a proposed agreement between the contractor and the finance company was discussed. A week later the Board were desperately seeking a loan from City Bank to pay the contractor and so prevent a stoppage of work. They failed on both counts.

A contract between the company and Henry Bond dated 1st December, 1862 placed him under an obligation to build the whole line to Ventnor for £126,000, reduced by £3,000 following the abandonment of the first 26 chains of railway at Ryde. By June 1865 he had supposedly completed most of the work but had received only £95,811 17s. 4d. in cash and shares leaving a balance of £30,188 2s. 8d. due to him. Henry Bond arranged to be paid off by the Warrant Finance Company, it taking possession of his plant and the obligation to build the line.

At the end of May the IWR Board met with representatives from the finance company when they concluded a fresh agreement for completion of the railway from Shanklin to

Ventnor. John Fowler and Mr Addison, engineers for the two parties, were left to agree the amount to be paid and time limits for completion of the contract. The IWR found some money for immediate payments and work recommenced under the control of a new contractor.

Warrant Finance Company had been formed in March 1864 as one of several investment companies that advanced money in exchange for shares and property. The financial upheavals of the 1860s, if not conducive to the raising of capital, gave ample scope for the acquisition of shares in railway companies throughout Britain. A significant holding of shares brought with it power and by 1869 the following railway companies had a Warrant Finance Company Director on their Board:

Brecon and Merthyr Tydfil Junction Railway Company - James Mann
Cambrian Railway Company - James Mann
Isle of Wight Railway Company - Joseph Bravo and Abraham De Pass
Neath and Brecon Railway Company - William McAndrew
Potteries, Shrewsbury and North Wales Railway Company - Joseph Bravo
Swansea Vale and Neath and Brecon Junction Railway Company - William McAndrew

At first Warrant Finance Company appeared to be something of a white knight as it continued to accept a mixture of shares and cash for work carried out. Within a short time, however, the price of this generosity became apparent. In August the finance company attempted to block the loan of £10,000 from City Bank and demanded four seats on the IWR Board, i.e. a majority. Naturally James Simpson wrote a letter of refusal. He did offer the four seats authorised in the Acts of 1863 and 1865 for the Central and Western Lines but they gave powers only to *advise* on matters relating the Eastern Section. Messrs McAndrew and Bravo were made Central Lines' Directors but they resigned as soon as their lack of control over the company's affairs became clear.

Throughout the remainder of the year the Board juggled with shares pledged with the bankers as security and then retrieved for issue either to investors or, more usually, in lieu of the many debts. Meanwhile the contractor made slow progress and in January 1866 the solicitor wrote to the finance company reminding it of the expiry time for completion of the contract. This met with a sharp response as the IWR was having difficulties in pledging or placing the remaining £24,000 preference shares to meet the contractor's instalment payments. Other shareholders were becoming concerned about the delays, and the Board only avoided the appointment of a Committee of Investigation in February by agreeing to fill the vacancies for two Central Lines' Directors.

As 1866 progressed the IWR Board became increasingly desperate. Here, more than any other time in the company's history, the Minute book hints at what faced the Board as they met, week after week, in smoke filled rooms wrestling with the overwhelming problems that engulfed them. The stress on individual Directors soon took its toll.

Despite having received £1,000 in overdue instalment payments for rolling stock in February, the Railway Carriage Company secured a judgement against the railway company; in March it had to be placated with a further £400 and a promise of further payments within weeks. George Porter, the solicitor, found £200 from his own pocket, the Board agreeing to pay him with interest as soon as the company could. To raise more money they gave instructions to sell surplus land at Brading Quay and some houses at Sandown by auction or private treaty; other money came from City Bank which agreed to increase its loan to the huge sum of £50,000. The finance company complained about delays in payment, but this time they were caused by the City Bank's reluctance to release shares because of the IWR's high level of indebtedness.

On 10th May, 1866 the finance house of Overend Gurney failed with liabilities of £10 million caused through dealing in unsound railway shares. The failure had a profound effect on railway investment throughout Britain. Railway company shares became virtually unsaleable overnight and those companies with over-extended capital were the worst affected. The crisis badly hit many individuals, including contractors working on new lines, and three railway companies actually became insolvent. Francis Player wrote another of his letters about the IWR to the railway press, part of which read:

> I know a few tradesmen here who have taken a £10 share as a business investment, but the bulk of the Shareholders seems a nonentity. Are contractors and finance Companies the holders, and shall we see a glut of the shares on the market when the line is finished?

Relations between the IWR Board and the finance company remained at a low ebb. William McAndrew criticised the state of the line from Ryde to Shanklin whilst the IWR, in turn, complained about workmanship on the remaining section to Ventnor - this proved justifiable when the Board of Trade inspector refused to sanction its opening. Warrant Finance Company claimed payments amounting to £7,600 for 'extras' and, in retaliation, the IWR claimed £6,215 for work not completed under the contract and damages. Meanwhile the finance company began to transfer some IWR shares to its Directors and employees. Soon afterwards a group of 'shareholders' inserted a notice in the *Isle of Wight Observer* calling for an extraordinary meeting. In a circular to shareholders the IWR Board wrote:

To the Proprietors of the Isle of Wight Railway Company
Mr James A. Mann, the Secretary of the Warrant Finance Company, having circulated to a number of the Shareholders a Statement containing misrepresentations of facts and figures, the Directors are reluctantly compelled to address the Proprietors and to request a full attendance at the Special General Meeting to be held on Friday the 8th June at 3 o'clock p.m. at 29 Great George Street Westminster.
They reserve any detailed reply to the Statements of Mr Mann until the Committee is appointed.
The Board have nothing to conceal and have no intention to resist inquiry. Their only object is a fair and impartial Committee and their reasons for mentioning this are as follows:-
The Requisition for the Meeting is signed by twenty-three Proprietors, twenty-two of whom are parties recently qualified by small parcels of Shares transferred from the Warrant Finance Company limited.
The Warrant Finance Company are the Contractors for the Works, and their object as avowed in writing is to obtain a majority of Seats at the Board.
The Warrant Finance Company were bound by deed to complete the Line to Ventnor by 1st January last. It is not yet finished and the present difficulties of the Company have mainly arisen from this circumstance.
Penalties to a considerable amount have been incurred by the Contractors by this default, and under such circumstances it cannot be for the interest of the one hundred and eleven Independent Shareholders in the Company that the Warrant Finance Company should compose a majority of the Board.
The Directors however do not desire to prevent the Warrant Finance Company being fairly represented on the Committee (and on the Board) but they desire that the Shareholders at large should have at least an equivalent representation and to the decision of a Committee so appointed, the Directors would pay every respect.
You are therefore requested to attend the Meeting on the 8th June in order to protect your Interests by securing the appointment of a fair Committee to represent all parties.
By order of the Directors
R. Hicks
Secretary

Company's Offices
4 Victoria Street, Westminster SW
Dated this 29th day of May 1866

Despite the Board's appeal, a majority of those attending the meeting at 29 Great George Street on 8th June, 1866 were employees of Warrant Finance Company. They passed a resolution setting up a Committee of Investigation chaired by William McAndrew - the other members were Messrs Bruce, Roberts, Norton and Russell Scott, most of whom had connections with the finance company. The committee interviewed the IWR's senior officers and prepared a report with financial accounts that differed significantly from those produced by the IWR Board. The main area of dispute was the manner in which the IWR Board had borrowed £50,000 from City Bank, as shares pledged as security were those issued to individual Directors but not paid for. Supporters of the finance company claimed the Directors themselves were liable for the debt.

On 31st August the half-yearly meeting of IWR shareholders took place at the Pier Hotel Ryde. Capt. Huish took the chair in place of James Simpson, who was ill, although professing that he himself was not in the best of health - the strain was beginning to tell! Sixty-two registered shareholders attended, far too many for the small room provided. The meeting began with a long wrangle between representatives of Warrant Finance Company and the Chairman over the bona fides of certain individuals and their right to speak and vote at the meeting. The shares transferred to the employees of the finance company had been struck off the share register and despite a heated discussion the Chairman and other shareholders refused to reinstate them. The meeting then adjourned to larger premises at the Victoria Rooms, where shareholders were presented with conflicting sets of accounts in the reports from the company and the Committee of Investigation. After much argument the meeting was adjourned so that the IWR Board could prepare a response to the committee's report.

The *Isle of Wight Times*, along with other local newspapers, reported the proceedings with much glee. They carried the accusation that Huish rendered incorrect financial statements and tried to deny Warrant Finance Company voting rights despite the fact it possessed almost 6,000 shares. Huish attempted to stop them from advancing money for shares by asserting the finance company had no right to hold IWR shares. Just to complicate the situation the contractor received payment in shares registered in the name of Warrant Finance Company. In addition the IWR was threatened with the Court of Chancery on the grounds it did not possess all the sureties given to the banks. The antagonists called another extraordinary meeting in London on 14th September, 1866 to consider the report of the Committee of Investigation, but only two representatives of the shareholders and three from Warrant Finance Company attended. They wanted to remove the existing IWR Directors and elect replacements from their numbers, but Mr Dovers, a solicitor, expressed the view that the meeting had been illegally convened so its proceedings and resolutions were null and void. This was hardly surprising as the IWR Board took no part, claiming that employees of Warrant Finance Company were trying to use the meeting to discredit them and gain control of the railway.

By October a number of court cases were under way - Mr McAndrew had taken action against Major Atherley and others, City Bank refused to advance more money and took Alexander More to court, whilst creditors took out actions against the company for an assortment of debts. There was a real possibility that a Receiver would be appointed and assets seized. In this climate the solicitor negotiated with representatives of Beyer, Peacock & Co. and the Railway Carriage Co. for them to become 'trustees for the protection of the Company's property'. They obtained judgements against the railway and during December two locomotives and two wagons were assigned to the Railway Carriage Company and hired back to the IWR. Within days the third locomotive, two carriages, office furniture and stores were assigned to Beyer, Peacock & Co. under the same arrangements. This prevented other creditors from seizing them.

Major Atherley was involved in several court cases and eventually took out two actions against the railway, probably to protect his own position. As deputy Chairman he had entered into various financial commitments on behalf of the railway and, although the Board indemnified him against any consequences, the IWR could not pay off the debts. He wrote a letter of resignation to James Simpson on 24th October that was put before the Board at its next meeting on 6th November. The Board accepted it 'with much regret, and beg to express their appreciation of the valuable services rendered by Major Atherley to the company since its formation'.

Equally, the IWR could neither pay the holders of debenture bonds their interest nor the capital when the bonds became due for repayment. Over a period of months the Minutes contained numerous requests for payment by debenture holders; the Board could only ask for an extension of the time and promise to meet the outstanding interest as soon as they were able. Even so some debenture bond holders took the company to court. Landowners also received nothing for property taken by the railway. Mr Griffiths, whose land at Ventnor had been occupied in 1862, issued a writ demanding £747 15s. 10d. for purchase, interest and costs; in the end he accepted a rent charge, an annual payment to be paid in perpetuity. Other court actions involved landowners along the abandoned railway to Melville Street, Ryde.

Following the death of Capt. Huish in early 1867 Alexander Beattie joined the Board. Mr Beattie was an experienced railway Director, having served as Chairman of the North London Railway and East and West India Docks Railway. He and James Simpson met with the Directors of Warrant Finance Company in February and March to hammer out an agreement between the two parties. An exchange of letters commenced with City Bank in the hope of stopping its court actions against the Directors. The railway's manager had the task of negotiating a fresh arrangement for payments to the Railway Carriage Company. During March Mr Bourne laid before the Board a proposed agreement together with an estimate of the railway's expected earnings each month during the coming year; there would be instalments in varying amounts according to the season of the year. Beyer, Peacock were given £2,700 preference shares as security in exchange for a similar arrangement in respect of the debt for the locomotives.

Meanwhile the next meeting of shareholders took place on 23rd February, 1867. Following the opening of the line to Ventnor the railway generated a healthy income, but this had been used to pay the immediate debts. The Directors 'lamented' that an agreement had not been concluded with Warrant Finance Company. Acceptance of the accounts could not be voted on and the meeting was adjourned to 30th May, 1867, when an agreement with the finance company was produced. The IWR and Warrant Finance Company shared costs of the Committee of Investigation, the latter receiving £5,000 in settlement of a £7,070 claim for extra work, whilst Messrs Simpson, Atherley, Young, Twynam and executors of the late Capt. Huish agreed to take up £28,280 in shares pledged to the bank. As a price for reaching the agreement two Directors from Warrant Finance Company joined the Board of the IWR; Messrs Twynam and More resigned in favour of Joseph Bravo and Abraham De Pass.

A number of shareholders voiced their contempt for the Board's actions. Thomas Webster was particular antagonistic towards George Young claiming that he and Alexander Beattie had links with the company's bankers to the detriment of the smaller shareholders; James Mann, the Warrant Finance Company Secretary, and George Young were also accused of being 'in league together'. In fact, George Young was one of the unsung heroes of the crisis; by 1868 City Bank, of which he was a Director, had loaned considerable sums and he personally possessed 12,000 shares, the largest shareholding of an individual in the company. One local resident later commented, with some truth, 'without George Young that line, I believe, would never have been made'.

On 12th August, 1867 Royal Assent was given to a Bill authorising a further increase in Eastern Section capital. Up to £50,000 ordinary or preference shares could be issued and £16,600 borrowed. Subject to the agreement of ⅔ of the ordinary shareholders, preferential shareholders had the right to vote at meetings; debenture stock paying up to 5 per cent per year could be issued that were not limited in length like the bonds they replaced. The company proposed to pay the six-monthly interest on the debenture stock by setting aside sums from weekly receipts in a trust account.

At a meeting on 11th June, 1867 the Board set up a sub-committee to report on the financial position. Abraham De Pass (as Chairman), Joseph Bravo, Thomas Norton and George Young met on several occasions during June. They drew up a list of creditors and prepared a circular letter asking them to accept preference shares or debentures in lieu of debts. A few claims, probably the more dubious, were referred to the solicitor.

The Board responded to demands for payment by offering a mixture of preference shares and debentures. Although many creditors accepted shares, the Railway Carriage Company insisted on its existing arrangements; after all, they received such preferential treatment that a £14,617 10s. 1d. debt had been reduced to £3,994 3s. 4d. by the end of 1868. By August the Board reported that overall, the company had raised almost £140,000 by the issue of shares and debentures during the previous six months. £28,000 had gone on the promotion of Bills before Parliament; land cost over £40,000 whilst construction costs exceeded £157,000.

Parliament watched the activities leading up to the financial upheavals of 1866 with some concern. A Select Committee sat between 1865 and 1867 and its recommendations prompted the passing of the Railway Companies Act of 1867. The Act prevented the seizure of rolling stock for debt and permitted companies to make arrangements with creditors, subject to the approval of shareholders. Even so, two debenture holders took proceedings against the IWR for unpaid debenture interest and in April 1868 the court appointed Joseph Bourne as Receiver. A further finance company Director, its Chairman Albert Ricardo, joined the Board in 1869 following the death of James Simpson; half the members of the Board had connections with the finance company, not a majority but almost so. This duality lasted for a number of years.

Meanwhile the Directors concentrated on reaching agreements with the banks and throughout 1868 the Board and City Bank continually exchanged letters - the bank insisted on cash payments of interest that the railway could not make. In exasperation City Bank recommenced action in December against the 'old' Directors but Alexander Beattie secured a further postponement. Two months later he set out the financial position in a lengthy letter to the bank. The IWR proposed to deposit a *Scheme of Arrangement* under the Railway Companies Act in the Court of Chancery, to convert £70,054 of unissued ordinary and preference shares and debenture stock into 'B' debenture stock paying interest at 5 per cent for issue to creditors, including the bank. The bank agreed to accept the debentures if they received £3,000 in cash owed by the late Mr Simpson and £3,500 by the late Capt. Huish - naturally this was refused.

The Board pressed ahead with its *Scheme of Arrangement* and later in the year secured the approval of shareholders at an extraordinary meeting. On 20th November, 1869 the Court of Chancery made an order confirming the *Scheme of Arrangement*. A special meeting of the Board took place on 17th December at the solicitor's office at 4 Victoria Street, Westminster, when Alexander Beattie and Joseph Bravo went through a list of claims for land purchase and other liabilities. Roughly 30 landowners were owed varying amounts largely for interest and legal costs. A few were granted a rent charge whilst others who owned land between St Johns Road and Melville Street at Ryde were content to cancel the purchase if their costs were paid. In addition, many landowners had expressed an interest in buying back surplus land; Joseph Bourne was instructed to make the necessary arrangements. City Bank was owed over £30,000, the National Provincial Bank almost £5,000, Beyer, Peacock a further £5,000 after deduction of £6,130 for which they held Preference shares, and the Railway Carriage Company £6,500 plus £1,375 10s. for additional rolling stock bought since the date of the original agreement. The Secretary dispatched letters to each holder of debenture bonds and debenture stock asking them to take 'A' debenture stock. Similar letters were sent to landowners and creditors offering 'B' debenture stock bearing interest at 5 per cent or, in the case of landowners, the option of receiving a rent charge paying 4 per cent, the latter to take precedence over 'B' stock in the payment of interest. Following an agreement with City Bank, in January 1870 the Board authorised the issue of £30,374 'B' debenture stock to the bank in exchange for 1,317 ordinary and 2,421 preference shares held as security. Soon afterwards the Board began considering the responses to the Secretary's letters and by the end of the year most claims had been settled. The debt to City Bank had been cut by 31st December, 1871 to £25,229 but the bank was owed interest of £2,421 2s. 6d. In response to yet another letter asking for interest payments, Alexander Beattie lamented its lack of co-operation and politely pointed out that if it was unwilling to accept IWR stock in lieu of interest there was no point

5. Break Power to Passenger Trains.—All Passenger Trains consisting of *eight or more* carriages, must have *two* Break Vans attached, one at each end, and such Trains must be worked by *two* Guards. When working *down* Trains, the Guard in charge, or Head Guard, will use the Break at end of Train, the Under Guard the Van next the Engine. On the *up* journey it will be the reverse, viz., the Head Guard will be next the Engine, and the Under Guard at the end of the Train. The Head Guard will give the signal to the Engineman, after having received one from the Under Guard and Station Master. The Head Guard will work the Luggage Van down to the Pier and back.

15. Special Engines and Trains.—The following is a copy of the Notice issued July 11th, 1871, in respect to the running of special engines and trains, and must be strictly carried out:—

" No engine or special train must be dispatched from " any station unless proper instructions have been received " from me, giving full particulars as to working, &c., of " same.

" In cases when I instruct the Inspector to work these " specials, engines, or trains, by telegraph, the Station " Masters before allowing them to leave their stations, " must request the Inspector to produce *his authority*, and " he has orders to *write out* each message. The Station " Masters must *carefully read*, and if found correct, *endorse* " *the same* and instruct the Telegraph Clerk to forward it, " but the engine or train must not be dispatched until the " message has been *repeated,* and the repeated message duly " signed by the Clerk has been handed to the Station " Master, who will then permit the engine or train to " leave his station, if all is right. The Clerks must only " forward such messages that are *countersigned* by the " Station Masters."

19. Stopping Trains at Stations.—Engine-drivers must bring their trains to a stand as near the shelter of the booking offices, waiting rooms, and platform coverings as possible, more especially in wet weather.

20. Crossing Trains.—Enginemen and Guards must have their trains well under control when having to cross another train at a station, and in wet or snowy weather they must use every precaution, so as to leave no possibility of their not being able to pull up at the platform. Cases have occurred of trains running through Sandown Station in wet weather, and only narrowly escaping accident.

Extracts from Isle of Wight Railway Rules and Regulations, 1st March, 1878.

in him remaining a Director! This seems to have had the desired effect as two weeks later the bank concluded a fresh agreement to pay interest in cash at various dates during 1872 and 1873. The IWR deposited £1,921 debenture stock with the bank as security, the stock being returned when payments were made.

Throughout all these problems Joseph Bourne had to keep the railway running. He had considerable problems in getting rails, sleepers and locomotive coal as suppliers were reluctant to accept further orders without payment of their accounts. On several occasions, the Board scrambled to rake up some money to satisfy a particular firm before badly needed supplies of spares and other materials could be obtained. During the quiet winter months Directors guaranteed loans from the bank to pay the most urgent bills or debenture interest. They took a hard view of demands for cash payments and tried to settle most bills by the issue of debentures.

Income during 1872 showed a healthy increase but there was still a lack of ready cash. The Board negotiated a loan of £1,500 from the National Provincial Bank guaranteed by Mr De Pass to pay interest due on 'A' and 'B' debenture stock. The Directors received more debenture stock in lieu of cash for their fees. That year the Board declared a dividend on its preference stock* although payment had to be made by the issue of additional preference stock. Further loans peppered the Minutes during 1873 and 1874, but were repaid out of the summer traffic receipts. In 1876 the IWR made an application to the Board of Trade for an order authorising another increase in capital. Hamilton Fulton, who was the first Engineer and the holder of £1,000 of ordinary stock, objected on the grounds that the issued capital was already excessive. The Board of Trade rejected this and the Isle of Wight Railway (Additional Capital) Certificate (BoT) 1876 authorised the creation of £50,000 ordinary stock. The Board immediately issued £30,000 by offering the shareholders £75 of new stock for every £100 they held of existing stock; shareholders took up over £20,000 and the remainder sold quickly at a premium. More was issued with a mixture of cash to pay off the remaining debts, including money owed for locomotives and rolling stock. Of course the company's future was not yet totally assured; significant capital expenditure continued for several years, both to improve the railway's capacity for handling traffic and in connection with junctions to other lines in the Island.

So, what conclusions can we draw from the crisis? Clearly, the promoters had no real idea of the costs of building and operating a railway. They may have quoted a low estimate to make the undertaking more attractive to prospective investors but it seems more likely that inadequate allowance had been made for land and construction costs. Without the experience of Capt. Huish, the Engineer John Fowler, the company's Manager Joseph Bourne, the deep pocket of George Young and others, matters would have been much worse. Perhaps the most remarkable aspect of this affair was the way lessons learnt by the IWR Board did nothing to put off promoters of other railways in the Island. The Isle of Wight (Newport Junction) and Freshwater, Yarmouth and Newport railways both encountered severe financial difficulties and were in the hands of receivers at various times. Perhaps they had that passionate wish to achieve in the face of adversity. Certainly, the Island's railways would have been much the poorer but for those Victorian entrepreneurs.

And what did the railway cost? The capital originally authorised was £125,000 in shares and loans of £41,600. By the end of 1876 the paid up capital amounted to £131,410 ordinary stock, preference capital of £67,210 and borrowings of £146,199 - over double the original authority. Despite this burden, the amount of traffic carried by the railway had grown to such an extent that the company could afford the 5 per cent interest on its preference and debenture stock whilst ordinary shareholders gained a dividend of 3½ per cent that year.

---

* In July 1870 the IWR converted its share capital into stock, a simple device that avoided the need to issue numbered certificates; for the purposes of this book the term shareholder, rather than stockholder, has been used throughout.

In 1871 the railway at Ryde was extended north over a level crossing to connect with the tramway to the pier. To the right of Terminus Hotel we see the level crossing complete with gates and one of the curious huts also used on the pier. *R. Brinton Collection*

2-4-0T *Wroxall* and its train seen at Ryde which has obviously been specially decorated with flags but for what event is not clear! It evidently required the attendance of quite a few people including the local policeman. *R. Silsbury Collection*

Chapter Eight

The 1870s

By 1871 membership of the IWR Board had changed noticeably from that which existed when the railway opened. Alexander Beattie was Chairman, actively assisted by Abraham De Pass and Joseph Bravo. Although the frequency of meetings had dropped to once a month, the Board remained preoccupied with money.

A number of accidents occurred in 1871, made more significant because passengers were injured. On 14th February the 11.20 am train to Ventnor came to a halt shortly after leaving Sandown with a brake failure. Another locomotive about to leave Ryde with the 12.10 pm train was dispatched to assist, but collided with the guard's van of the disabled train as it rounded the curve just south of Sandown station. The Board instructed Joseph Bourne to dismiss the driver and visit the injured passengers, several of whom were quite badly shaken.

A more serious accident took place on 15th April when two trains collided near Sandown. The IWR operated the staff and ticket system with Sandown as the crossing point, supplemented by the use of a telegraph that on this occasion led to the accident. On 15th April the Chairman, Alexander Beattie, made a tour of the railway with a well-known relative Joseph H. Beattie, locomotive superintendent of the London & South Western Railway. Together they visited the workshops at Ryde where favourable comments were made on the enlarged facilities. They were provided with a special train to Shanklin but a telegram to the station master at Sandown so confused him that he dispatched the next up train when it should have waited for a down train carrying the train staff. Fortunately the drivers were alert and managed to slow their trains to walking pace before the collision took place in a cutting just north of Sandown station. During his enquiries into the incident Col Yolland of the Board of Trade established that trains crossed at Brading or Shanklin if they were delayed by the late running of steamers from the mainland - a frequent occurrence. Equally additional trains might be run under the control of the telegraph without the benefit of the single line staff or ticket! The trains suffered only minor damage - a broken buffer beam on one engine and a damaged drawbar on a carriage. Some of the passengers were not so lucky and Mr Cooper, a first class passenger, was thrown across his compartment and suffered head injuries when one of the armchairs ended up on top of him. Col Yolland insisted they be fastened to the sides or floor of the carriage in future and aptly summed up the situation with the caustic comment, 'the train-staff regulations have been habitually set at nought on this line'. Accidents were not confined to passenger trains for Joseph Bourne reported that two wagons had left the rails on 22nd August - just one of numerous minor derailments in the early years.

The IWR paid £2,238 0s. 5d. in compensation to injured passengers during 1871, most of it borrowed on a short-term basis guaranteed personally by Directors for which they received debenture stock as security. This included £1,000 for Mr Cooper, but only after he had taken the company to court. Miss M. A. Reed of Ryde received injuries in the accident on 14th February, 1871 and following a lengthy wrangle over compensation she settled for an annuity of 12s. 6d. per week (paid monthly) and £65 for medical, legal and personal expenses. Miss Reed proved most resilient as the railway had to wait until her death on 16th June, 1898 before being released from its commitment - an event important enough to justify an entry in the Minute book!

Given the numbers of accidents, it might be thought local personalities would be reluctant to travel over the railway - not so, as the Board continued to receive requests for free passes. Those issued with passes in 1871 included R. J. H. Saunders in his capacity as Engineer of the Isle or Wight (Newport Junction) Railway, C. F. Fisher the Ventnor solicitor, the Manager of the National Provincial Bank at Ryde and Messrs Mew, Hollier and Young, Sandown, Shanklin and Ventnor omnibus proprietors. In November 1871 the IWR Board authorised the issue of passes for the Directors of the Ryde Pier Company, the IWR Directors receiving passes over the tramway in exchange. A month later a further exchange of passes took place with the Directors of the Portsmouth Steam Packet Company.

On 7th August, 1871 the Ryde Pier Company opened an extension of its horse tramway to connect with the IWR at St Johns Road. Joseph Bourne took on the management of the tramway in addition to his existing duties, and in the following November the IWR Board granted him a gratuity of £25 'in consideration of Mr Bourne's increased labor [sic] and anxiety of late in connection with the opening of the Tramway'. The pier company paid for the use of IWR luggage vans, guards and porters; IWR permanent way men looked after the track. All this helped smooth the operation of the tramway but did nothing to alleviate the inconvenience of a slow, crowded journey and change of carriage. Access to the former IWFC quays at Ryde created another route by which parcels and goods traffic might travel over the IWR. If traffic payments are anything to go by, parcels and lighter goods were routed via Ryde whilst coal and other minerals continued to be landed at Brading Quay. The opening of tramways in Portsmouth and Ryde prompted a further increase in the numbers of visitors to the Island.* A contemporary report recorded that a passenger rarely completed a journey from London to Ventnor in under five or six hours - clearly the four hours quoted in 1866 was somewhat optimistic. The scramble at Portsmouth and Ryde for seating accommodation was not an agreeable experience. With a party of children, nurses with luggage, perambulators and bath tubs, a man needed to be something of an organiser to get them to their destination without losing his temper and some of their belongings! Inevitably complaints appeared in IWR Minutes relating to lost baggage. One such individual, a Miss Blurton claimed damages for the loss of 'her box'; the Board instructed the Manager to contact the LSWR as it was thought to have been lost on its line, but some time later a curt note recorded that it had been 'found at a station on the Brighton line' and the Board instructed the solicitor to 'communicate to' the LBSCR on the matter. On another occasion a bag belonging to a Mr Ash disappeared at Ryde and, whilst the Board agreed to pay £3, they ordered the station master and booking clerk to find the remainder of the £8 compensation themselves!

Just as the completion of the railway allowed travellers to reach Ventnor somewhat more easily, so residents were prompted to travel in the opposite direction. In June 1871 the IWR Board received a 'memorial from the Inhabitants of Ventnor' asking that an early train be run from Ventnor to connect with the 7.40 am steamer from Ryde. They also asked that the last evening train be from Ryde to Ventnor during the summer; it seems they did not get their trains. Following complaints, a notice was issued on 12th September, 1871 instructing booking staff not to show undue preference when issuing through tickets to London over the LSWR or LBSCR: 'Much dissatisfaction is caused by Booking Clerks pushing a certain route'.

On occasions the elements contrived to upset the working of the railway. On 3rd October, 1871 the Manager reported that a wagon-load of malt had been damaged by rain and a signal post at Shanklin had blown down. The Board approved of his method of disposing of the malt but ordered that signal posts be checked so that a repeat of the incident could be avoided. In November a particularly gruesome accident resulted in the death of five sheep valued at £13 10s. by their owner, a Mr Brown. Their mangled condition meant that Joseph Bourne could sell the carcasses for only £1 7s. 6d. so the Board had to issue a cheque for the balance.

On 19th January, 1872 another accident occurred when the 3.15 pm train from Ryde ran into a siding under construction at Wroxall, after a turnout had been left wrongly set following the shunting of a wagon of stone. The train collided violently with the wagon badly injuring a labourer unloading it. Passengers were shaken but otherwise uninjured; fortunately the engine sustained no damage and the train continued its journey after about 20 minutes.

A tradition that has long-since disappeared was the reproduction of railway timetables in local newspapers. Details of IWR trains published in the *Isle of Wight Chronicle* on 4th July, 1872 showed that the service differed little from previous years although it carried more passengers. The Directors, in their report to the shareholders' meeting on 29th August, concentrated on the achievement of an agreement for through booking from London and

---

* The introduction of the August bank holiday in 1871 may also have been a factor.

other places on the LSWR and LBSCR, the purchase of a locomotive and more rolling stock. Six months later the Board had to tell shareholders that overall income declined in 1872 because the railway carried fewer first class passengers, despite a considerable increase in those travelling second and third class. This reflected a shift in the type of visitor travelling to the Island to middle-class families who went second class; although growing, the numbers of third class passengers were still tiny when compared with the other classes. The tonnage of goods rose significantly as the returns to the Board of Trade show - these were not isolated rises. But all this additional traffic took time to crystallise into profits.

Year ending	Passenger traffic Numbers carried			Season	Goods traffic Minerals	General	Gross receipts Passengers	Goods	Working expenses	% of receipts
31st Dec.	First	Second	Third	tickets	tons	tons	£	£	£	
1871	92,773	291,921	36,075	160	14,968	22,823	20,071	3,577	17,232	73
1875	92,386	383,071	82,446	647	24,919	26,749	26,708	5,305	15,085	47
1880	68,194	333,608	115,487	106	21,780	31,763	25,159	7,464	16,172	50

Shareholders watched the improving financial position with frustration. Debenture holders received their interest but other shareholders received nothing. At a six-monthly meeting on 25th August, 1871, Hamilton Fulton, the company's first Engineer, complained of a 'want of zeal' in the executive to reduce working expenses. A year later he proposed that a committee of shareholders be set up to investigate the affairs of the company, but this was rejected after a vote. This was not without irony as the finance company used this device in 1866 - now shareholders sought their revenge! That year the Board declared a dividend on preference stock but there was still nothing on ordinary shares. The August 1873 meeting took place at Ventnor instead of in London. Again the numbers of passengers showed an increase but the extra income had been swallowed up by higher employee and material costs. Expenditure on the capital account included an engine shed and related alterations to the workshops at Ryde. The 'independent' shareholders, i.e. those with no connections with Warrant Finance Company, resented the power wielded by finance company Directors who had occupied four of the six seats on the Board since 1870. In February 1874 they passed a resolution setting up a committee of shareholders to consider how expenditure could de reduced. Chaired by Capt. H.F. Twynam, its members consisted of J.D. Baldry, J.B. Denton, A.T. Simpson, R. Scott, H.H. Fulton and Col Atherley. The committee met the Board on 4th June, 1874 and agreed that appointments to the Board would maintain the balance between representatives of the finance company and other shareholders. The Directors agreed to take half their fees until a dividend could be paid on ordinary stock - significantly the Board declared a dividend in 1875! They also agreed to the removal of the audit office from London to Sandown with the aim of simplifying the accounts and saving money. The move took place in August 1874, but to accommodate the extra staff £150 had to be spent in 1875-1876 on extending the Sandown offices. A Board room and offices for the Secretary were retained at 122 Cannon Street in London.

Early in 1874 the Directors' report to shareholders contained a brief but significant entry. Against the advice of the auditors the IWR Board decided not to establish a fund to pay for the eventual renewal of assets. Although the decision permitted the payment of a dividend to shareholders it proved rather short-sighted as the Board later discovered. At the shareholders meeting on 31st August, 1874, Joseph Beattie announced his decision to retire from the Board. Shareholders passed a resolution approving the appointment of William McAndrew (a Warrant Finance man), in place of Albert Ricardo, and Col Atherley (from the committee), who took the seat vacated by the resignation of Alexander Beattie; Joseph Bravo became Chairman of the Board. At the shareholders' meeting a year later, the Board reported the death of Thomas Norton. An uneasy truce reigned as the Board turned to more pressing matters.

Following abandonment of the IWR extensions in 1867 other promoters sought to fill the gaps in the Island railway network. In 1868 the Isle of Wight (Newport Junction) Railway

The earliest known view of the station building at Brading was taken from the second platform and is probably dated between 1870 and 1877. Above the door to the booking office can be seen the station clock, the profusion of posters and signs is also obvious.   *R. Silsbury Collection*

This photograph, probably dated between about 1875 and 1879, shows the station building at Wroxall in its original state with an excellent collection of notice boards. Mr Grant's hotel and refreshment room is the two-storey building in the background.   *R. Silsbury Collection*

secured an Act of Parliament for a railway from Sandown to Newport followed by the Ryde & Newport Railway in 1872, much to the consternation of the IWNJ Directors who expected theirs to be the only railway linking the IWR with Newport. The IWR gained an appreciable amount of traffic when materials used in the construction of the IWNJ and RNR lines were transported by rail from the quay at Brading.

The RNR began at a junction with the IWR about a mile south of Ryde station near Smallbrook, to which point the IWR built a second line of rails for the exclusive use of RNR trains. Barely had the RNR been formed than its Directors asked the IWR to work their line and that belonging to the Cowes & Newport Railway, to which the IWR Board responded positively. The Boards of the companies accepted terms but the agreement collapsed when it was put before an IWR shareholders' meeting on 26th February, 1875; shareholders were anxious not to jeopardise their dividend and could recall a declaration by their own Directors three years earlier that they 'adhere to the policy . . . of avoiding all extensions or engagements calculated to weaken or diminish the value of your property'. The RNR opened for traffic in December 1875 worked by locomotives loaned by Henry Martin, the contractor working the CNR; six months later a Joint Committee of the two companies took over the operation of their railways.

Several months earlier, in February 1875, the IWNJ finally gained Board of Trade approval to begin carrying passengers from Sandown to Shide on the edge of Newport. Joseph Bourne became Manager and the IWNJ made 'temporary' use of the offices at Sandown. Ryde Works maintained IWNJ locomotive and rolling stock and loaned additional stock when require, at a modest cost, of course! The IWR Directors explained their involvement by emphasising that the line was worked 'under the Direction of Mr Bourne'; more truthfully, an 1878 edition of the IWR rule book treated the IWNJ line as part of the IWR system.

The idea that the Island railways should be worked as one entity by the Joint Committee of the LSWR and LBSCR was gaining support. In December 1875 *Herapath's Railway Journal* reported a rumour that the mainland companies had offered to work the Isle of Wight railways for 50 per cent of gross receipts and claimed that such a course would be profitable to all concerned. They reckoned without the IWR shareholders who knew their company already cost less than 50 per cent to operate and, being the most profitable of the Island railways, an agreement of this nature would benefit other companies at their expense.

The growing traffic prompted the purchase of a further locomotive and more rolling stock. Accommodation at stations was improved, particularly for coal and other goods. Ventnor was typical: Thomas King was allowed to use 'the excavation' at the station for coal storage in 1869 and thereafter other merchants took out leases allowing them to use excavations in the cliff for stores or offices - the permanent way men provided an additional siding. During the 1870s G. Smith rented coal stores and in 1874 H. & P. Owen took some space - their sign faced the station yard atop a former ticket collector's hut that had done duty on the Ryde Pier tramway. Most merchants appeared to be individuals operating on their own account, but an exception were the executors of Col Hargreaves who rented land for coal storage at Brading Quay in 1874 and 'portable' stores at stations. It seems Hargreaves had some private-owner coal wagons as IWR Minutes recorded a decision to pay 3d. a ton whenever it borrowed any! The firm gave up its accommodation in about 1885.

During 1875 the Board imposed a round of fare rises claiming that increased costs made them inevitable. Predictably the Board received letters of complaint and in June 'a memorial from the Clergy on the line', together with a letter from Mrs Margaret Huish opposing the running of cheap Sunday trains. They met with the usual response.

Two fatalities to gangers occurred at Truckells in December 1876. Apparently it was the practice of gangers riding on a trolley to hitch a lift by hanging on to the last vehicle of a train. Naturally steps were taken to end this dangerous practice whilst £10 was ordered to be paid 'to the poor woman and her young family'. On 31st May, 1877 the 7.27 am train from Ryde was approaching Shanklin when two locomotive boiler tubes burst leading to an inrush of water into the firebox and putting out the fire. The *Isle of Wight Times* recorded: 'Ventnor

A view of Sandown station taken sometime between 1875 and 1890. A mirror image of that at Shanklin, the station building has been extended at the south end to accommodate the company's offices. The short lived wooden footbridge leads to a rather makeshift up platform with its short covering. The signal box can be glimpsed beyond the footbridge as can the IWNJ locomotive shed. To the right, the goods yard occupies the site of the original crossing loop. According to the rule book, the up starting signal was a modern repeater for the main signal towering over the station on the left.   IWSR Collection

passengers were delayed for about half an hour whilst another locomotive was procured'. On 22nd January, 1878 the 3.10 up train from Ventnor left the rails as it approached Sandown station; the *Isle of Wight Chronicle* reported that the train was well spread about and three carriages damaged, one turned over and another had an end smashed in. The company claimed there were no severe injuries and somehow the accident escaped the attention of the Board of Trade.

On 1st March, 1878 replacements for the 1864 rule book came into use. One version incorporated traffic matters usually printed by larger companies as a separate Appendix to the working timetable. Some entries gave a useful insight into operating practices. Station staff received lengthy instructions on the manner in which station clocks were to be kept to time, how cash and surrendered tickets had to be remitted to the offices at Sandown and in the handling of luggage, parcels and goods traffic. Goods staff were exhorted to clean wagons after use, whilst guarding against the stealing 'in considerable quantities' of grease from the axleboxes of rolling stock. A reproduction of a notice issued on 11th July, 1871 gave a rather convoluted instruction about the running of special trains - clearly a consequence of the accidents that year. A further paragraph warned permanent way men not to attach trolleys to the rear of trains. Amazingly, for an additional charge, wagons could be left on the main line for unloading at a spot convenient to the customer!

During the years 1875 to 1879 Joseph Bourne managed the IWNJ as part of the IWR system, although a constant shortage of money exasperated the IWR Board who expected prompt payment of bills. In 1878 the two companies fell out over a debt of £400 for rolling stock repairs and rent for the use of Sandown station. Joseph Bourne was dragged into the dispute and his services as IWNJ manager dispensed with from April 1879, shortly before the line opened to a joint station at Newport. Perhaps the IWR, and Joseph Bourne in particular, could be forgiven for harbouring some feelings against its unpredictable neighbour.

The 1¼ mile tramway between the railway at St John's Road and Ryde Pier proved quite incapable of coping with large numbers of travellers during summer months, and many proposals were put forward for the construction of a railway. Eventually the local authority concluded an agreement with the RPC, LSWR and LBSCR for a railway passing under the Esplanade. Delegations of residents from Ryde, Newport, Sandown, Shanklin and Ventnor attended meetings with a Joint Committee of the LSWR and LBSCR when they voiced the desire of the Island population for a proper railway at Ryde; in the face of such lobbying the two mainland companies decided to construct the link themselves.

Preliminary surveys were carried out in the Autumn of 1876 and a Bill was placed before the 1877 session of Parliament for powers to build a pier and railway to St John's Road. There was still a great deal of suspicion of the motives of the mainland companies, especially when it became known that they planned to operate their own trains - land to the west of St John's Road station was earmarked for locomotive sheds. At a hearing before Parliament the LBSCR General Manager explained that the company would work its own trains to the IWR station at St Johns Road, with carriages being taken forward by Island companies' locomotives. Representatives for the IWR voiced its alarm that the LBSCR, in particular, planned to buy the other railways and promote an alternative route to Ventnor. The IWR asked for the opportunity to become a partner in the undertaking because it had been given that option when the tramway was built. The mainland companies, however, convinced Parliament that they would treat the Island railways equally, and instead of operating their own trains conceded running powers to the IWR and RNR. Construction began during 1878 and took two years to complete. A bridge over the railway replaced the level crossing at St John's Road and a LSWR-design signal box was provided about 50 yards to the north to serve the tracks at this point. Col Yolland rejected the proposed track layout because of the large number of facing connections and a different arrangement had to be installed. IWR trains began working to Ryde Esplanade station in early 1880 and to Pier Head in July; the horse tramway was cut back to serve just the pier. Although the railway carried parcels there were no sidings or other accommodation for goods traffic. Moreover, the approaches to the tunnel under the

In this view of Ventnor station, it has received its permanent station buildings but lacks the goods shed added in 1876, nor has the bay road been connected with the turntable. The hillside is being quarried away in the vicinity of the tunnel mouth.   *R. Silsbury Collection*

Ventnor station seen in the late 1880s showing the turntable that, at this date, gave access to no less than four tracks. The platform coverings stop well short of the goods shed whilst the island platform lacks all adornment.   *R. Brinton Collection*

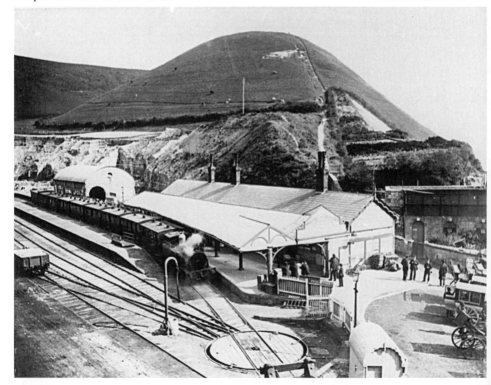

Esplanade passed through the former IWFC dock and, apart from a small quay adjacent to Esplanade station, the docks were swept away. By then, however, the opening of railways to Newport had created alternative routes for goods. Most traffic came via a railway jetty on the River Medina that was closer to the mainland and therefore more convenient for shipping than Brading or St Helens. This represented a threat to the IWR's monopoly of traffic to Sandown, Shanklin and Ventnor - we shall see more of this in later chapters. The mainland companies wrote asking that the IWR double its line between Ryde and Sandown but after Joseph Bourne gave details of the likely cost to the IWR Board in July 1880 a decision was deferred, never to be reconsidered.

Connecting Portsmouth and Ryde was a ferry service operated by the Port of Portsmouth and Ryde United Steam Packet Company, an amalgamation of numerous competing companies over the years. All bar the ferry company itself had a poor opinion of its services, and in 1879 the LSWR and LBSCR secured an Act authorising the raising of £50,000 each to begin a competing service. The ferry company bowed to the inevitable and in 1880 sold out to the two companies.

A number of employees left the IWR to work on other railways:

C.B. joined the IWR in October 1874 as a clerk but resigned in May 1877 having 'joined the R.N.&C. Rly. Co. as Stores Clerk'.

J.H. started as a cleaner on 2s. 6d. a day in July 1875; he joined the Ryde Pier Company to 'drive the Steam Tram' in June 1879 but came back to the IWR in September 1882 as an engineman - he stayed with the IWR until retirement many years later.

J.W. was an engine cleaner but was fined 3s. for 'not getting engine out in time on 13th December, 1874'. J.W. 'Joined Newport Junction Railway on 19th January, 1878'.

W.V. joined the IWR on 4th August, 1864 as a porter earning 10s. a week. He was promoted to cleaner in 1866 and fireman shortly afterwards. He collected a couple of fines: 1s. for coming on duty with 'dirty clothes and flesh' and on 20th November, 1865 6d. 'for neglecting to put scotch across the line'. They did him no harm as W.V. was promoted engineman in May 1874. Two months later he joined the 'Sandown & Newport Railway' but in June 1882 moved to the Brading Harbour Railway. He retired from the IWR in September 1921.

To finish this chapter, details should be given of two more accidents. On 17th August, 1880 the 9.16 am passenger train from Ryde ran into the dock siding at Brading where it collided with eight or nine wagons. The train consisted of a locomotive, eight carriages, a passenger guard's van, a luggage van and an empty carriage truck. As a result of the accident 13 passengers complained of injury. The engine and two carriages left the rails, one wagon was totally demolished and two others damaged, including one driven over the buffer stops. At the time a gang of 15 men were relaying a section of track on the single line between Ryde St John's and Brading. The foreman of the gang attempted to attach four timber trucks to the previous up train but the rope tying them to the train broke and the wagons free-wheeled back into the siding. He, the permanent way inspector and the station master all failed to ensure that the points had been reset for the main line. The Board of Trade inspector held the foreman responsible for causing the accident and blamed the station master for neglecting to check the points before clearing the signals. None were interlocked and Col Rich, the Board of Trade Inspector, naturally called for this to be done.

Col Rich reported on another accident in the early hours of 28th August, 1880. A goods train from Ventnor consisting of 23 wagons and a brake van had reached Brading where 13 or 14 were being shunted on to the branch to Brading Quay. Four wagons derailed on the spring-loaded connections to the branch. Again the Colonel called for the provision of a signal box and proper interlocking.

Chapter Nine

Consolidation - The 1880s

The improvements evident in the company's financial position continued into the 1880s. The IWR purchased additional locomotives, carriages and goods stock, stations were improved and renewal of track could be readily afforded. Many shareholders, however, saw the continued expenditure as money that should rightly come to them as increased dividends. In the 1880s there was a clash between these viewpoints just when the railway's income reached a plateau.

The IWR Board met monthly at the Secretary's office at 122 Cannon Street, London with Joseph Bravo in the chair and Directors A.D. De Pass, W. McAndrew, G. Young and Col. Atherley. When Mr Bravo died in 1881 William McAndrew took over the reins of Chairman but his combative nature was not appreciated by all he met; John Bailey Denton, a chartered surveyor, joined the Board. Joseph Bourne remained in the manager's seat assisted by Robert Hicks as Secretary.

At Ryde, the opening of the LSWR/LBSCR joint railway in 1880 meant that passengers no longer had to endure a slow journey by tram and the change to a railway carriage at St John's Road. Instead they could board a Ventnor or Newport train immediately after disembarking from the steamer. The IWR Directors welcomed the opening of the railway, but could not pass up an opportunity to claim compensation for the 'injurious' effects of the railway on IWR property at St John's Road. To construct the approaches to a road bridge the mainland companies purchased two small plots of land and provided a new entrance to the station yard. The IWR employed Mr Binfield Bird, a surveyor and land agent of West Cowes, who recommended the company claim £3,058 principally for the loss of business by the refreshment rooms. The rooms attracted trade both from railway passengers and passers-by; a considerable amount of house building was in progress nearby. The IWR claimed that passing trade would decline as the bridge blocked the view of the building! Naturally the LSWR and LBSCR were much offended by the IWR's greed and resisted the claim. The IWR obtained several valuations of the 'loss' and Mr Piper, the tenant, had to provide details of his takings. George Pownell, a Director of the North London Railway, acted as arbitrator and eventually awarded compensation of £1,033. Within a few months Joseph Bourne wrote to the two companies asking to rent arches below the road bridge as offices and stores at a nominal rent and suggested the Joint Committee fit them up at a cost of no more than £150. The Joint Committee brusquely responded that the IWR had received its compensation! But after more correspondence the two sides agreed to share the cost of fitting them up and the IWR had its arches - they are still used as railway stores today.

Relations were little better with the Ryde, Newport & Cowes Joint Committee mainly because the RNR and IWNJ terminated at IWR stations and were obliged to pay rent that the latter deducted from traffic receipts; disputes continued well into IWC days and the payments remained a bone of contention right up to the start of the Great War in 1914. The opening of the IWNJ through to Newport encouraged the development of goods traffic across the Island from Medina Jetty to Sandown, Shanklin and Ventnor. This traffic travelled only a short distance by the IWR so Joseph Bourne imposed a 'terminal charge' for station accommodation and other services; the effects were such that traders claimed it was cheaper and more convenient to cart goods by road. The IWNJ took the IWR before the Railway Commissioners who ruled on 19th July, 1882 that the IWR could only charge a mileage rate, much to the disgust of Joseph Bourne and his Board.

Any failing on the part of an IWR employee in a matter involving a 'foreign' railway was calculated to bring down the wrath of the General Manager:

G.H. joined the company on 14th July, 1864 as a 'policeman' and progressed through the ranks until promoted in July 1871 to station master at Shanklin. On 11th September, 1880 the Manager fined him £2 9s. for returning a full truck of goods to Newport as an empty wagon; at that time he received a salary of 25s. per week. On 25th May, 1881 he was fined one month's pay (£5) for neglect of duty in allowing a train to enter a siding and derail. He then had an uneventful career until retiring on 29th March, 1913 when the Board granted an allowance of 10/- per week.

In 1880, 1881 and 1882 considerable sums were spent in alterations and extensions to the stations at Sandown, Shanklin and Brading, the latter being in readiness for the opening of the railway to Bembridge (*see Chapter Eleven*). At Shanklin J. Jolliffe had the contract for work that, if instalment payments are anything to go by, must have proved quite extensive; F. Bradley supplied ironwork for the platform covering that alone cost £159 15s. At the six-monthly meeting on 23rd February, 1882 the Directors obtained shareholders' permission to issue the remaining £20,000 capital authorised by the Board of Trade in 1876.

The need to pay for improvements to the railway was of continuing concern to the Board and shareholders alike. Without a renewals fund the Directors had to raise capital by the issue of stock and debentures, investors being attracted by the potential dividends or, in the case of debentures, a regular fixed interest payment. Naturally the company had to generate enough income to service its debts, a simple task when times were good. To give an example, Board of Trade returns gave details of total income and expenditure for the three years 1881 to 1883:

Year ending 31st December	Income £	Expenditure £	Net profit £	% expenditure in relation to income
1881	33,210	16,968	16,242	51
1882	35,880	18,240	17,640	51
1883	33,789	17,787	16,002	53

To balance this, during 1883 there were the following liabilities:

	£	s.	d.
Due in January 1883 - Six months interest on the 'A' Debenture stock at 5%	1,661	12	9
Ditto on 'B' Debenture stock	1,637	13	9
Ditto on 'C' Debenture stock	160	0	4
Six months interest on Preference stock at 5%	1,629	9	10
	5,088	16	8
Due in August 1883 - Six months Preference and Debenture interest	5,088	16	8
Due during 1883 - Dividend of 4¾% on the Ordinary stock	6,927	1	5
Total	17,104	14	9

Expenditure on the capital account continued at a high level into 1883. In February 1883 Joseph Bourne submitted a list of work he considered necessary during the current six months. Totalling £3,900, it included machinery and tools at Ryde Works (£300), a carriage shed at Ryde (£500) that was never built and an additional locomotive. Mindful of this, the Directors ordered that all further outlay on the capital account had to be submitted to the Board before being incurred. This embroiled them in the vexed question of what additional machinery was necessary for the workshops and the purchase of permanent way materials. At the end of July Mr Bourne's revised estimate of expenditure necessary before the end of the year amounted to £1,207 10s., including the provision of a gas supply to Ryde Works piped along the railway from the nearby gas works. Joseph Bourne also reported that the roof of the locomotive shed at Ryde needed repairs before the next winter - naturally the Board had to agree!

Changes in legislation led to a reappraisal of insurance cover and the Minutes for April 1883 covered the matter in some detail. The whole railway was valued at £23,835 for which the Lancashire Insurance Company asked a premium of £35 15s. per year; a year later the IWR took out additional cover for its employees in compliance with the provisions of the

Employers Liability Act. Some working practices were rather dubious as an entry for August 1882 showed: Joseph Bourne reported that the Royal Insurance Company required the construction of a frame over a boiler on which sleepers were being dried as at the time the railway creosoted its own sleepers. He was instructed to discontinue drying the sleepers on the boiler - one wonders what this practice had been doing to the health of employees working nearby!

Shareholders' dissatisfaction with the management of the IWR continued to simmer despite the declaration of the highest-ever dividend on the ordinary stock. At a six-monthly meeting on 21st February, 1883, Horace F. Tahourdin, an accountant, complained that running costs were too high. Apparently he owned stock in two other railways and the IWR compared unfavourably with both. That year the percentage of expenditure in proportion to receipts rose to 53 per cent; this was a quite unacceptable figure to shareholders who naturally wanted the highest possible dividend. No doubt they remembered Capt. Huish's comment that they would be poor managers if running costs ever exceeded 50 per cent. Another shareholder pointedly remarked that this had not been the first time that Mr Tahourdin had spoken at length about the company's performance. Of the Directors Tahourdin said 'they are taking £500 a year for looking after this property'; small wonder he made himself unpopular with the Board. In response to the complaints William McAndrew disclosed that the company had '. . . half the line laid down in steel rails - we are gradually completing the whole bit by bit every year . . .' There had been only one delay to trains of ten minutes when '... a train had left Ventnor without the Staff and the man had to go back for it . . .'!

Horace Tahourdin and other shareholders continued to press for changes. On 4th June, 1883 the Board voted out a resolution from J. Bailey Denton to halve Directors fees and authorised the issue of a further £3,300 'C' debenture stock to pay for some of the capital expenditure. Mr Denton was a distinct thorn in the side of the Board. In November 1883 he returned half his Directors' fees for the preceding quarter and kept this up until February 1884, when the Directors resolved to reduce their fees to £300 per annum until a 5 per cent dividend per annum could be paid on ordinary stock. Mr Denton accompanied his battle with a barrage of suggestions and requests for statistics. The Board ordered that the giving of any information had to take second place to the clerks' ordinary work; similar requests from Mr Tahourdin received the same response. Although no record exists of the shareholders' meeting on 15th August, it was evidently as lively as those during the 1860s. There was then a gap in the Minutes until the following November. In the intervening time Horace Tahourdin, Arthur T. Simpson and John Bailey Denton issued a circular calling for an extraordinary meeting of shareholders, to appoint 'a Committee to enquire into the working and general management of the railway and the means of reducing the working expenses'. In response the Board instigated a brief action in the courts but failed to prevent the meeting.

The extraordinary meeting went ahead on 27th November, 1883 at the City Terminus Hotel, London but without the three named shareholders. William McAndrew, as Chairman, held sway and maintained that the 1874 committee's recommendations had been implemented as far as practicable. The working expenses of the Secretary's office had been reduced to £150 per annum and he criticised John Bailey Denton, who wanted the office closed, for circulating the shareholders contrary to the Board's wishes. In a reference to the running costs McAndrew stated that increased numbers of passengers forced the running of more trains. Irregular working of the ferries often forced the company to lay on extra trains - a provision that shareholders had asked for many years before. Clearly the purchase of the ferries by the LSWR and LBSCR had yet to bear fruit! He also agreed that seating accommodation for first and second class passengers was out of proportion to their earnings. In a reference to the stability of the company, however, a shareholder commented that ordinary stock which 10 to 12 years ago was worth £25 to £30 had lately been selling at £129.

The bitterness had to end. On 7th January, 1884 an important meeting of the Board took place at 122 Cannon Street, London. Present were W. McAndrew (Chairman), Col Atherley, A.D. De Pass, J. Bailey Denton, G. Young, H.F. Tahourdin and Capt. H.F. Twynam. Col

Atherley had clearly been unhappy with the activities of the Board and submitted a letter dated 7th November tendering his resignation as Director; he was replaced by Horace Tahourdin. The Board elected John M. Stobart to fill the existing vacancy. George Young decided to follow Col Atherley and wrote (on 7th January) to the Board; Capt. Twynam took his place. At the following meeting on 4th February the Board decided to implement the programme of the committee of 1874. More controversially, costs of the court action totalling £232 9s. 9d. were debited against the Directors instigating them (Messrs McAndrew, De Pass, Young and Atherley), because the action had never been sanctioned in Board Minutes. William McAndrew objected to this and soon afterwards he resigned from the Board, Horace Tahourdin was appointed Chairman and Francis W. Slade became a Director.

The Board immediately set up a 'General Committee' as evidently the new Directors were not satisfied with Joseph Bourne's management. For the February Board meeting Mr Bourne estimated that capital expenditure would total £500 during the current half-year and a further £4,000 in the future - clearly not to the liking of the Board. He had an interview with the committee on 20th May but within days Horace Tahourdin corresponded with James Connor, brother of Mr B. Connor, locomotive superintendent of the Caledonian Railway. Mr Connor began work on 22nd July and in their report to the next shareholders' meeting on 27th August, 1884 the Board disclosed that: 'The Directors not having been able to make satisfactory arrangements with Mr Bourne, have terminated his engagement with the company, and have appointed Mr James Connor, Engineer and Traffic Manager'. The local press more diplomatically reported Joseph Bourne's 'retirement'.

The Minutes for the months following James Connor's arrival contained little information of the changes wrought by the new General Manager, and we have only returns to the Board of Trade to indicate how he brought expenditure under control. During the year ending 31st December, 1885 the percentage of working expenses to income dropped to 44 per cent, capital expenditure ceased and economies were made in renewal of the permanent way.

In February 1884 the Board resolved to appoint Mr Mackay, an accountant, to advise on the best means of reducing paperwork and amalgamating the Secretary's office in London with the office at Sandown. Meetings of the Board were transferred from 122 Cannon Street, London to Horace Tahourdin's office at 9 Victoria Chambers, Westminster. The Secretary received £25 as a contribution to his removal expenses to the Isle of Wight. His office at Sandown came into operation on 24th June, 1885.

The opening of the Joint Railway at Ryde, and purchase of ferries by the LSWR and LBSCR heightened expectations amongst Isle of Wight residents that there would be significant improvements in services connecting the Island with London. Neither of the mainland companies attempted to compete for Portsmouth traffic and their fast trains were inferior to those going to other destinations. Improvements in the quality and reliability of the ferries took time and there were many complaints about high fares. One reason for this discontent was the 3d. toll paid to the RPC for each passenger booked to any station in Ryde. (The IWR and Ryde Station Company had agreed a 4d. toll but the failure of the latter made it void.) Later a court action established that the toll had to be paid by passengers travelling from the mainland *and* those from stations in the Island. IWR shareholders voiced their concerns at their six-monthly meetings and the Secretary tried to negotiate improvements, particularly concerning fares. In June 1884 the IWR Board noted that through fares had not been revised in time for the summer season, about which 'complaints had been made loudly by visitors to the Island' and naturally passed on by hotel keepers!

Representatives of the local authorities never stopped demanding a greater availability of third class fares and seating accommodation. They received suitably robust replies but the Board did gradually ease the restrictions of past years. On 28th May, 1885 the Board agreed to a proposal revising the fare and ticket arrangements; from 1st July to 30th September return 'Tourist' tickets were issued on weekday mornings and all day Sundays at a rate of 1½ times ordinary first or second fares. For journeys between Ryde Pier Head and Ventnor, fortnightly tickets cost 35s. first class and 28s. second; monthly tickets were 48s. first class and 40s. second.

Third class return tickets, including 'Market' fares, were abolished with the exception of those issued by agreement with the IWNJ. Officers and Privates in uniform received tickets at 'Military' rates consequent on the passing of the Cheap Trains Act in 1883 that obliged railways to carry troops and military stores at fixed rates. Following a deputation a year later, the IWR Board decided to make third class single and cheap second class return tickets available on the first two trains each day. This was not enough for some residents; a Mr Wood wrote:

> Even on Whit Monday this ridiculously mismanaged railway made no exception whatever in favour of third class passengers. They advertised what they called a 'cheap' second class return between Ryde (but from St John's Road only) and Ventnor, 11½ miles, at half a crown. To call this cheap is a strange misuse of the adjective, quite peculiar to the Isle of Wight Railway managers. They seem to have no conception of the wants and means of the people. Let us imagine a working man at Ryde wishing to treat his wife and two or three children to a day's outing to Ventnor and the Undercliff. It is to be supposed he could afford ten shillings for the railway fares only. If it had been a third class trip at half the fare, scores of working men would have availed themselves of the opportunity; they and their families would have had a happy day, and the Railway Company's receipts would have been several pounds heavier. But no, the directors have not the common sense to see it.

Other complaints received by the Board included one from Ventnor Local Board about the lack of footwarmers: passengers had to make a specific request to get one and even then they were not always supplied. The carriages also lacked hat racks and were not always lit when the train passed through Ventnor tunnel. Not all people were honest, as in February 1884 the Manager informed the Board of the conviction of a Mr J. before the magistrates for selling the return half of a ticket at Bembridge - he was fined 1s. and ordered to pay 9s. costs. Goods traffic was not ignored and during 1885 the IWR spent small sums constructing two private sidings. After years of delay the Shanklin Gas Company began receiving deliveries of coal at its own siding, built by IWR workmen for £139 15s. 7d. A siding for the cement works at Brading Quay cost somewhat less at £47 14s. 6d. Coal merchants and builders preferred to rent space in the goods yards.

During the years 1883 to 1887 there were numerous attempts at amalgamation of the Island railways, including attempts to lease or sell them to the LSWR and LBSCR. When a LSWR Bill was before Parliament in 1883, Joseph Bourne informed the latter's General Manager the 'price' the IWR Board might expect for the sale of its railway. It seems the IWR had an inflated idea of its value to the two mainland railways. Joseph Bourne ensured his efforts were acknowledged in a resolution of the IWR Board on 5th February, 1885:

> . . . in the event of the Railway being sold to any of the Mainland Companies under powers obtained in the sessions of 1885 or 1886 the Directors would upon sale recommend the Shareholders to vote Mr Bourne the sum of £2,000 . . .

During 1884 Roderick MacKay, a Director of the RNR and an auditor for the IWR, proposed an amalgamation of the CNR, RNR, IWNJ and IWR. The IWR attitude is best illustrated by this entry in the Minute book for 11th November, 1884: 'An application from the lateral Island Lines for an amalgamation with this Railway was considered, and the Secretary was instructed as to a reply'. Although a Bill went before Parliament, it was withdrawn when the CNR, RNR and IWNJ failed to reach terms. On 17th November, 1886 the IWR Minute book mentioned a meeting between the IWR and IWNJ Boards concerning a working agreement or amalgamation. The IWR Board sanctioned a draft agreement, but on 14th December the Chairman reported that the IWNJ disputed the terms for amalgamation alleging that the interests of debenture holders were not sufficiently protected - one IWNJ Director held a significant number of debentures. The IWR had already placed a Bill before Parliament for a comprehensive amalgamation of the Island companies (including the Shanklin & Chale and Freshwater, Yarmouth & Newport companies), and containing powers for their sale or lease to the LSWR and LBSCR. Much offended by the rebuff from the IWNJ, the IWR withdrew its Bill and petitioned Parliament in opposition to another Bill for an amalgamation of the CNR, RNR and IWNJ. Originally it contained provisions to include the IWR and Brading companies, but correspondence suggests that the Boards of the other Island companies, particularly the IWNJ, imposed conditions unacceptable to the IWR. Fearing a loss of tolls for the use of the station and line at Ryde, the IWR succeeded in the insertion of clauses requiring the running of at least seven passenger trains a day (except Sundays) between Ryde and Newport.

A minor but regular irritation for the IWR Board was the management of the refreshment rooms at Ryde and Sandown. In 1880 Mr Pritchard lavished £1,550 on the construction of an impressive building at Sandown for use as a refreshment room. Together with that at Ryde, it was leased to a Mr Clarke, the refreshment contractor for the LSWR, for £200 per annum plus 12 per cent of gross receipts over £400. The Board also considered providing rooms at Shanklin but, after making a provisional agreement with Mr Clarke, the idea had to be abandoned after the justices refused to grant a drinks licence. Following the opening of the joint railway at Ryde, income from the rooms at St Johns Road station declined and Mr Clarke soon asked to be released from his commitments. In December 1885 the IWR Board accepted the surrender of the lease upon payment of £1,000, although part of this sum was offset by the sale to the railway company of the furniture, crockery, etc. for £45. In August 1886, after rejecting several potential tenants, the Board ordered that the Ryde refreshment rooms be closed and the Sandown rooms kept open under the management of Mr Connor, but 'that the Manager give his attention to economy in the meantime, that no fancy or needless stock be purchased' - it was soon re-let.

On 19th November, 1886 the first of several incidents occurred which brought into question James Connor's management. He reported that £14 0s. 5d. sent for payment of wages at St Helens Quay had been lost. Naturally the Board expressed their displeasure and ordered that future movements of money be signed for and receipts given at each stage in the journey. The following month he had to explain why £20 2s. 6d. was expended for a valuation of furniture and utensils at Sandown refreshment rooms without first obtaining the Board's approval. On 6th June the Board criticised the tardy sale of old rails - iron was fetching a good price at this time. During the summer there were repeated complaints about late working of trains so the Chairman insisted that all delays exceeding 20 minutes be reported to him personally. Two farmers shared £61 for burnt crops and seven sheep were killed by a train at Winstone. Finally, in December 1887 Fraser and White billed the company for £469 2s. 8d. for coal allegedly supplied but not accounted for. Messrs Tahourdin and Stobart saw Mr Connor on 29th December and told him that the Board were resolved on his dismissal - he was given the option of resigning. The departure of the Manager was quickly followed by that of the permanent way inspector as the Board was very critical of the way the track had been maintained.

Like his predecessor, James Connor had been expected to operate the railway single-handed whilst communicating with a Board sitting miles away in London, and whose members made only occasional visits to the Island. The Board took steps not to repeat the problem and on 7th February, 1888 promoted two existing employees. Henry Day was appointed interim Traffic Manager; he had joined the IWR on 28th May, 1868 and graduated through the offices as clerk, book keeper, audit clerk, chief clerk and cashier. Henry Brent, who had begun as a fitter in January 1870, became permanent way manager, locomotive superintendent and manager of Ryde Works. The works foreman, Mr Thornton, took charge of the workshops in Henry Brent's absence. To help share the load, the Secretary managed the wages and a Mr C. U. King was retained on a part-time basis for a few months to supervise the workshop and permanent way departments, his fare from London being paid by the company. The appointments were made permanent on 31st July, 1888 when the Board settled Henry Day's pay at £200 per annum and Henry Brent £150. Mr Day took on the 'Quarry Superintendence' and the duties of the Secretary when Mr Hicks fell ill in 1890. Both Henrys went on to serve the company with some distinction for many years.

The installation of Horace Tahourdin as Director and Chairman of the IWR in 1884 heralded a golden age for the shareholders. The Board had tight control of capital expenditure and income was higher than ever before. True, the numbers of first class passengers declined but this was more than balanced by increased income from second class and third class travellers. Much of this was attributable to the attractions of the growing resorts of Sandown and Shanklin. Goods traffic had also shown a satisfactory increase.

Isle of Wight Railway

From October 1888 until further notice

Down trains

WEEKDAYS

Station		1,2 & 3 *	1,2 & 3	1,2 & 3 *	1,2 & 3	1 & 2	1 & 2	1 & 2	1 & 2	1 & 2	1 & 2	1 & 2	1 & 2	1 & 2
Ryde Pier Head	dep		8.0	9.16	10.22	12.5	1.10	2.10	3.15	4.12	5.25	6.38	7.50	9.0
Ryde Esplanade	"		8.4	9.20	10.26	12.9	1.14	2.13	3.19	4.15	5.29	6.42	7.54	9.5
Ryde St. Johns Rd.	"	7.25	8.10	9.24	10.30	12.15	1.18	2.16	3.22	4.19	5.33	6.46	7.58	9.10
Brading	"	7.33	8.19	9.32	10.39	12.23	1.26	2.24	3.30	4.27	5.41	6.54	8.6	9.18
Sandown	"	7.40	8.25	9.38	10.45	12.28	1.32	2.29	3.35	4.33	5.46	7.0	8.12	9.23
Shanklin	"	7.45	8.31	9.45	10.51	12.36	1.38	2.36	3.42	4.39	5.53	7.6	8.18	9.29
Wroxall	"	7.51	8.38	9.53	10.58	12.43	1.45	2.43	3.50	4.46	6.0	7.13	8.25	9.25
Ventnor	arr	7.56	8.45	10.0	11.4	12.49	1.51	2.50	3.56	4.52	6.6	7.20	8.32	9.40

SUNDAYS

Station		1,2 & P	1 & 2	1 & 2	1 & 2	1,2 & P	1 & 2	1 & 2	1 & 2
Ryde Pier Head	dep	9.25	1.0	3.0	7.40	10.10	1.50	4.10	8.35
Ryde Esplanade	"	9.29	1.5	3.4	7.44	10.16	1.56	4.16	8.40
Ryde St. Johns Rd.	"	9.33	1.10	3.8	7.48	10.22	2.2	4.22	8.47
Brading	"	9.41	1.18	3.16	7.56	10.28	2.8	4.28	8.53
Sandown	"	9.47	1.24	3.22	8.2	10.34	2.14	4.34	8.59
Shanklin	"	9.53	1.30	3.28	8.8	10.44	2.22	4.44	9.7
Wroxall	"	10.0	1.37	3.36	8.15	10.48	2.26	4.48	9.11
Ventnor	arr	10.5	1.43	3.42	8.22	10.52	2.30	4.52	9.15

Up trains

WEEKDAYS

Station		1,2 & P	1 & 2	1 & 2	1 & 2	1 & 2	1 & 2	1 & 2	1 & 2	1 & 2	1 & 2	1 & 2 S	1 & 2	1 & 2	1 & 2 S
Ventnor	dep	7.25	8.5	9.20	10.25	12.10	1.12	2.10	3.15	4.15	5.25	6.42	7.55	8.40	9.45
Wroxall	"	B	8.11	9.25	10.31	12.15	1.18	2.16	3.21	4.20	5.31	6.47	8.0	8.45	9.50
Shanklin	"	7.35	8.18	9.32	10.38	12.22	1.25	2.23	3.28	4.27	5.39	6.54	8.6	8.51	9.57
Sandown	"	7.40	8.25	9.38	10.45	12.28	1.32	2.29	3.35	4.33	5.46	7.0	8.12	8.56	10.2
Brading	"	B	8.31	9.44	10.50	12.33	1.38	2.36	3.40	4.38	5.51	7.5	8.18	9.1	10.7
Ryde St. Johns Rd.	"	-	8.39	9.52	10.57	12.41	1.45	2.44	3.43	4.46	5.59	7.13	8.26	9.10	10.15
Ryde Esplanade	"	7.55	8.44	9.56	11.2	12.45	1.50	2.48	3.52	4.50	6.3	7.17	8.30	9.14	
Ryde Pier Head	arr	7.58	8.48	10.0	11.5	12.48	1.54	2.52	3.56	4.53	6.6	7.20	8.34	9.18	

S Saturdays only.

* Parliamentary between Ryde, St. Johns Road and Ventnor and intermediate stations.

B Calls to pickup passengers for Portsmouth, London and Brighton.

BRADING HARBOUR RAILWAY

WEEKDAYS

Station		1,2 & P	1 & 2	1 & 2	1 & 2	1 & 2	1 & 2	1 & 2
Bembridge	dep	8.5	10.28	12.12	1.15	3.18	5.30	7.55
St. Helens	"	8.10	10.32	12.17	1.20	3.23	5.35	8.0
Brading	arr	8.15	10.37	12.22	1.25	3.28	5.40	8.05
Brading	dep	8.32	10.51	12.35	1.40	3.41	5.52	8.20
St. Helens	"	8.37	10.56	12.40	1.45	3.46	5.57	8.25
Bembridge	arr	8.42	11.1	12.45	1.50	3.51	6.2	8.30

SUNDAYS

Station		1,2 & P	1 & 2	1 & 2	1 & 2	1 & 2
Bembridge	dep	1.5	2.5	3.5	4.22	7.45
St. Helens	"	1.10	2.10	3.10	4.27	7.50
Brading	arr	1.15	2.15	3.15	4.32	7.55
Brading	dep	1.20	2.15	3.18	4.35	9.0
St. Helens	"	1.25	2.20	3.23	4.40	9.5
Bembridge	arr	1.30	2.25	3.28	4.45	9.10

Year ending 31st Dec.	Passenger traffic Numbers carried			Season tickets	Goods traffic Minerals tons	General tons	Gross receipts Passengers £	Goods £	Working expenses £	% of receipts
	First	Second	Third							
1881	66,527	359,712	119,002	105	22,226	29,961	25,197	8,013	16,968	51
1885	57,035	368,063	173,272	120	46,750	23,175	25,480	8,595	15,114	44
1890	51,023	368,987	278,114	117	47,385	25,251	27,590	9,796	15,719	42

The shareholders could look forward to a regular dividend as high as any paid by a railway company in Britain. But the differing classes of debenture and their advantage in income over ordinary and preference stock continued to exercise their minds. So that holders of ordinary and debenture stock might receive a more equal share of the profits, in 1889 the company placed a Bill before Parliament to consolidate and rearrange the capital - it received Royal Assent on 25th July, 1890. Ignoring that authorised by the IWR (Steamers) Act 1865, which was never issued, the total authorised capital became £402,312 and borrowings £196,911. The Act authorised the issue of £185,000 in debenture stock bearing interest at 4 per cent in place of £148,000 in existing debentures paying 5 per cent, i.e. £68,536 in 'A' debenture stock, £67,548 in 'B' debenture stock and £11,916 in 'C' debenture stock.

Work put in hand at stations included a 'new verandah' at Sandown whilst a platform covering for Ventnor cost £575. Although residents of Lake were repeatedly refused their own station, in 1889 the company spent £14 7s. 10d. on the construction of a 'platform at Lake' adjacent to the County Cricket ground; it was ready for use by 17th August when the *Isle of Wight County Press* carried an advertisement:

Volunteer Sports at the County Cricket Ground, Shanklin.
Visit of HRH. Prince Henry of Battenburg, Monday August 19th
Cheap return tickets (first and second class) will be issued to Shanklin by all trains up to 6 pm. The 1.12 and 2.10 pm trains from Ventnor and the 1.15 and 2.20 pm trains from Ryde will convey passengers to the platform adjacent to the ground, and passengers will be taken up from the same platform by the 6.42 and 7.50 pm trains from Ventnor, and 6.38 and 7.42 pm trains from Ryde.
H.K. Day, Traffic Manager, General Offices, Sandown. August 1889.

A week later the *County Press* reported:

Regimental Sports of the Island Volunteers
at the Isle of Wight County Cricket Ground, Landguard, on Monday 19th
A considerable number of spectators assembled on the highway at the bridge across the railway outside the ground, from which a fair view of the proceedings could apparently be obtained. By arrangement with the Isle of Wight Railway several trains daring the day stopped at the special platform connected with the ground, and Mr H.K. Day, the manager, personally superintended the traffic arrangements, which were completely satisfactory.

A year later the IWR concluded an agreement with Col. Hartopp, Secretary of the Isle of Wight County Cricket Club 'to make an easy slope to their cricket ground' - they also granted Col Hartopp a first class season ticket at second class rate in lieu of a free pass over the railway. Members of the press also received free passes:

A. P. Meggs, Reporter	*I. W. Journal*, Newport	first class
F. Moor, Proprietor	*I. W. Advertiser*, Ventnor	first class
Mrs Butler, Proprietor	*I. W. Observer*, Ryde	first class
W. H. Dann, Reporter	*I. W. County Press*, Newport	second class
G. H. Brannon, Manager	*I. W. County Press*, Newport	second class
H. J. Tresidder,	*I. W. Press*, Ventnor	second class
G. Mearman, Proprietor	*I. W. Chronicle*, Sandown	second class
D. Rogers, Proprietor	*I. W. Guardian*, Shanklin	second class, upon the withdrawal of the letter he had written!

The IWR Directors gained from the issue of free passes by other companies. Of two passes issued by the LSW, one was used by the Chairman and the other by his colleagues in rotation!

1892	Capt. Twynam	1894	Mr Stobart
1893	A.D. De Pass	1895	Mr Slade

In November 1889 the company purchased a cottage called Simeon Lodge, Sandown from Mr Pritchard for £25; it had been rented for many years as a home for the station master. More trivial matters mentioned in correspondence included a reply to an enquiry from a Ventnor hotel quoting rates for placing adverts in passenger carriages; £12 per annum first class and £6 6s. second, the existence of third class compartments was not mentioned. Cheap tickets at a rate of 3s. 6d. first and 2s. 8d. second were offered for travel between Portsmouth and IWR stations over the Easter weekend, 19th to 22nd April, 1889. A Sunday service was operated on Good Friday and Easter Sunday but with an extra working leaving Ryde Pier Head at 11.15 am and returning from Ventnor at 12.00 noon, plus a return trip from Brading to Bembridge leaving at 10.20 am and 11.30 am respectively. Various firms rented space at stations for amusement or other slot machines; in 1890 so many new agreements were made that one wonders how much space remained for passengers:

Automatic Weighing Machine Co. - four machines at £10 per annum.
Automatic Amusement Co. - ten machines at £30 per year.
Sweetmeat Delivery Co. - after being in arrears, the rent for their machines was reduced to £35 per annum.
Automatic match machines - certain stations at a minimum rent of £13 10s. per year.

In June 1890 the *Isle of Wight County Press* announced a change in the time of arrival of the national newspapers:

We are glad to learn that the agitation of the Island local authorities for an earlier newspaper train and boat has been successful, and that on and after the first day of next month, the train will bring on the London papers direct to Stokes Bay, from whence they will be conveyed across the Solent by a boat put on to meet them. At Ryde Pier the 9.16 am train will bring them on to all stations on the Isle of Wight Railway.

A surprisingly lengthy down train is seen passing a family enjoying an outing on the river just south of Brading station.   *R. Silsbury Collection*

Chapter Ten

Board of Trade Regulation

Before 1889 Government legislation placed relatively few demands on the IWR. The regulation of management and operation of Britain's railways was channelled through the Railway Department of the Board of Trade; they had powers to demand returns of the amount of capital issued, details of a company's income received from passengers and freight and a summary of all manner of expenditure. Board of Trade Inspectors would inspect a new railway and sanction opening if it was not a danger to the public using it. Parliament extended their powers in 1871 to cover alterations to stations, junctions with new lines and to report on accidents. Amongst other requirements, signals had to be interlocked with points whenever a company submitted a railway for inspection but they were not obliged to upgrade lines already in use. This had tragic consequences when an accident took place at Armagh in Ireland in 1889. A lengthy excursion train was parted after the locomotive stalled on a steep gradient and, due to inadequate brakes, most of the carriages ran back to collide at speed with a following train, resulting in the loss of some 80 lives. Such were the effects of this tragedy on public opinion that Parliament quickly passed a Regulation of Railways Act to force companies to upgrade their lines. The Act empowered the Board of Trade to order companies to comply with certain requirements within set times. It sent such an order to the IWR on 29th November, 1890, giving one year to install block working systems and 18 months to interlock signals and fit continuous brakes to passenger locomotives and trains.

Block signalling between 'Brading and St John's, and also along the whole line' had been proposed in October 1875. Preece's Block Instruments were installed between Ryde and Sandown when a signal box came into use at Brading in 1882. A previous order in 1885 relating to unsafe cast-iron structures required the replacement of four underbridges that had cast-iron girders; the last iron girders in an overbridge at Lake were replaced on 19th September, 1891.

The first tangible changes in response to the Regulation of Railways Act were noted by the local press in April 1891, when trials began between Sandown and Brading with the Webb & Thompson Patent Combined Electric Train Staff; by September the whole line from Ryde to Ventnor had been so equipped. In January 1892 the IWR Board decided to fit the Westinghouse air brake at an estimated cost of £1,740. The quick-acting brake was a particularly good choice for a railway such as the IWR with six stations in 11¼ miles. In order to bring the signalling up to date, the IWR Board accepted a tender from Messrs Saxby & Farmer on 11th November, 1891 for alterations at Shanklin. This was followed by a second order on 15th January, 1892 for more modest improvements at Ryde, Hyde, Apse, Winstone, Wroxall and Ventnor; the last included the resignalling of No. 2 departure road for use also as an arrival road. Major-General Hutchinson visited the Island on 11th June, 1892, when he inspected and approved the changes at Ryde St John's Road, Shanklin and Ventnor.

The alterations at Shanklin were quite extensive. Although a second platform had been constructed in the 1870s, trains were not officially permitted to cross at the station and all could use the down platform. The latest Board of Trade Regulations made double track working essential and required the provision of a footbridge or other safe means of crossing the line. The company built a subway to give access to the second platform and employed Saxby & Farmer to resignal and interlock the station. On the up platform they erected a signal box to one of the firm's standard designs, but to give adequate sight of the station it was placed high up above the platform coverings; the signal box had 20 levers of which five were spare.

Sandown also lacked modern signalling but there changes were more complicated. A subway to replace the wooden footbridge between the platforms had been suggested as long ago as November 1883, but the Ryde, Newport & Cowes Joint Committee refused to pay more than the cost of routine maintenance. The existence of a level crossing and footpath across the line at the south end of the station restricted the length of the platforms, but after lengthy arguments the IWR and IWC obtained Parliamentary powers during 1890 to buy land to divert the crossing and build a subway. Plans of the proposed works were sent to the IWC in June 1891, but correspondence passed to and fro for months as the companies argued about the cost and their respective responsibilities. It was not until 25th February, 1893 that the *Isle of Wight County Press* reported that work had just begun. Platforms were extended and connections provided to give IWC trains direct access to and from Shanklin - a rarely-used facility before Southern Railway days. The up platform was widened, and new waiting rooms and a veranda roof provided, with a raised Saxby & Farmer signal cabin containing 32 levers of which four were spare. A subway between the platforms replaced the footbridge. Major General Hutchinson gave approval to the alterations on 18th May, 1893, subject to some minor alterations to the interlocking.

The signalling equipment purchased by the IWR were standard items supplied by signalling firms. Signals had wooden posts and lower quadrant arms but each supplier had their 'house style', principally in the design of embellishments to the tops of posts. As a result the products of Messrs Stevens and Saxby & Farmer became somewhat mixed at locations such as Ventnor and Ryde, where alterations were carried out at different dates. Home and distant signals had red arms - yellow arms to the latter did not appear until after the IWR ceased to exist in 1923.

The Regulation of Railways Act permitted railway companies to raise additional capital to pay for the improvements, subject to the sanction of the Board of Trade. The IWR wrote to the Board of Trade on 19th April, 1893 stating that £4,953. 10s. 4d. had been expended in complying with the Act authority was given to issue an additional £4,900 debentures.

Another provision of the 1889 Regulation of Railways Act was a requirement to display the fare on tickets. In certain circumstances railways could be exempt from this provision if the fare included extras such as the Ryde Pier toll. In the case of the IWR, it continued to issue its Edmundson-style printed tickets that had probably changed little since the railway opened. As late as 1903 IWR through tickets were not displaying the fare because one passenger wrote a letter of complaint to the Board of Trade on the matter. Although not required to do so, it seems the IWR then began issuing tickets printed with the fare plus the entry 'including 3d. for Ryde Pier toll'; colours of first, second and third tickets were respectively cream, blue and yellow. During the 1893 season the IWR was issuing 'Tourist' tickets giving unlimited travel for a week between stations on the railway at a cost of 7s. 6d. first class and 5s. 6d. second class. The tickets themselves measured about 3¾ in. by 2½ in. and were light green in colour. Each bore the name of the IWR and Brading companies and had provision for the insertion of the passenger's name and period of validity before issue. In an attempt to minimise fraud, the company demanded a deposit of 1s. that would be refunded if the bearer surrendered the ticket within one day of expiry and signed the back. Similar blue coloured tickets were issued for travel to all Isle of Wight stations (except Ryde Esplanade and Ryde Pier Head) priced at 16s. first class and 12s. second class; they were identical except for the heading which included the names of the Central and Freshwater companies. Timetables and fares were publicised in a 78 page book giving details of connecting train services and fares from numerous locations on the mainland.

The popularity of Ventnor as a winter resort for invalids led to the introduction of a special train in the Autumn of 1891. The LBSCR operated a fast train that left Victoria station in London at 12.0 noon and connected at Portsmouth with a ferry to Ryde. At 3.15 pm an IWR train left Ryde Pier Head on a non-stop journey to Ventnor. Dubbed the 'Invalids' Express' for obvious reasons, the timetable allowed 21 minutes for the journey but the train crew and station staff entered into the spirit of the occasion, and on the first run on 2nd November, 1891 reached Ventnor in 19 minutes; later trips achieved the journey in 18½ minutes. Given the need to change single line tokens *en route* this was a creditable achievement. Usually the train consisted of four carriages and a van - a light load even with a full complement of passengers. If stories about the train are to be believed, it travelled through stations considerably faster than officially allowed and train crews made full use of judiciously placed sand bins for the exchange of single line tokens; on occasions the train reached 60 mph. At first the heavier locomotives *Brading* and *Bonchurch* were used but later the smaller 2-4-0Ts were found more suitable. The express train much pleased Ventnor Council who passed a vote of thanks to the railway; what the passengers thought of the experience was not recorded! The train, which ran non-stop only in the down direction, appeared in the timetable until 1903 when it began calling at Shanklin - it ceased running altogether in 1908. The fast train could be identified by a round disc bearing a red cross on a white ground on the locomotive smokebox door. Other IWR trains carried a disc with a green centre and at night a lamp with a green lens; Bembridge branch locomotives carried a lamp all day. The introduction of special headlamps and discs probably followed the opening of the LSWR/LBSCR railway at Ryde when signalmen had to differentiate between Island companies' trains.

Apart from the addition of the fast train, advertised timetables differed little from those in previous years. In the winter of 1894-1895 there were 12 return workings to Ventnor increasing to 16 on Saturdays in summer. Their timing was dictated largely by the working of the steamers between Portsmouth and Ryde and a need to connect with London trains operated by the LSWR and LBSCR. Most journeys were slow, as in August 1895 a passenger leaving Ventnor on the first up train at 7.30 am would not expect to arrive at London Bridge until 10.50 am or Waterloo at 11.22 am. The IWR engine for the first up working would have come from an unadvertised early morning down mail and goods train.

Traffic carried by the railway continued the trend of previous decades. The numbers of first and second class passengers dropped, but those travelling third class exceeded all records. Goods traffic reached a peak in 1896 and then steadily declined until after the beginning of the next century.

Year ending 31st Dec.	Passenger traffic Numbers carried			Season tickets	Goods traffic Minerals tons	General tons	Gross receipts Passengers £	Goods £	Working expenses £	% of receipts
	First	Second	Third							
1891	49,604	363,491	301,255	109	49,147	27,438	27,525	10,217	15,173	40
1895	46,125	309,311	309,311	133	56,027	34,240	28,101	11,296	16,204	41
1900	48,007	263,950	526,937	151	35,805	24,270	29,973	11,740	19,845	48

The figures for third class included an increased number of workmen's tickets. The IWR ran no trains specifically for workmen (unlike the IWC) but issued tickets that were valid for one return journey each day by any train. During 1899, 322 monthly, 131 fortnightly and 362 weekly workmen's tickets were issued. There were strict rules governing their issue as an applicant had to give details of his full name, employment and employer; they were not available to 'master men', persons working as salesman or the self-employed.

The growth in the numbers of workmen's tickets and goods traffic was influenced by a increasing resident population in towns served by the railway - more residents wanted to travel and they also created a greater demand for goods, particularly coal. Whilst Brading declined in importance, the populations of Sandown, Shanklin and, to a lesser extent, Ventnor increased appreciably in the latter half of the 19th century. As the figures for 1927 show, this growth was not maintained in the remaining years of the company's life:

	1869	1894	1927
Ryde	9,269	10,952	11,294
Brading	3,709	1,560	1,696
Sandown	-	3,592	7,661
Shanklin	479	3,277	7,368
Ventnor	3,208	5,816	6,059

Reductions in the amount of goods carried between 1895 and 1900 were partly attributable to a wholesale revision of goods rates. Traders complained that neighbouring railways often charged a different rate to carry the same goods; this was hardly surprising as they had been fixed by numerous Acts of Parliament passed over a period of many years. The Board of Trade swept away the old charges and replaced them with a standard series of charges on a geographical basis. One set of rates applied to all railways in the Isle of Wight; the relevant

ISLE OF WIGHT RAILWAY.
CHEAP TOURIST TICKETS

ARE ISSUED AT THE UNDERMENTIONED FARES

ON WEEK-DAYS BY ALL CONNECTING TRAINS UP TO AND INCLUDING the 2.10 p.m. from VENTNOR and the 2.15 p.m. from Ryde.

And ON SUNDAYS BY ALL TRAINS.

FROM	VENTNOR 1R	2R	WROXALL 1R	2R	SHANKLIN 1R	2R	SANDOWN 1R	2R	BRADING 1R	2R	RYDE ST. JOHN'S ROAD 1R	2R	RYDE ESPLANADE 1R	2R	RYDE PIER HEAD 1R	2R	ST. HELENS 1R	2R	BEMBRIDGE 1R	2R	NEWPORT VIA SANDOWN 1R	2R	COWES VIA SANDOWN OR RYDE PIER 1R	2R	FRESHWATER and YARMOUTH VIA SANDOWN 1R	2R
VENTNOR			0 7	0 5			1 10	1 6	2 6	1 8	3 0	2 0	3 6	2 5	4 0	2 10	3 1	2 7	3 3	2 9	3 8	2 8	4 0	3 0	5 1	4 3
WROXALL	0 7	0 5			0 11	0 8	1 1	0 10	1 7	1 1	2 1	1 5	2 5	1 8	2 10	2 0	2 7	1 11	2 9	2 0	3 5	2 6	4 3	3 1	5 4	3 1
SHANKLIN	1 1	0 11	0 11	0 8			0 8	0 5	1 3	0 11	1 7	1 1	2 1	1 3	2 6	1 8	2 3	1 8	2 5	1 8	3 1	2 6	4 3	3 1	5 4	3 1
SANDOWN	1 10	1 6	1 7	1 1	0 8	0 5			0 8	0 5	1 3	0 11	1 8	1 3	2 1	1 8	1 9	1 3	1 15	1 0	2 8	2 0	3 6	2 7	4 7	3 5
BRADING	2 6	1 8	2 1	1 5	1 3	0 11	0 8	0 5			0 8	0 5	1 0	0 8	1 3	1 0	1 0	0 7	1 4	1 0	2 0	1 6	3 0	2 0	...	...
RYDE (St. John's Road)	3 0	2 0	3 0	2 0	1 7	1 3	1 3	0 11	0 8	0 5			0 7	0 6	1 0	0 10	0 7	0 6	0 10	0 7	2 8	2 0	3 6	2 6	...	...
„ (Esplanade)	3 6	2 5	3 6	2 5	2 1	1 3	1 8	1 4	1 0	0 8	0 7	0 6			0 3	0 2	0 9	0 7	1 11	1 3	...	...	...	...	...	...
„ (Pier Head)	4 0	2 10	4 0	2 10	2 6	1 8	2 1	1 8	1 3	1 0	1 0	0 10	0 3	0 2			1 3	0 11	2 5	1 9	...	...	...	...	...	...
ST. HELEN'S	3 1	2 7	2 7	1 11	2 3	1 7	1 9	1 3	1 0	0 7	0 7	0 6	0 9	0 7	1 3	0 11			0 5	0 4	3 2	2 6	4 0	3 0	5 10	3 10
BEMBRIDGE	3 3	2 9	2 9	2 0	2 5	1 9	1 15	1 0	1 4	1 0	0 10	0 7	1 11	1 3	2 5	1 9	0 5	0 4			3 4	2 6	4 2	3 1	5 3	3 11
ALVERSTONE	2 3	1 10	2 0	1 5	1 10	0 9	1 0	...	0 7	...	2 0	1 10	2 3	2 0	2 5	2 0	2 0	1 5	2 1	1 10	1 10	1 4	...	...	...	...
NEWCHURCH	2 8	2 1	2 5	1 11	1 10	1 0	1 6	1 0	0 11	0 7	2 3	1 8	3 2	2 3	3 8	2 8	2 11	2 1	2 3	1 6	1 6	1 0	2 3	1 7	...	...
HORRINGFORD	3 0	2 4	2 9	2 0	2 0	1 3	1 10	1 0	1 10	1 3	3 0	2 0	3 6	2 6	4 0	2 11	3 9	2 6	2 7	1 11	0 10	0 7	1 10	1 4	...	...
MERSTONE	3 4	2 8	3 1	2 3	2 5	1 7	2 2	1 3	2 2	1 7	3 2	2 6	3 6	2 8	4 4	3 3	3 9	2 9	2 11	2 1	1 0	0 9	1 3	1 1	...	...
BLACKWATER	3 8	3 0	3 5	2 7	3 0	2 2	2 6	2 1	2 6	2 11	3 6	2 10	...	...	4 8	3 7	4 0	3 0	3 4	3 9	0 9	0 6	0 11	0 9	...	...
SHIDE	4 2	3 3	3 11	2 10	3 2	2 0	2 7	2 2	3 0	2 2	...	...	...	...	...	...	4 3	3 2	3 7	2 6	0 2	...	0 9	0 7	...	...
NEWPORT	4 3	3 5	4 0	3 1	3 1	2 6	2 8	2 0	3 0	2 7	2 8	2 0	...	...	...	...	4 0	3 0	3 4	2 6	...	...	0 7	0 5	3 1	...
COWES	4 6	3 5	4 3	3 1	3 6	2 7	3 6	2 7	3 6	2 7	3 6	2 7	...	...	...	...	4 0	3 0	4 2	3 1	0 7	0 5			3 6	3 0
CARISBROOKE	4 5	3 5	4 4	3 1	3 6	2 7	2 11	2 1	3 1	2 7	3 0	2 0	...	...	...	...	3 11	3 0	3 0	3 1	...	...	...	...	...	...
CALBOURNE	5 8	4 1	5 5	3 9	4 8	3 3	4 8	3 3	4 8	3 3	4 8	3 3	...	...	...	...	5 2	3 8	5 4	3 9	...	...	...	...	...	...
NINGWOOD	6 2	4 7	5 11	4 3	5 3	3 9	5 3	3 9	5 3	3 9	4 8	3 3	...	...	...	...	5 8	4 2	5 10	4 3	...	...	...	...	...	...
FRESHWATER AND YARMOUTH	5 7	4 3	6 1	4 3	4 7	3 6	4 7	3 5	4 7	3 5	5 1	3 10	...	...	...	...	6 1	3 10	5 3	3 11	...	...	3 6	3 0		

☞ See Page 7 for Cheap Return Tickets between Ryde and Ventnor.

These Cheap Tickets are available to return by any train on day of issue only, except those issued on Saturdays and Sundays. They are only available to and from the Stations named thereon, which are available for return up to the following Monday night.

TICKETS AT SPECIAL REDUCED FARES

ARE ISSUED TO

SCHOOL, PICNIC and PLEASURE PARTIES,

Consisting of 10 First Class or 16 Third Class and upwards.

Apply to Station Agents, or to the Traffic Manager, Sandown, a day or two in advance.

Extract from Summer 1893 timetable booklet

legislation rejoiced in the title 'Railway Rates and Charges No. 9 (Isle of Wight Railway & c.) Order Confirmation Act 1892'.

Other matters affecting the railway were relatively minor compared with the changes wrought by Government. The winter of 1890-1891 was notable by its severity and a severe blizzard struck the South of England on 9th March, 1891, causing disruption to train services. On the IWR, the night goods train stuck in a drift just south of Wroxall derailing four wagons and delaying the first two passenger trains on the morning of 10th March. Another derailment took place on 6th November, 1891 when a locomotive and truck left the rails on a siding under repair in Ryde yard. The Board ordered that rules be tightened and the signalman and ganger, the latter in particular, be reprimanded for their carelessness.

Staff relations on the IWR received relatively little attention (in print). During the 19th century, if a man stayed out of trouble, he could expect a modest increase in his pay every year or so. There seemed to be no formal pay scale but seniority was acknowledged and there were distinct differentials between grades. Hours of work were very long, although it must be said that the IWR was no different from any other railway in this respect. Even before events that gave rise to the Regulation of Railways Act, the Railways Department of the Board of Trade had taken an interest in the hours of work of railway employees. They required railways to submit returns; that from the IWR in respect of July 1886 showed:

| | No. employed | Occasions when duty exceeded 12 hours by | | | | | |
		1 hour	2 hours	3 hours	4 hours	5 hours	6 hours
Passenger guards	3	19	-	-	-	-	-
Goods guards	2	1	-	2	-	-	-
Drivers and firemen	10	97	4	-	2	6	1
Signalmen	6	50	13	19	14	6	1

In case the reader might think these conditions existed only during the summer season, a return for January 1887 was no better and for the drivers and firemen slightly worse! In 1893 the Board of Trade and Railway & Canal Commissioners were given powers to force a reduction in the working of excessive hours and thereafter IWR employees enjoyed the luxury of shorter hours. The misdemeanours of one individual appeared with some regularity in staff records:

J.L. joined the IWR as a porter but was later promoted to signalman. He received a fine of 2s. 6d. 'for leaving the points in Ryde yard leading from main line to the upper part of the carriage siding unlocked on 14th August, 1880'. He had a further 2s. 6d. deducted on 10th September, 1881 'for causing a slight collision in Ryde yard between a passenger and goods engine thro' wrong shunt'. In August 1893 he was suspended for eight days for causing the 'Central Company's' engine to leave the track on points in Sandown station. He lost another 2s. 6d. on 24th March, 1894 for leaving his signal box 'thereby causing delay to 5.12 Special Train'. He last offence took place on 7th November, 1894 when 'drunkenness' led to a 14 day suspension and a reduction to the grade of Ryde goods porter.

The death of the Secretary, Robert Hicks, was reported in April 1893; he had been ill for four years and Henry Day had long since merged the Secretary's duties with his own. Other members of management and Board were more robust and, apart from the death of Abraham De Pass in 1897, continued to serve the company into the next century.

Henry Brent secured the Board's approval for some limited expenditure beyond normal renewals. In 1890 the company bought a house at Sandown for use by the station master, and stations had their platform coverings extended. From 1894 onwards locomotives received extensive repairs and overhauls and, towards the end of the century, additional rolling stock was purchased. For accounting purposes, costs of renewals were spread over a period of several years. On 7th August, 1895 Henry Brent wrote to the Board of Trade giving details of some minor changes in signalling arrangements at Ryde St Johns Road station. Col Addison made an inspection on 13th September and reported that a pair of up inner home and shunt signals had been installed. The remaining spare levers in the South signal box had been

One of the Beyer, Peacock 2-4-0Ts hustles its train along the line from Brading towards Sandown sometime between 1882 and the turn of the century. In the background can be discerned Brading chalk quarry served by a siding from the station.   *R. Brinton Collection*

Photographers loved to take views of locomotives at their 'home' stations. This is *Sandown* seen at Sandown not long after the rebuilding of the station in 1893. The wooden buffer beam to the locomotive carries a screw coupling for passenger vehicles and a five link loose coupling for goods use. The metal object on the footplate on the right is a lifting jack.

G.M. Miskin/T. Cooper Collection

utilised and some complicated interlocking added to the North box. The changes allowed trains to approach Ryde whilst an engine continued shunting in the station. Col Addison had doubts about the unusual signalling arrangements:

The Station Cabin now contains 34 levers, all in use, and the interlocking of the points and signals appears to have been correctly carried out. I must however point out that the plan here adopted of releasing the inner home signals by the advance slots and the outer by the inner home signals is not one which usually commends itself to the Board of Trade Inspection Officers. The station is however used jointly by the Isle of Wight and the Isle of Wight Central Companies and there are reasons for adopting the arrangement referred to which are not generally to be found and under the circumstances no objection need perhaps be raised.

The accounts show this work cost £120 so the company took care not to incur any further expense in altering track and signalling. Also in 1895, the Board of Trade had another bee in its bonnet when it asked for a return giving details of station nameboards - apparently travellers had difficulty in distinguishing station names from amongst a welter of advertisements. The IWR merely responded that nameboards were situated clear of adverts whilst station names were painted on seats and 'other suitable positions'. Frequent use was made of enamel signs, bought in from signal firms whose catalogues advertised a range of standardised station fittings in addition to their principal products.

The Diamond Jubilee of Queen Victoria in 1897 was an occasion for much celebration in the Isle of Wight and reflected a fondness that lingered for years after her death. The shareholders voted 50 guineas each to the Indian Famine fund, the National Hospital for Consumption and the Isle of Wight Infirmary. The IWR Board entered in to the spirit of the occasion by giving donations to the organisers of funds 'for providing Treats to the Children and aged poor' in towns served by the railway; Ryde, Sandown, Shanklin and Ventnor each received £5, Brading, Bonchurch, St Helens, Wroxall and Bembridge £2. The Board showed a similar generosity towards employees when they resolved to give each person one day's paid holiday to be taken on 22nd June, the day declared as a holiday to celebrate the event; a few essential staff worked on Jubilee Day but they received a day off in lieu. Locomotives and rolling stock were decorated with flags for the occasion.

The introduction of the Invalids' Express prompted a complaint about the lack of a footbridge across the railway at Brading - passengers had to use a foot crossing south of the platforms to gain access to the up platform and a footpath along the railway to Yarbridge. On 30th June, 1897 the Board of Trade received the following letter which they passed on to Henry Day for his comments:

> 5 Winton St
> Ryde
> 28 June 1897

Sir,

I. Wight Railway

Brading Station on this line is a junction Station for the S. Helens & Bembridge Branch Line and has *great need* of a bridge or sub-way.

Twice every week day an express train goes *down* to Ventnor & Sandown not stopping at Brading. Soon after these trains respectively pass Brading Station the line, a single one, is used for trains which stop there & to get to the Station, the up side, passengers from Yarbridge must cross the line *on a level*. No doubt most of the people who cross the line know of these trains, but I think the fact that it is a junction station ought to be sufficient reason for your department to insist on a sub-way being supplied, that is if they have the power to insist.

Traffic increases, & there are more trains, & unless some step is taken there will be I fear loss of life some day.

I am Sir,

your obedient servant
C.W. Moody

The pair of starting signals and the bracket over the tunnel mouth can be discerned in this view taken during shunting at Ventnor. On the left can be seen the IWR's varied collection of wagons. An additional spur and kickback siding have been added on the right.   *R. Silsbury Collection*

The lengthy line of carriages in the island platform includes some of the 1882 carriages with their higher roofs. The goods yard is crowded with wagons. Some further quarrying has taken place.
R. Silsbury Collection

Henry Day wrote a suitably robust reply:

> Isle of Wight Railway
> Engineer's and General Manager's Office
> Sandown
> 24 July 1897

Sir,

I have submitted to my Directors your letter of 28th June together with the copy letter from Mr Moody referred to therein having reference to the alleged necessity for a Bridge or Subway to be provided at Brading Station and in reply I have to point out for the information of the Department that strictly speaking there are no express trains on the Company's Railway. It is only a Single line and altho' certain trains do not stop at intermediate stations they all have to slow down when approaching and passing thro' stations to enable the Train Staffs to be exchanged by hand: consequently so far as the speed of the trains are concerned it is practically the same for both stopping and non stopping trains.

The traffic to be dealt with at Brading is small but should it reach such proportions as to necessitate a Bridge or Subway my Directors will provide one or the other as they have done at all other stations where the Traffic has called for it.

I may add that we have had no representation whatever from the public as to the want of a Bridge or Subway at Brading Station which was Inspected and passed by an Inspector of your Department when the small junction line to St Helens and Bembridge was constructed.

> I am Sir
> Your Obedient Servant
> H.K. Day
> Secretary

The Board of Trade passed the reply to Mr Moody adding that '. . . the Board of Trade have no power to compel the Company to construct a Bridge or a Subway at the Station.' Mr Moody would not let the matter rest and in April 1898 complained '. . . I am certain that in the case of any fatal accident the Railway Company will not escape the Censure of a jury.' Even before his letter, however, the IWR Board had asked Henry Brent to prepare an estimate of the costs of providing a footbridge or subway. Given the proximity of the River Yar that might easily flood a subway the Board wisely decided on a footbridge, and on 5th November, 1897 awarded a contract to W. Bain & Co. for its supply and erection; IWR staff built the foundations and the final bill was just short of £250.

Brading was the location of a little Yuletide humour:

Scene: Railway Station Platform (not 100 miles from Brading) during the busy season.

Strange Gentleman (to Station Master bustling about platform): 'You seem to have plenty to do here, Station Master.'

Station Master: 'Do, Sir; what with trains coming this way and trains coming that way, besides attending to passengers' luggage and goods traffic, I do have something on my mind.'

Strange Gentleman: 'Yes, I know something of what it is, being Station Master at Clapham Junction.'

Exit Station Master as train arrives: 'B.... Junction. Change here for B...., &c., &c.'

Sir,

Doubtless the festivities of Christmas assisted the vivid imagination of the person (late Station Master at Clapham Junction) who invented and inserted in your last issue the remarkable conversation said to have passed between himself and me at my station. I flatly deny uttering the words he attributed to me either to him or to anyone else, and shall feel obliged if you will, in your next impression insert this my denial, and if he will condescend to reply, be candid enough to add his name and address.

> I am, Sir,
> Yours obediently,
> GEO. CORBETT
> Station Master

[*Isle of Wight County Press* 27th December, 1890 and 3rd January, 1891]

Shanklin station seen after the alterations made in the 1890s. The top of the signal box can be seen above the platform covering on the left. The main building and its later extension have acquired ornate ridge tiles. The wooden structures nearest the camera cover stairs to the subway.   *R. Silsbury Collection*

The disc on the smokebox shows that the train speeding through Shanklin sometime between 1892 and 1900 is the Invalids Express. The profusion of metal signs and wooden poster boards is typical of IWR stations.   *R. Silsbury Collection*

On 11th October, 1899 war broke out in South Africa between Britain and the Boers. The Minute book first mentioned it on 31st March, 1900 when Henry Day informed the IWR Directors that Porter 'D', who had worked on the railway since 1894 and was a reservist, had been called for service with his regiment in South Africa. They agreed to keep his job open and pay half his wages to his wife. Porter 'D' was one of several employees to see military service and he survived to return to the Island but left the railway in 1908. Such was the war 'fever' sweeping the country at the time that even the IWR joined in:

A correspondent writes that on the arrival of the Ventnor train at Brading yesterday morning warning was received that 'Boers' were in possession of the line at Smallbrook.

Precautionary measures were adopted on nearing the spot, the brakes being applied and a scout sent out in the person of the stoker, who found four big 'porkers' in occupation.

With the assistance of the guard the enemy, after showing a stubborn resistance, was driven back, and the train was able to proceed in safety.

[*Isle of Wight County Press* 25th November, 1899]

After the end of the main campaign in South Africa in the Autumn of 1900, the commander, Field Marshall Earl Roberts, returned to Britain and landed at Cowes on 2nd January, 1901 before travelling to Osborne House to see the Queen, barely three weeks before her death. In connection with his visit, the IWR arranged for a train of army 'Volunteers' to travel from Ventnor to Whippingham. In a letter to Henry Brent, Mr Day wrote: 'The Central Co want both Carriages and Engine to go thro - I see no objection to the former but I don't like the latter. What do you say? The load would be about 12 coaches in all'.

In this view of Ventnor, the platform covering has been extended towards the goods shed and the island platform possesses light standards. One of the Oldbury three-compartment saloon composites stands on the right. At the rear of the line of wagons to its left is IWR goods brake van No. 1. *R. Silsbury Collection*

A wealth of detail can be seen in this view of the sluice gates under construction at St Helens in 1879. On the left is the nucleus of the north quay complete with locomotive shed.
R. Brinton Collection

The route of the Brading Harbour Railway.

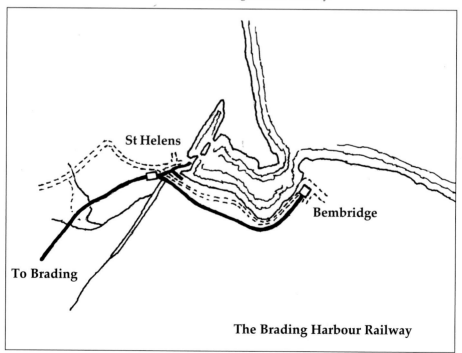

St Helens

Bembridge

To Brading

The Brading Harbour Railway

Chapter Eleven

Brading to Bembridge

For centuries Brading Haven provided a safe anchorage for sailing vessels. At one time the sea entered the haven both from St Helens and Sandown Bay. In 1388 Sir William Russell of Yaverland constructed a causeway and bridge at Sandown Bay to prevent the sea flooding adjacent low-lying land. The Oglander family reclaimed Brading north marsh in 1562, and in 1594 embankments were constructed near Yarbridge to recover a further acreage. This work prevented vessels from berthing close to Brading High Street and a replacement stone quay was constructed, a short distance east of the town. There followed one failure: Sir Hugh Middleton built an embankment between St Helens and Bembridge in 1622 to reclaim the remainder of the haven; in 1630 the sea breached it and the land was inundated.

By the 19th century the haven had become badly silted and only vessels with a shallow draught could anchor or land goods at the town quay. Despite this, during the 1860s the IWES built a spur railway to its own wooden structure nearby. In 1863 the local press mentioned proposals for a branch from Rowborough to St Helens and via a causeway to Bembridge; it met opposition, probably from Sir Henry Oglander who owned much of the land. When the Bembridge Railway, Tramway and Pier Company obtained its Act of Incorporation in 1864 it included powers for a railway on a different route, beginning with a junction with the IWR near Brading station and following the south shore of the harbour to Bembridge Point where there was to be a pier. The Act also authorised a tramway to Culver Down, together with reclamation of the salt marsh and mud flats to the landward side of the railway. The realisation that the pier would have been in an exposed position beyond Bembridge Point resulted in the placing of a Bill a year later for changes in the route of the railway, to replace the tramway to Whitecliffe Bay by a railway, the construction of an embankment between Bembridge and St Helens Mill with wharves at St Helens and reclamation of Brading Harbour. This time local residents overwhelmingly opposed the embankment and wharves, the whole scheme was abandoned, no capital was raised and the original powers lapsed.

Ten years later fresh proposals emerged. A Bill was placed before the 1874 session of Parliament by which the Brading Harbour Improvement Railway and Works Company would construct an embankment between St Helens and Bembridge, quays near St Helens Mill and a railway along the north edge of the harbour to a junction with the IWR goods' branch near its quay. The Engineer, Richard J.H. Saunders of Ventnor, estimated the cost of the line at £15,000 plus £25,000 for the embankment and quays, the amount of capital subsequently authorised. Sir Henry Oglander, who had bought the haven from the Earl of Yarborough in order to preserve the view from his house at Nunwell, died during the passage of the Bill through Parliament. Lady Oglander's request for £10,000 compensation was probably not met, but she would have been relieved of the burden of maintaining the 16th century embankments. There was no other opposition and the Bill became law on 7th August, 1874.

Little is known of the proceedings of the BHIR because no Minute books and few other papers have survived. According to the Act of Incorporation the first Directors were William H. Saunders, a solicitor with connections with the Isle of Wight (Newport Junction) Railway and William A. Mansell - the link with the IWNJ was reinforced by the employment of R.J.H. Saunders who was also Engineer of that company. In 1875 a Mr A. C. Bruce wrote on the company's behalf to the IWR asking if it would guarantee part of the expenditure; naturally the IWR refused to accept such a commitment. That year control of the BHIR effectively passed to the House and Land Investment Trust Company Limited, one of the 'Liberator' group of companies run by Jabez S. Balfour MP and funded by the Liberator Building Society. The group were responsible for building the Hotel Cecil, Whitehall Court and various large office blocks in London. By 1879 Balfour had become Chairman of the BHIR and in 1882 Henry S. Freeman was said to be his deputy.

By the end of 1874 Richard Saunders had been replaced as Engineer by James Walker. Scott & Edwards of Melmerby, Yorkshire was appointed contractor and the company had served notices for the purchase of land. Soon afterwards the contractor began work on the erection of a barrier between St Helens and Bembridge; this involved the transportation of thousands of tons of chalk, clay and other rubble from Bembridge Down and Portsdown Hill behind Portsmouth. Sluices were constructed at St Helens to control the flow of water from the River Yar. Progress escaped the attentions of the local press until May 1877 when they reported that the railway works were proceeding briskly. That year station buildings at the two stations were erected (rather prematurely as it proved) and, after a court action, the St Helens Oyster Fishery Company received £8,000 compensation for loss of business.

For a shareholders' meeting on 29th August, 1878 the IWR Board wrote that the line from Brading to St Helens opened for traffic on 1st August, but the Directors failed to mention that only goods traffic was being carried. Six months later the IWR Board predicted the opening of the BHIR to Bembridge during the summer of 1879 and stated that steamers were already calling at a small pier there. The few returns to the Board of Trade by the BHIR gave details of traffic carried in 1880 and 1881; for 1882 and later years, the information was included in returns made by the IWR.

Year ending 31st Dec.	Goods traffic Minerals tons	General tons	Merchandise £	Minerals £	Misc. £	expenses £	% of expenditure
1880	13,185	6,950	449	329	13	989	125
1881	13,573	8,249	357	468	825	576	69

BHIR goods rates were mentioned in a letter from Henry Day accepting an offer for the purchase of some scrap metal - one sentence read:

In addition to the above you would have to pay the Brading Harbour Company's charges of 6d. per ton for carriage over that Company's Railway from Brading to St Helens and a further 6d. per ton for unloading from trucks to vessel - in all 1s. per ton.

Desperate attempts were made to complete the embankment between St Helens and Bembridge. The company's property had already been mortgaged to its financiers on 14th September, 1879 in return for capital. The BHIR's returns to the Board of Trade recorded only details of BHIR authorised capital, far less than the expenditure incurred by the House and Land Investment Trust with which BHIR finances were entangled - small wonder that bricks used in building Bembridge station were said to have cost a £1 each!

Attempts to complete the barrier across the harbour were frustrated when the sea broke through at the Bembridge end, and for weeks workmen battled with the elements in a vain attempt to seal the breach. In February 1880 they achieved victory after building a row of piles and a second short section of embankment at an extra cost, said to total £10,000. By then time limits for completion of the railway had expired, so a further Act had to be secured for an extension of time, powers to raise additional capital and permitting the company to provide and work steam vessels between Brading Harbour and Hayling Island, Portsmouth, Southampton and other ports. According to a Board of Trade return the costs of securing the 1874 Act had been £4,500 and that in 1881 £750.

By June 1881 the BHIR was in the hands of a Receiver, the Manager Mr Freeman. That month an excursion train took local children to Ryde to celebrate the centenary of the Robert Raikes Sunday-School movement; scaffolding had to be erected to allow passengers to board the train as the station platforms were incomplete. The BHIR gave notice that its goods service between St Helens and Brading would be discontinued; lengthy discussions resulted in a fresh agreement but whether the IWR took over working the goods trains in 1881 is not clear - the IWR Board again put off making the necessary extensions at Brading station to accommodate the Brading company's passenger trains.

In an agreement dated 28th February, 1882 between Henry Freemen (for the Brading company) and the IWR, the latter undertook to operate the line as part of its system for 50 per cent of the gross receipts. The IWR used two locomotives, *St Helens* and *Bembridge*, owned by the BHIR, but provided rolling stock, station and maintenance staff - Joseph Bourne collected an additional £10 per month for managing BHIR train services. Mr Freeman wrote to the Board of Trade on 24th April, 1882 giving notice that the railway was ready to open for passenger traffic. Precisely one month later, Col Yolland, the Board of Trade inspector, inspected an enlarged station at Brading, the IWR goods branch to Brading Quay and the BHIR line to St Helens and Bembridge. The first of two reports read as follows:

Railway Department
Board of Trade
1 Whitehall
25 May 1882

Sir,

I have the honour to report for the information of the Board of Trade that in compliance with the instructions contained in your minute of the 16th Instant, I have inspected the Brading Harbour Railway which commences in an end on junction with the Brading Branch of the Isle of Wight Railway near Brading Quay and terminates at Bembridge, a length of 2m 14.3 chains.

The line is single throughout with sidings at a Brick Yard, at St Helens Station and at Bembridge.

The land has not been purchased nor any arrangements made for an additional line at any future period. The width of the line at formation level is 20 feet, the gauge is 4 ft. 8½ inches and the width between the line of the sidings is 6 feet.

The line is laid with steel rails flat bottom that weight 72 lbs. per linear yard in lengths of 21, 22 and 24 feet on cross sleepers of Baltic Timber rectangular, the smallest scantling 9 in. x 5 in. and the average 10 in. x 5 in. in lengths of 9 feet placed 2 ft 6 in. apart except at the joints where the distance is 1 ft. 10 inches.

The joints of the rails are fished with two plates and four bolts. The rails are fastened to the cross sleepers by fang bolts at the joints and at some intermediate sleepers by dog spikes.

The ballast is shingle and is stated to be 1 ft. 6 inches in depth below the under surface of the sleepers.

There are stations at St Helens and at Bembridge, the Terminal Station. The fencing consists partly of continuous iron wire 4 feet high with 5 wires and the distance between supports 7 feet, and straining posts at intervals, and partly of larch posts and rail fencing with 4 rails 4 feet in height with intermediate brick posts.

There are no bridges over or under but there are two low viaducts, one of three yards, and the other of four yards in length, entirely constructed of timber - sufficiently strong. There are no level crossings.

The steepest gradient on the line has an inclination of 1 in 100 and the sharpest curve has a radius of 12 chains.

At the siding at the Brick Field there is a wooden frame with four levers and with the points locked by Annett's key kept at St Helens Station.

At St Helens Station the signal box contains a Locking Frame with 10 levers, none spare, and at Bembridge there is a similar box with the same number of Levers, none spare. The interlocking is correct.

The line is constructed partly alongside the River Yar and partly alongside of land reclaimed from the sea. I have pointed out on the ground where fencing is required alongside the River Yar, and also alongside of the Brick Field, and this fencing is at once to be put up.

The guards outside the rails on the viaduct are fixed too far from the rails and are to be brought to within 7 or 8 inches of the rail so as not to interfere with the Rolling Stock. This is to be done at once.

I am informed that the line is to be worked by the Isle of Wight Railway Company and that only one Engine in Steam carrying a Train Staff is to be used between Brading and Bembridge.

An undertaking to this effect, signed by the Chairman and Secretary of the Company should be sent without delay to the Board of Trade and I can recommend the Board of Trade to Sanction the opening of the line for traffic as soon as this undertaking has been received.

I am.......

W. Yolland
Colonel

A separate report was written concerning the IWR's line, a length of 43 chains. It differed from the Brading company's line in several respects. Ballast was sandstone 15 in. deep and there was just one culvert. Rails were partly steel flat bottom in 21 and 24 ft lengths, weight 70 lb. per linear yard, fixed to sleepers by fang bolts and partly in double-headed rail of similar lengths weighing 75 lb. per yard and carried in 36 lb. iron chairs held in place by oak keys placed outside the rails, the chairs being fastened by spiked treenails. Rail joints were fished using iron plates 18 in. long and ¾ in. thick fastened by four ¾ in. bolts. Sleepers measured 10 in. by 5 in., 8 ft 11 in. long spaced 2 ft 10 in. apart except at joints when they were 1 ft 10 in. The steepest gradient was 1 in 150 and the sharpest curve 12 chains.

Brading station had been altered to provide a bay platform and run-round loop on the opposite side of the down platform. Behind the branch loop a signal box was erected to the same design as that at Ventnor with wooden upper works on a brick base. Stevens supplied a 30-lever frame (it had two spare levers), upgraded the signalling and interlocked the signals, they also equipped the BHIR line. At a level crossing near the site of Brading Quay was a signal box containing eight levers all in use - the tracks to the quay were not mentioned. Apart from minor comments about the locking in the box and the absence of a name board at Brading, Col Yolland reported favourably on the works.

The railway opened to passenger traffic on 27th May, 1882 ready for the Whitsun holiday when it was said 300 St Helens and Bembridge villagers took advantage of a free trip to Ryde. Just as the local press largely ignored the construction of the line, so its opening received only a brief report in the *Isle of Wight Times* for Thursday 1st June, 1882:

> BRADING Harbour new railway is in a fair state of completion. The line was inspected by Colonel Yolland RE, Her Majesty's Inspector of Railways, and found to be in a sufficiently satisfactory condition to warrant his passing the line for passenger traffic. On Saturday passengers were conveyed over the line for the first time.
>
> At Brading a suitable station has been erected, platform widened, a new siding constructed and a handsome signal station adorns the eastern embankment. Arrangements have been made for working the new line of railway which will be under the management of Mr J. Bourne.

Situated across the road from Bembridge station the Royal Spithead Hotel opened on 15th July; it was another lavish 'Liberator' project and is alleged to have cost £10,000. A special party with Jabez Balfour at the head travelled from London to Portsmouth where they boarded the vessel *Alexandra* for passage direct to Bembridge. On the railway a special 'saloon' train hauled by the engine *Bembridge* decorated with flowers and bunting ran from Bembridge to Brading. At Brading a military band and other guests joined the train to return to Bembridge for lunch. The local press reported that the embankment was lit from end to end by fairy lights.

The spur to Brading Quay and Bembridge left the main line at Brading by means of a trailing connection to the down loop. Passenger trains used the bay platform and run-round loop allowing locomotive and stock movements to be separated from the main line. A short siding from the loop usually accommodated a spare carriage. Bembridge trains could be signalled to arrive or depart from the down main platform if required. The down platform was provided with a lengthy covering that nethertheless gave little real shelter in windy weather. The IWR claimed to have spent £3,164 on extending the station for the Brading company, of which £940 18s. 11d. went to Stevens & Co. for the signalling, etc.

Upon leaving Brading the railway briefly followed the main line to Ryde before executing a curve to the right. Shortly afterwards it straightened and separated from the goods branch just before a level crossing (64 chains from Brading). The quay line continued curving to the right before crossing an embankment built in 1630 to end on a wooden quay. Immediately beyond the level crossing were sidings on land rented to a firm of coal merchants managed by the Executors of Col Hargreaves - they complained in June 1879 that the construction of the BHIR cut off their access to the sea. A cement works on the site was first mentioned in the IWR Minutes for 1884 and 1885, when an agreement was concluded with a Mr Jolliffe to provide a siding. The works had closed by 1905 when a Mr Gosling, who planned to reopen them, unsuccessfully asked for a reduction in the rate of 1s. a ton for the carriage of coal from St Helens and cement in the reverse direction. Correspondence lapsed after Mr Gosling failed to obtain agreement with the owner of an old quarry just south of Brading station to supply chalk. In January 1907 a Mr Charles Lingham also tried to gain a reduction in rates and enquired if the IWR would sell land, a cottage and store adjoining the works. The store and some adjoining land already had a tenant, but the IWR Board offered the remainder on a 14 year lease at £40 per annum plus 3d. per yard royalty on any material quarried there. In 1912 a Mr Greville rented the land on behalf of the Isle of Wight Cement Company and the works reopened soon afterwards; it lasted only a short time, as on 30th December, 1914 Henry Day reported that the company had become insolvent owing money for freightage and rent. In 1921 the cement works again resumed production but it appears to have lasted only a short time; the SR used the siding to store spare sets of carriages during winter months.

After leaving the Brading Quay branch, the BHIR followed the banks of the harbour towards St Helens. Halfway along this stretch a spur led to a brick works built in 1880 and known as Carpenters or Faithfull's siding. The siding was the site of an accident on 12th June, 1885 when guard A. G. was crushed between a wagon and a coal shed during shunting operations; he died in the Infirmary five days later. The IWR renewed the agreement with Mr O. Faithfull in 1902 and the siding remained in intermittent use until removed in 1946.

A short distance beyond, the railway reached the only intermediate station at St Helens (1 mile 55 chains). The station building dated from 1877 and matched that at Bembridge and just beyond the platform was a small signal box and water crane. The line to Bembridge curved sharply to the right throwing off a spur to St Helens Quay that continued straight on across the embankment road, before bifurcating into sidings on the north and south quays. The north quay was the oldest part of the complex and predated completion of the line to Bembridge. A stone-built locomotive shed capable of accommodating two small locomotives dated from these early days - it ceased to be used for locomotive purposes in October 1921. An ornate water tank over a small smithy adjoined the shed. Across the road behind the quay was a gas works built in 1891 to 1892 to supply St Helens, Bembridge and Seaview; small skips of coal were wheeled by hand across the road to the gas works on a short length of narrow gauge track added in 1903. The IWR later built a transhipment shed for use by Chaplin's at the far end of the quay. A track branched to the right across the entrance to the Eastern Yar to reach sidings on the south quay; it handled mainly mineral traffic and had a transhipment crane running the length of the quay on its own track.

Between St Helens and Bembridge lies the roughly 'L' shaped embankment that excludes the sea from the harbour. Along its top is the road over which the BHIR and its successors extracted a toll from users. After leaving St Helens station, the railway rose slightly as it curved sharply to the right. It then crossed the Eastern Yar just upstream of sluice gates that controlled the output of water to the sea. SR records refer to the existence of three separate bridges; St Helens bridge measured approximately 113 ft in length on 13 spans built with timber piles, girders and decking. The adjoining Embankment Road bridge had been rebuilt in IWR days with four spans 77 ft long in reinforced concrete piles, girders and decking. The Wharf bridge leading to the south quay had a length of 94 ft on eight spans, all in timber. The line then headed across reclaimed land on its own low embankment as it paralleled the road towards the terminus at Bembridge (2 miles 65 chains). Between the two an area of marsh, commonly called Bembridge lagoon, became home to a sizeable population of wild fowl; part of the area was used for gravel extraction at one time.

The station building at Bembridge differed from that at St Helens only in being the opposite way round in relation to the access road and railway - at St Helens the facade and windows faced the village but the opposite applied at Bembridge. As the building predated the track by several years it has been suggested that the layout differed somewhat from that which had been intended. If the deposited plans are anything to go by, it was not originally intended to provide a road along the embankment. The railway line would then have approached the station closer to the shore and passed on the opposite side of the building.

Reproduced from the 25", 1908 Ordnance Survey Map

St Helens station and quays.

A view of St Helens station taken in April 1951, it had hardly changed since IWR days.
C. G. Woodnutt/T. Cooper Collection

Chaplin & Co.'s barge *Excelsior* stands alongside the north quay at St Helens in IWR days. The rudimentary shelter for unloading was later replaced by a larger purpose-built shed at the far end of the quay. The water tower and roof of the engine shed can be discerned to the left whilst the large building in the background is Edward Way's flour mill. *R. Brinton Collection*

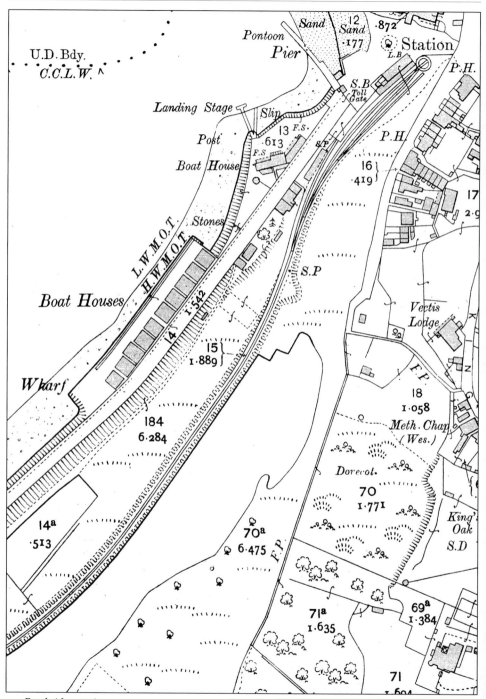

Bembridge station.   *Reproduced from the 25″, 1908 Ordnance Survey Map*

The track layout at Bembridge was a model of simplicity: a 16 ft 5 in. diameter turntable gave access to the platform road and a run-round loop. Coal and coke were dealt with at a siding and wharf at the Brading end of the station, just across the road from a pier built to serve the Brading company's steamers. A second siding was added parallel to the run-round loop after the IWR bought the line. The station buildings at St Helens and Bembridge were arguably the most impressive railway buildings in the Island. Built principally in red brick, the ornate style of finish to the eaves, chimneys and dormer windows to the upper storeys lifted them well above the ordinary. This served to set them apart from their more austere cousins on the IWR, whilst that at Bembridge made a perfect foil for the grandiose hotel across the road. There was an office for the booking clerk, accomodation for passengers, the remainder of the building being living accommodation.

The first station master of Bembridge was a young man of 24 years, a Mr William Weeks. He joined the IWR in July 1874 as a ticket collector at Sandown and soon gained promotion to parcels and goods clerk at Ventnor before becoming a station master in May 1877 at the smallest station, Wroxall. In April 1882 he transferred to Bembridge; a slight reduction in pay was offset by the provision of living accommodation, a decided advantage over Wroxall for a man with a wife and young family. But life was not kind to William Weeks as after nine years at Bembridge he died of 'a long and painful illness' on Sunday 8th November, 1891. His coffin was conveyed to its last resting place by train and borne by a group of platelayers, several heads of department represented the IWR and five of its eight station masters attended. An obituary notice in the *Isle of Wight County Press* for 14th November, 1891 described him as 'the respected station master at Bembridge'.

The railway was only a by-product of the activities of the BHIR and its parent company, the House and Land Investment Trust. Roughly 800 acres had been reclaimed but a decline in the value of farming land meant that it had little apparent value. The completion of the hotel was followed by the development of a golf course on the Duver and other recreational activities designed to attract the wealthy to the area. Of the railway's effects on the villages it served, this can best be illustrated by a quote from Capt. de Boulay's 1911 book *Bembridge Past and Present*: 'Bembridge found all the blessings of modern civilisation showered on it as if by a magician's hand'.

For the BHIR itself, the financial position did not improve and in April 1883 the IWR Board decided to charge interest at 7½ per cent on the capital expended in enlarging Brading station for the BHIR. At an IWR Board meeting on 2nd July, 1883 the Directors read correspondence concerning the activities of steamers operating from a wooden pier opposite the station at Bembridge to Seaview, Portsmouth and Southsea. Apparently the Board had not anticipated their operation when the working agreement was drawn up and ordered Joseph Bourne to report on the extent to which the railway suffered from this competition. In May 1885 the IWR bowed to the inevitable and agreed to run additional trains to meet the steamers and issue special fares between Bembridge and Ventnor.

As if the BHIR were not a sufficient speculation, proposals for the introduction of a train ferry between the mainland and St Helens came to public attention in 1881. Samuel L. Mason, General Manager of the North British Railway from 1867 to 1874, promoted the idea of a train ferry between the mainland and the Isle of Wight. At times he acted as an expert witness for the LBSCR and convinced the company of the scheme's merits. The North British Railway operated two train ferries across the Rivers Forth and Tay, of which one from Tayport to Broughty Ferry ceased running in 1881. In November 1881 Mason bought an 1858 vintage steamer *Carrier* along with moveable cradles and winding engines for £3,400. He made agreements with the LBSCR, the Receiver of the BHIR and others to secure rights to parts of the foreshore at St Helens and at Langston near the Hayling Island branch. On 14th February, 1884 the Isle of Wight Marine Transit Company Limited was formed with a capital of £30,000 in £10 shares. Jabez S. Balfour MP became Chairman and finance came from his group of companies. The Transit company agreed to buy the benefits of the agreements for £28,425 including £7,000 for *Carrier* although part of the payment was in shares. *Carrier* could carry

We have included this photograph because it clearly shows the platform of Bembridge station and signal box before the construction of the canopy. The ivy has grown a little but there is evidently a lack of siding space as dumb buffered wagon No. 35 stands on the loop road whilst being unloaded.   *R. Brinton Collection*

This delightful view of Bembridge station amply demonstrates the towering presence of the hotel. A gathering of staff have had their picture taken with the branch locomotive *Bembridge* and the Golden Valley carriages, possibly soon after the stock arrived in 1887.
                                                        F.N. Broderick/R. Brinton Collection

up to 14 wagons on two tracks, each having a maximum load of four tons. Ramps to allow wagons to be run on and off the vessel were installed at Langston and St Helens, the latter being just beyond the south quay. Services began on 1st September, 1885, patronised by the LBSCR which repeatedly invited the London & South Western Railway to join in the venture. The Rector of Carisbrooke presumably bought some shares in the Transit company as he was prompted to write: 'The operations of the Transit Company give the promise of a great boon to the Isle of Wight'. Despite this accolade *Carrier* had difficulties in operating successfully in the exposed waters of the Eastern Solent, but the LBSCR was persuaded that the undertaking was a worthwhile investment and bought the company in 1886. The service operated at a considerable loss until it ended on 31st March, 1888. The gear at St Helens lay about until August 1900 when Mr Brent reported an offer of £65 for the remains - the Board insisted on payment of £75 cash before removal!

The other schemes were more low key. In 1882 Frank Caws, builder of a chain pier at Seaview, promoted a Bill for powers to construct a tramway from the pier to a terminus close to the old abbey tower at St Helens, a length of 1¾ miles; the tramway would have been single except for two passing loops. Three years were allowed for completion and motive power could be 'animal, steam or mechanical'. The local population opposed its construction and Parliament threw out the Bill. In 1899 Mr Caws promoted a scheme a light railway from Ryde to the pier at Seaview, but this time powered by electricity. An application for a Light Railway Order was made to the Light Railway Commissioners who held an inquiry at Ryde Town Hall on 20th October. Again the residents of Seaview almost unanimously opposed the scheme and convinced the Commissioners that the line should not be built.

In 1892, after some dubious dealings, the heart of Jabez Balfour's empire, the Liberator Building Society, suspended payments. Balfour fled to Argentina but was captured and handed over to the British authorities in April 1895. After a trial for fraud he served his prison sentence at Parkhurst jail. In May 1895 the United Realisation Company was created to take over the assets of the Liberator Building Society and associated companies including the BHIR. The BHIR had continued to require the services of a succession of Managers and Receivers; those named on surviving documents included Francis M. Coldwells, in 1893 C.J. Stewart, and a year later S. Wheeler; E. du Boulay, the harbour master, was described as the 'local manager'.

In 1894 the Brading company gave notice that it proposed to apply for an Act to define the limits of Brading Harbour, construct an extension to the quay at the northern edge of the harbour at St Helens, operate steamboats and tugs and levy tolls. It also proposed a change of name to the Brading Harbour & Railway Company and powers to raise a further £30,000 by the issue of debenture stock. The Bill encountered significant opposition to the harbour proposals and had to be withdrawn. In December 1895 the Brading company had placed a fresh Bill before Parliament, similar to but less controversial than that a year earlier. The Bill became law on 14th August, 1896 authorising a change of name to the Brading Harbour and Railway Company (BHR) and, although the Act did not benefit the railway, it did clarify the extent of the harbour and the company's rights to tolls, etc.

Meanwhile the IWR and BHR had been in desultory correspondence mainly concerning the condition of the track and the engine *Bembridge*. Suddenly, a special meeting of the IWR Board was called for 3.0 pm on 24th November, 1896. The Chairman reported that the United Realisation Company had offered to sell the railway and quays for £10,000. He recommended they offer £8,500, plus a contribution to the costs of gaining the necessary Parliamentary sanction. Negotiations were left in his hands.

The companies needed to obtain Parliamentary approval for the sale and the process began when the BHR placed a Bill before the 1897 session; the Bill failed possibly because it attempted to authorise additional capital for the IWR. On 10th June, 1897 the two companies agreed to share the costs of promoting a fresh Bill that the IWR placed before the 1898 session. The Isle of Wight (Brading Harbour and Railway) Act dissolved the Brading company and transferred ownership of the harbour and railway to the IWR for £16,500; it also gave authority to the IWR for the raising of an additional £30,000 in stock and £10,000 in debentures, subject to the sanction of its shareholders. An agreement attached to the Act listed numerous conditions and provisions, mainly to safeguard the rights of local residents.

The Autumn of 1898 was taken up with legal matters. The date of transfer of ownership was 31st July, but until the purchase money could be paid over, the IWR was obliged to pay interest of 4 per cent. An IWR shareholders meeting took place on 1st September when the Directors obtained authority to issue £23,100 as ordinary stock, the additional capital counted for dividend purposes from 1st January, 1899. Existing shareholders were given the option of buying the stock, most of whom did so. Mr Beale, the company's solicitor, paid the full purchase price and interest to the United Realization Company on 31st October; all assets of the Brading company were in the hands of the Realization company who held the BHR's entire share holding.

The purchase of the railway included the harbour, quays, a sizeable acreage of land and equipment such as the steam cranes on the quay and the locomotive *Bembridge*. The complexity of the sale led to one plot of land adjoining the gas works at St Helens being conveyed to the IWR in error, and the solicitor had to transfer it back again! The United Realization Company held a land sale at Bembridge on 20th September, 1898 when over 50 more parcels of land were disposed of, including St Helens gasworks and numerous buildings at St Helens and Bembridge. The Chairman with one of the Directors attended and purchased some lots on behalf of the company. In total the IWR paid about £1,500 for various bits of land adjoining the railway. In the following weeks there ensued some complicated negotiations with other purchasers as each sought to exchange parcels of land until everyone ended up with what they wanted. The Board wisely declined an offer to buy the BHR steamers - the Royal Spithead Hotel had been sold in 1894.

Naturally the IWR had to spend more money on the railway it purchased. In June 1899 extensive repairs were made to one of the steam cranes at St Helens at a cost of £125 including £42 10s. for a new boiler. In the following October, the Board authorised work to repaint the stations and enlarge the booking offices by the construction of brick single-storey lean-tos; one such extension at Bembridge was added to the end of the station building close to the turntable. On 4th August, 1902 a Mr J. Allen fell whilst alighting from a carriage that had 'overlapped' the short platform at St Helens; the Board ordered a lengthening of the platform by 81 ft and additional fencing. Wheeler Bros of Ryde successfully tendered in February 1903 for the construction of a gate keeper's cottage at Brading Quay and repainting of cottages and Ferry House, and in May 1904 for covering the platforms at the two stations. To reduce the amount of coal dust flying around, a cover to the coal wharf at Bembridge was provided. The importance of Messrs Chaplin's traffic to the railway at St Helens was acknowledged by the expenditure of £80 on providing a transit shed for their use.

Inevitably the permanent way on the branch needed renewal. By December 1899 some chaired track had been laid between St Helens and Bembridge but this applied only to running lines, sidings and the run-round loop at Bembridge remained in flat-bottom rail, although the opportunity was taken to add a second siding at Bembridge and rearrange those on the quay. More permanent way bought second-hand in 1907 permitted the replacement of the remainder of the line; it came from the LSWR and LBSCR Joint Railway that was being retracked.

Other tasks included fencing, additional moorings in the harbour and the extension of a breakwater using redundant rail and sleepers. Buildings were constructed for rent to local businesses, one for a sailing club plus an office with stores at Bembridge and numerous boat houses. They were situated on a wharf close to Bembridge station. A small hand-crane was provided for lifting boats in and out of the water; it ran along a length of standard gauge track unconnected with the railway. Just as the BHR had been, the IWR became more a property company than a railway. The Board ordered the opening of an 'Estate Account' with an initial balance of £962 10s. in order to keep its property interests separate from railway matters. Near Bembridge station an office was built for Mr Freeman who acted as agent for the collection of rents, etc. Henry Brent had to provide three dozen boards advertising plots of land for rent.

So much property was owned by the IWR in the neighbourhood that St Helens Local Board demanded £225 towards the cost of making up of Station and Latimer Roads.

The company continued to let out land for numerous pastimes. On one occasion the Secretary asked £3 3s. per year for 'sporting rights' over land and a stream opposite St Helens station. He offered a plot measuring 40 feet by 25 feet for a 'Racquet Court' at Bembridge on a lease for 7, 14 or 21 years at a rent of £3 per annum, an old tennis court 110 feet by 80 feet for seven years at £7 per year - even a rifle club was proposed. Golf was popular with both sexes and there existed separate clubs for gentlemen and ladies on land leased from the railway. In 1883 that for the gentlemen acquired royal patronage and a change of name to 'The Royal Isle of Wight Golf Club'; the IWR granted reduced fares to members and ran extra trains for their benefit. In December 1897 it agreed to issue season tickets to members of golf and sailing clubs travelling to St Helens and Bembridge from Ventnor at a rate of £6 6s. per annum and from other stations at £5 5s.; presumably special tickets were printed. This led to protests from members of golf clubs in Sandown, Shanklin and Ventnor that they should receive similar concessions! Eventually the IWR Board gave way and in June 1905 season ticket rates for golfers were quoted as:

	First six months		Second six months	
	Ladies	Gents	Ladies	Gents
Ryde to Sandown & Bembridge	£3. 0. 0	£4. 0. 0	£2. 0. 0	£2. 0. 0
Ryde to Sandown, Shanklin and Bembridge	4. 0. 0	5. 0. 0	3. 0. 0	3. 0. 0

Special golfing events had been taking place for several years; one such occasion led to the following letter on 12th April, 1901 from Mr Day to Mr Wetherick at St Helens:

Please note about 16 golf caddies will travel to Ventnor on Monday the 15th inst. and Tuesday the 16th inst. at a fare of 1s. each for the 3rd class return journey. They will probably pay their own fares, but should they inform you that the same will be paid by Major Gordon, please accept this statement and issue without payment, and in that case we will collect from this office.

Issue blank tickets for whole No. on both days, endorsed 'Golf Caddies' and quote reference to this letter thereon.

The ladies' golf links adjoined the railway near St Helens station. On 20th May, 1904 the branch train hit a cow belonging to a local farmer that had strayed from the golf course; the farmer demanded £15 compensation but Henry Day refused any payment as the golf club had settled the claim. As a consequence the IWR Board gave notice to the club that the lease was for golf purposes only and the cattle must be removed. When the lease came up for renewal on 25th December, 1904, the club tried to secure grazing rights, but the IWR Board demanded improved fencing and an increased rent rising from 10s. to 15s. per acre. This proved excessive and an annual tenancy was later offered at £25 per annum without grazing rights. When the club asked permission to use a horse when cutting the grass, the IWR Board agreed provided it was tethered when not performing its duty! Another accident took place on 24th July, 1911 when the branch train had a slight disagreement with a Mr Gilbert Nugent's motor car parked on the level crossing leading to the ladies' golf links and water works. Sadly the club folded after the outbreak of the Great War.

The golfers repeatedly asked for additional trains to connect with fast trains to and from London, but without a guaranteed traffic the Board initially refused. They gave way in 1903 and during the summer agreed to introduce trains from Brading at 12.35 pm and 7.5 pm on weekdays to connect with the 9.10 am and 3.35 pm trains from Waterloo, the 2.2 pm departure was altered to 2.45 to connect with the 11.35 am Victoria train; another train left Bembridge on Sundays at 7.5 pm to connect with London trains.

The dredging of Bembridge harbour was fraught with difficulties. Fraser & White, a local firm of coal merchants, wanted various areas dredged so that vessels with a deeper draught could use the quay. At first the IWR acquiesced and went so far as to ask for tenders for the

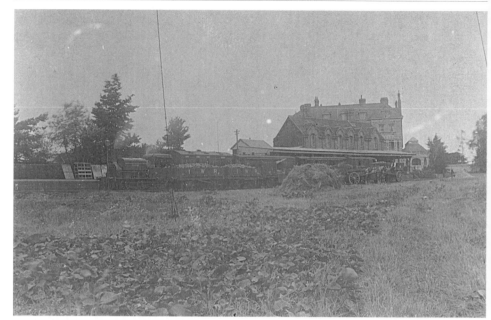

Bembridge, Oldbury composite No. 35 and the Golden Valley vehicles stand behind a long row of IWR wagons occupying the new siding.   *IWSR Collection*

The branch locomotive *Bembridge* has acquired its unusual additions in this photograph said to have been taken in 1911. The train is formed with the Golden Valley vehicles and a five-compartment Oldbury third. The signal box lurks behind the all-enveloping platform covering.
                                                                                          IWSR Collection

work. When the harbour master Capt. du Boulay was consulted the Board discover that dredging the channel at the entrance of the harbour would cost considerably more than first thought. Mr Gilbert, a Director of Fraser & White, refused to guarantee any additional traffic so the IWR had to seek some other way of funding the dredging. Letters were sent to the Admiralty and Board of Trade asking for authority to dredge, and unsuccessfully seeking to interest the Navy in using the harbour as a torpedo station so they might then be asked to contribute to the cost!

In the hope of improving the arrangements for unloading coal at St Helens Quay, the Directors, Henry Day and Henry Brent visited Phoenix Wharf, Southampton on 30th December, 1903 to see the cranes there at work. Mr Brent's report gives a useful insight into the existing and proposed unloading arrangements at St Helens:

The proposal is to substitute two powerful Steam Cranes, with ample margin of range and power, in place of the 3 small ones now in use, and to substitute 'Grabs' (nominal 1 ton) for the ½ ton skips which are filled by hand. The lowest tender is that of Messrs J.H. Wilson of Liverpool who have made special adaptations to suit our work.

	£
Their tender for two cranes (£500 each) amounts to £1,100	
Freight to St Helens and putting in position	22
Erecting same which is not included in Contract, Estimated at	18
Work on Jetty to suit Crane outriggers	20
Strengthening Jetty to carry the extra Weight of Crane	35
Wages in Slewing over the Wagon roads to meet extra size of Cranes	8
Two No. 6 Hones Patent Grabs of 29 Cubic feet capacity,	
or 1 Ton Approximately each @ £118 each	236
Extra Chair for same, and a method of releasing, say	24
Contingencies 2½%	37
	£1,500

Modes of Working Compared

Under present arrangement the time taken to discharge 480 tons of Coal is 15 working hours, on which 15 men take £10 or 13s. 4d. for each man which is a little under 10¾d. per hour, this gives a cost of 5d. per ton for labour.

Under proposed working 12 men would earn £5 in 8 hours, which is at the rate of 1s. 0½d. per hour, with less fatiguing work, but they would take only 8s. 4d. each for the job, this reduces the cost by one half viz.: to 2½d. per ton.

Men to be paid on the tonnage.

As now, each of the 3 Cranes lift about 10½ tons per hour of house Coal, rather more of Gas Coal and less of Steam Coal.

As proposed, each of the two New Cranes is taken to lift 30 tons of house Coal per hour and would thus discharge the *Allerwash* (480 tons) in 8 working hours.

Saving in Cost of Working

On men in holds and on trucks 25,000 tons @ 2½d. per ton say	260. 0. 0
On Cranemen 12s. 6d. per week	32. 0. 0
On Coal & General Stores &c.	25. 0. 0
Total gain	£317. 0. 0

In the absence of the branch engine, one of the smaller 2-4-0Ts would work the branch. The lady seems to have little interest in the locomotive on the turntable.   *R. Silsbury Collection*

Expenditure

£1,500	Cranes, Grabs &c
500	New trucks

£2,000		
Interest at 4%		80. 0. 0
Upkeep of the extra trucks		40. 0. 0
Additional Engine working consequent on rapid unloading half day per Cargo, 15s. per week		39. 0. 0
		£159. 0. 0

The Board accepted a tender for new cranes and within a short time Henry Brent had inspected and purchased 20 additional wagons. Soon afterwards the Board received a complaint of damage by a crane grab to the hatch of the coal barge *SS Allerwash*. Barely had the first claim been settled than another incident occurred. This time the Board instructed Mr Brent to carry out the repair, the 'Damaged plate to be preserved'.

In November 1904 a Mr Rawson from the Industrial and Engineering Trust attended the meeting of the Board and asked for an option to purchase about 60 acres of land at St Helens, south of the railway, including the ladies' golf links. The Board offered the land for immediate sale at £100 an acre or £150 on an option of 18 months. A shocked Mr Rawson refused saying that he had hoped that 'having regard to the enormous developments the Trust would bring about in St Helens' the IWR would have given the land for nothing or a free option for 18 months at £25 an acre!

There were still problems with the harbour at St Helens as late as July 1912. The Secretary attended a hearing before the Commissioners of Trinity House in Southampton following complaints about the frequent grounding of *Ellington*, *Allerwash* and other barges whilst being piloted into the harbour. The incidents were attributed to the silting of the marked channel and the IWR had to carry out some dredging and provide an additional buoy. A few months later the IWR Directors were much excited by a possible contract to supply stone from Ventnor Quarry, via St Helens, to contractors working at Keyhaven near Hurst Castle. In December 1912 the IWR quoted for the supply of 100,000 tons of ballast at a rate of 200 yards a day - they asked 2s. 1d. per yard. The contract would have brought in over £10,000 for an outlay estimated at £3,000 for 50 additional wagons plus the cost of a tip cradle at St Helens - it is possible that the construction of additional wagons in 1913 was linked to the Board's hopes from this contract. The quotation was evidently too high as the contractors went elsewhere for their supplies.

Meanwhile the Bembridge steamers continued to work, albeit intermittently, during the summer months. Following their sale by the United Realization Company, the vessels passed from one company to another as each slipped into financial difficulties. Eventually the *Alexandra* and *Lord Kitchener* ended up in the ownership of Fraser & White in lieu of debt and in 1913 Percy Gilbert and his family set up the Bembridge & Seaview Steamship Company Limited to continue the service. The outbreak of the war saw an end to it, and following unsuccessful attempts to re-establish a service in the early 1920s the pier at Bembridge was condemned and removed in 1928.

Finally, we should mention a minor but long-lived matter. At a meeting in October 1909 the Board was asked to find a site near Bembridge station for a memorial to the Revd J. Nelson Palmer, a local minister. An elaborate drinking fountain subsequently appeared close to the Royal Spithead Hotel on land leased from the railway for a nominal sum. The monument outlived both hotel and railway and is (as at 1998) still there.

The IWR station at Ryde seen at the turn of the century. The island platform was redecked in 1892 but the station is otherwise largely unchanged since the 1870s. The footbridge and road bridge date from the opening of the Joint Railway to the pier in 1880. The carriage shed has received a lean-to extension outside which can be seen two NLR carriages. The windmill drove a pump to supply water from the company's well. *Locomotive Publishing Company*

Chapter Twelve

A New Century

For Britain, and the Isle of Wight in particular, the start of the 20th century marked the end of an era. The Isle of Wight's most famous resident, Queen Victoria, still reigned but she had barely a year to live and once King Edward VII had been crowned the Island slipped into the shadows.

Horace Tahourdin remained Chairman of the Board of the Isle of Wight Railway assisted by his fellow long-serving Directors: John Stobart, Capt. Henry Twynam and Francis Slade. On 7th December, 1902 John Stobart died and two months later Alfred F. Slade took his place. The Board were informed of Capt. Twynam's death on 26th June, 1903. New blood came in the shape of the Hon. Gilbert Rollo who became a Director in December 1903 and Percy W. Gilbert in March 1904, a Director of coal firm Fraser & White. Two years later Alfred Slade died and in March 1908 Francis Slade retired due to ill health. His son Charles F. Slade joined the Board, followed in 1910 by Capt. Walter Waring MP and Percy Mortimer JP. Percy Mortimer was Chairman of the IWC and became a Director of the IWR at a time when the two companies were on reasonable terms. Under a reciprocal arrangement Horace Tahourdin joined the Board of the IWC, but both men resigned when the Willmott family took over the Central in 1911. Management of the IWR remained in the capable hands of Messrs Day and Brent. The stations, permanent way, locomotives and rolling stock were all in good order, if a little elderly, but nothing to worry about.

Queen Victoria died quietly in her bed at Osborne House on 22nd January, 1901. Her coffin was taken to Gosport on 1st February by the royal yacht *Alberta* and then by train to London. The Island railways took no part in this but the IWR did run a special train for local people to Whippingham as this letter to Henry Brent disclosed:

Dear Sir,   31st January, 1901
Burial of the Queen
Enclosed notice
Will you please arrange for a third Engine to be on the Main Line on Friday at 7.45 am to take light train to Ventnor at 8.12 or 8.20 as the case may be. This Engine will work the 9.32 Special to Ryde St John's Road and pass thence to Whippingham. I have asked the Central Co. to provide a Fireman from St John's Road.

We will not want a fourth Engine as the thro train is taken off and only two Engines will be required on Saturday for the same reason.
    Yours Truly
    H K Day

The coronation of King Edward VII was an event on a par with Queen Victoria's Jubilee. Employees received a day's paid holiday and the IWR subscribed £2 to each town towards funds to commemorate the coronation. Other payments to local organisations in 1901 included Ventnor and Ryde National Schools, Isle of Wight Infirmary, County Rifle Association, Rose Society, Shanklin Horticultural Association and regattas at Ryde, Sandown, Shanklin, Ventnor, Bembridge and St Helens. Contributions were also made to illustrated guides printed by the towns extolling the virtues of taking a holiday in the Island. Having secured their fare in getting to the Island, the IWR did its best to tempt visitors to use the railway during their stay; by 1902 it offered an amazing range of Tourist and Excursion bookings. Those from Shanklin included special rates by all trains to every station in the Island, cheap tickets to Portsmouth and Southsea, with weekend tickets to London. There were also weekly tourist tickets and 'half holiday' tickets on Wednesdays to IWR stations, cheap evening 'market' tickets on Saturdays and excursions to Alum Bay, Totland, Blackgang, Round the Island, Bournemouth, Weymouth, Worthing and Brighton. This ignores reduced rates granted to various groups including members of the golfing fraternity. In March 1904 the IWR Board approved the sale of books of first class tickets valid for a year for £1 12s., equivalent to 1½d. a mile - apparently the scheme was similar to one operated by the North Eastern Railway.

Ryde St Johns.   *Reproduced from the 25", 1908 Ordnance Survey Map*

Staffing matters were always calculated to generate considerable correspondence. Equally an eagle-eyed Henry Day at Sandown could be relied upon to come down heavily on an errant employee:

5th March, 1901
This morning a Commercial holding a 3rd class single fare for Shanklin for which he had paid *two pence* joined the 8.5 am with four cases of luggage which was labelled and passed without comment by Porter D. receiving I have no doubt a tip.
Failing a proper and satisfactory explanation from D. of this neglect to perform the duty for which he has been paid by the company, that is the collection of Excess Luggage Charge, suspend him from his duty and report to me.
Unless there is some reasonable excuse forthcoming there is only one term to be applied to the transaction, that is barefaced robbery.

A few hours later Mr Day had calmed down:

Commercial Luggage   5th March, 1901
Porter 'D's reply is not satisfactory but I will fall in with your wishes and accept in the hope that he will in future do his duty honestly and protect the company interests in such cases.
Have an excess ticket made out for 1s. 3d. and send me, *collecting from D.*

The need to operate with flexibility was an essential feature for a small company such as the IWR. Numerous opportunities for extra traffic included special events at Lake and elsewhere:

18th January, 1901
Please arrange for the 2.10 pm up and 4.40 pm down trains to be stopped at the County Ground tomorrow Tuesday the 19th inst. to put down and pick up a County team.
Guard to secure tickets.

To Mr C. Brading:

Return of Issues   4th February, 1901
I don't understand your reply unless the lad S. is trying to hoodwink you in order to hide his neglect. Surely it is known at Brading station that I require a return of issues in connection with every special event? If it is not known you had better advise them now.

To Mr Wetherick, St Helens:

22nd February, 1901
Your memo of the 21st re Football Team to Newport tomorrow.
We will arrange for a Special to leave St Helens at 12.15 pm. Issue 3rd returns to Newport at a fare of 2s. 6d. each - not less than 10.

In 1902 the sports ground at Lake was sold and along with it went a useful source of traffic. However, the halt was not abandoned as in 1893 the IWR Board had agreed to a request from a Mrs Harvey to stop one train a day 'for the convenience of persons using the New Convalescent Home' - they are said to have used the halt until the Great War. The home, paid for by Mrs Harvey, was formally opened by the Duke and Duchess of Connaught on 20th May, 1893.

On 25th May, 1904 the Board heard of the death of J. Thornton, the Ryde Works foreman. Mr Thornton joined the IWR in December 1866 as a fitter and became foreman in November 1874. The Directors expressed their condolences to his widow and recorded their appreciation of his long and faithful service. The search began for a replacement and at the next meeting on 22nd June it was proposed that the Chairman's son, Horace D. Tahourdin, be appointed to the vacancy at a salary of £2 10s. per week. His employment began 'in about a fortnight or so soon as Mr Gilbert can spare him' - clearly he had been in the employ of Percy Gilbert in

George Corbett, long-serving station master at Brading, is pictured at the door to his booking office; retirement at age 65 had yet to become the norm.   *R. Brinton Collection*

some capacity. H. D. Tahourdin actually commenced his employment with the IWR on 18th July. He seems not to have been enamoured with his salary and 12 months later unsuccessfully applied for the position of locomotive superintendent with the IWC.

Some of the obligations in the Railway Employment (Prevention of Accidents) Act 1900 came into effect in 1904, mainly affecting the working of goods trains. In August instructions were given for the provision of lighting in goods yards so that shunting could continue in the hours of darkness. Most station platforms and buildings had been equipped with gas lighting quite early in the life of the railway, the exceptions being at Brading and Wroxall where oil sufficed. Five gas lamps were provided in the yards at Ryde, three each at Sandown and Shanklin, two at Ventnor and three at St Helens Quay where gas lighting was also installed in the station, the Brading company's stations not being equipped. Other requirements in the Act included the provision of lookout men to safeguard men working on the permanent way, and the outlawing of ropes to tow wagons into and out of sidings. Revised instructions were issued as tow-roping was apparently a common practice at Sandown and Shanklin.

At a Board meeting on 21st July, 1905 the Manager reported the occurrence of an accident to Inspector William Wheway whilst delivering excursion handbills near Niton. He had been thrown from a van when the horse stumbled and received such severe injuries that his left leg was amputated below the knee. The Board ordered the issue of a letter of sympathy, a cheque for £5 to meet immediate expenses and his full wages. Negotiations were instigated with the insurers to ensure adequate compensation and the company paid for an artificial leg! Mr Wheway had joined the company on 28th July, 1864 as a guard and was said to have been the guard on the first trains from Ryde to Shanklin in 1864, and through the tunnel at Ventnor two years later. Despite his injury, Mr Wheway took over as a station master at Brading following the death of George Corbett in 1911 and remained there until the company ceased to exist in 1923; he died in 1927 at the age of 87.

Mr Corbett had been station master at Brading since the 1870s. George Humby was appointed station master to Shanklin in July 1871 (he had joined the company on 14th July, 1864 as a 'Policeman') and remained there until retiring in March 1913. There was also William Wetherick, who joined the IWR on 1st April, 1865 and had a chequered career before and after becoming station master at Ventnor in 1876; he was pensioned off in 1907.

Returns to the Board of Trade show the relentless increase in the numbers of third class passengers and an equally dramatic reduction in those travelling first or second class. Goods traffic gradually returned to its 1896 levels and remained buoyant until the beginning of the Great War.

Year ending 31st Dec.	Passenger traffic Numbers carried				Goods traffic		Gross receipts		Working expenses	% of receipts
	First	Second	Third	Season tickets	Minerals tons	General tons	Passengers £	Goods £	£	
1901	49,010	271,347	528,173	178	34,813	24,657	30,138	11,481	19,163	46
1905	49,120	241,645	621,644	233	57,887	6,838	31,044	11,824	19,655	45
1910	45,642	206,247	729,959	244	56,454	8,448	32,837	11,599	21,111	47
1912	40,365	184,331	725,978	237	57,196	8,310	32,322	11,623	20,746	47

The sale of stone and other building materials from a quarry in the vicinity of Ventnor station was first mentioned in 1867 when Joseph Bourne was given the sum of £60 with which to begin commercial exploitation. Quarrying eventually opened out the areas each side of the tunnel mouth, and in 1896 the IWR paid £1,200 2s. 6d. for more land adjoining the station for a new road and so that quarrying could continue. In March 1902, to encourage trade, the IWR Board ordered that a price list be printed and a notice board exhibited in the station yard carrying the wording 'St Boniface Stone Quarries'. The quarry was let out shortly before the start of the Great War and although business declined soon afterwards it remained in use until 1923 when the undertaking was wound up.

Numerous requests were received from firms anxious to rent sites for their slot machines on station platforms. Cigarette machines had been in place since 1893 and during the early years of the century agreements were made with the following: in April 1901 the Mutoscope Co. at £22 10s. per annum, in February 1903 the Anglo Egyptian Trading Co. selling tooth powder for

This view of Brading station from the north dates from 1910 and shows *Brading* about to leave with an up train. *Shanklin* is working the Bembridge branch, some spare carriages occupy the siding; the signal box on the left presides over proceedings.   *Real Photographs*

Bonchurch stands in the down platform at Brading in 1913 at the head of an assorted collection of Oldbury carriages. A considerable growth in hedges and trees has cloaked the station.
                                                                                    IWSR Collection

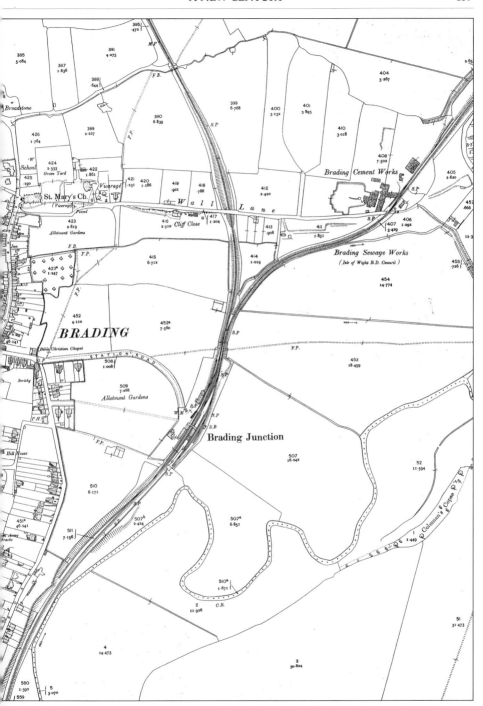

Brading Junction.   *Reproduced from the 25", 1908 Ordnance Survey Map*

Looking from Sandown's down platform towards Brading. The crossing loop has been extended, the IWNJ locomotive shed has gone and the IWR goods yard has gained an additional siding.
IWSR Collection

The signal is off for a Ventnor-bound train to leave Sandown in 1910. The imposing tree soon had to be removed as it blocked the signalman's view! Note the unusual design of the refreshment room building.
G.M. Miskin/T. Cooper Collection

£20 per year, and in 1905 the Sweetmeat Auto Delivery Co. which agreed to pay 30 per cent of gross takings and £75 a year for the privilege of placing sweetmeat and weighing machines.

W.H. Smith retained charge of the bookstalls and advertising for which they had to pay rent and a percentage of profits.

In 1904 several houses in Grove Road, Sandown came up for auction. Anxious to enlarge the goods yard, Nos. 9 and 10 were bought for £550 so that the gardens could be shortened by 30 ft. The IWR promptly let the houses but resold them two years later for £570, less the land taken for the goods yard! A use for the money was soon found as, whatever the adverts may have said, more protection for passengers from the elements was desirable. In November 1905 the Board authorised an extension of platform coverings at Shanklin. This was followed in August 1906 by similar work at Ventnor; 200 ft of the island platform received a covering, whilst that on the main platform was renewed and extended 72 ft along the front of the goods shed.

Whereas the provision of a gas supply to towns in the Island had been a child of the 1800s, attention now turned to schemes for the provision of electricity. In December 1897 the company entered into an agreement for the sale of a plot of land adjoining Ventnor station to Messrs Edmundson & Co. for £800 for a proposed 'Electric Station'. The IWR gained some income from the installation work as contractors used the railway to ship cable and other materials to sites at stations. Private sidings were proposed to an electric light works at Lake and to a new gas works - the latter foundered when the gas company proved unable to buy the necessary land. The Ryde Electric Light Company applied in March 1902 for a turntable and siding to its proposed works at St John's Road. The IWR offered to lay the siding for £150 if the turntable from Ventnor was used, or £206 if a new one had to be purchased. The electric company was expected to pay the cost of providing the siding and enter into a lease for 7, 14 or 21 years at £15 per annum. The scheme failed when the Ryde Electric Light Company reported its inability to get adequate foundations on the intended site and had to build the works away from the railway. In 1904 the Isle of Wight Electric Light & Power Company Limited, as the Ventnor company had become, offered £10 a year for permission to lay an electricity cable through Ventnor tunnel to supply Wroxall - it is still there.

In 1906 the National Telephone Company provided telephone 'call boxes' for the use by the public at Sandown, Shanklin and Ventnor. However, the stations themselves were not equipped and several were not connected to the network until SR days.

The appearance of motorised road transport and an increase in operating costs prompted a number of railway companies to investigate the possibilities of operating steam rail motors, or the use of oil or electricity instead of coal. The Metropolitan, District, Brighton and South Western companies each electrified parts of their systems, principally to counter competition from street tramways and motor omnibuses. The IWR Board wanted to reduce fuel costs and these means of propulsion were seen as possible ways of achieving this. Rail motors could stimulate traffic by operating frequent passenger services on lightly-used lines. This was, however, a double-edged sword as railmotors had limited seating accommodation and most could haul only a single light trailer. They were also difficult to maintain and had to be kept away from the smoke and dirt of locomotive running sheds. In May 1904, whilst the Chairman and Henry Brent visited the North of England to inspect some second-hand wagons, they took the opportunity to ride on an 'electric railway motor' between Newcastle and Benton on the North Eastern Railway and view a petrol motor 'not yet at work or perfected'. They evidently realised such vehicles would be a liability on the IWR where any engine could work goods trains between passenger services. Despite this, on 25th October, 1904 the Board asked the two Henrys to investigate the costs of employing a road or rail car between Sandown and Shanklin. This was in response to the activities of the Isle of Wight Express Motor Syndicate, formed to operate the first 'Road Motors' in the Isle of Wight. Not everyone welcomed the motor buses as a letter published in the *Isle of Wight County Press* on 19th August, 1905 showed:

One hears many uncomplimentary remarks about the railway companies and expressions of gratitude for the advent of the motor bus. The fares charged by the Isle of Wight Express Motor

In 1893 the island platform at Sandown was rebuilt and provided with a signal box high in the roof of the platform covering. The down platform has also received its covering.

IWSR Collection

On the down platform at Sandown, passengers wait for the next train. The station clock and Nestles chocolate machine jostle for attention amongst auctioneers' posters.

G. M.Miskin/T. Cooper Collection

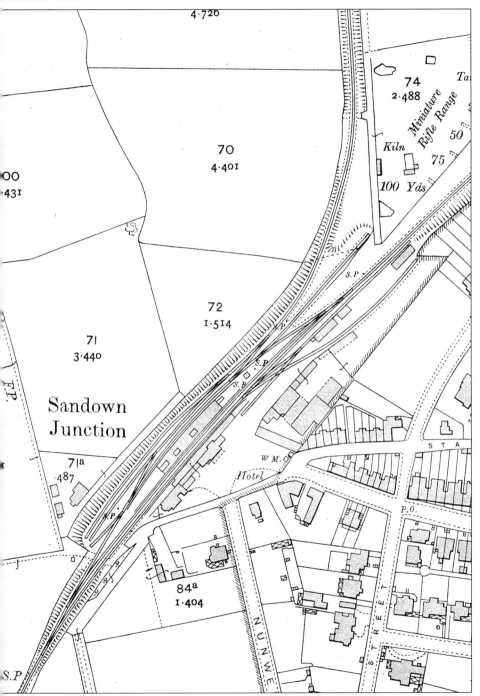

Sandown station.

Reproduced from the 25", 1908 Ordnance Survey Map

The full extent of the station building at Sandown can be seen in this *c*. 1910 view. Access to the offices on the first floor was gained by the exterior staircase to the left of the building.

IWSR Collection

The lack of motorised transport is evident of this view of the station yard at Sandown in 1910. A horse bus belonging to the Sandown Hotel waits for passengers whilst another horse is hauling a White & Co. container to its destination. A sign identifying the entrance to the booking office perches on top of a rather fragile covering to the pavement.

G.M. Miskin/T. Cooper Collection

Syndicate are, to say the least, rather tall. For instance, a visitor wanting to make a return trip from Sandown to Ryde by motor-bus, will have to pay at least 2s., yet the much-abused railway company would be happy to oblige him for 9d. After the novelty of this new form of transport has worn off, I predict most people will prefer to travel a little more cheaply, even if they have to revert to the more ancient, but less snail-like, method of transport.

At a shareholders' meeting the Chairman, Horace F. Tahourdin, pronounced that the IWR had not suffered much from such competition and went so far as to suggest they be prohibited from the Island altogether! It was not long, however, before such thoughts were replaced by a sober appreciation that railways on the mainland were losing trade to road transport. The railway gained a brief breathing space when the omnibuses proved unreliable but they reappeared in 1906, and when introduced between St Helens and Bembridge the IWR imposed a hefty 1s. toll over the toll road; there followed a predictable and robust exchange of letters with the bus operators. Soon afterwards the Board instructed the Engineer to report whether the speed of omnibuses should be limited over the road bridge at St Helens and keep a record of any damage - in 1908 a 12 mph speed limit was imposed on all motor vehicles but by then the bus service had ended. Cheap tickets at a rate of ¾d. a mile were introduced. Second class tickets issued at the time bore the notation 'SF' (Special Fare) and more significantly 'No Lge'; they had a rather fetching colour combination in pink and red.

On 4th June, 1903 the Board took up an offer from a Mr Fitzmaurice, agent to the Petroleum Product Company, of a free trial of their 'Patent Liquid Fuel'. A steam crane at St Helens was equipped and set to work on 22nd August. When this proved satisfactory, on 29th October the Board authorised further trials on a 'goods engine', actually *Bembridge*. Oil fuel proved cheaper than coal but the cost of converting the remaining locomotives and constructing storage tanks made the scheme uneconomic. The possibility of using electricity first surfaced during May 1899 when there was an exchange of letters with the British Electric Traction Company. In 1906 Ventnor UDC attempted to persuade the County Council to purchase the Island railways, electrify and operate them as one undertaking; this followed complaints principally about high fares and goods rates to the town. The IWR Board, in reply to a letter from a Mr T. C. Chapman, made their views clear:

Dear Sir,   24th April, 1907
                        Isle of Wight Railways Electrification

With regard to yours of the 15th instant my Chairman has submitted the correspondence he has lately had with you to my Board and I am desired to say that the proposals therein made are so unsatisfactory and indefinite and show such a want of knowledge of the nature of the Traffic to be dealt with in the Isle of Wight that they do not consider any good purpose would be attained by continuing the correspondence.
        Yours faithfully,
        H. K. Day, Sec.

Between December 1908 and January 1910 correspondence passed between the IWR and various people including a Mr Dawson, Mr Marshall and the Electric Railways Syndicate. Mr Marshall, a mechanical and electrical engineer, prepared a detailed report claiming that the Island railways could be purchased and electrified for £1,200,000. Of this, £310,000 represented the cost of electrification on the single phase high tension AC system fed via overhead wires - the same as that adopted by the LBSCR. Sadly the merits of the scheme were diluted by fanciful suggestions for 'halt stations' and extensions including one to Seaview, a connection between the two stations at Ventnor, and from St Lawrence to Freshwater. A frequent service was proposed:

Shanklin station has changed somewhat in this view of the station frontage. Horse buses were a common feature prior to World War I; this one belonged to the Royal Spa Hotel.

IWSR Collection

Views of goods trains on the IWR are quite rare so we had to include this print of *Bonchurch* leaving Shanklin with a down goods in June 1910. The train includes a Chaplin & Co.'s container carried on one of the company's low sided wagons. *R. Silsbury Collection*

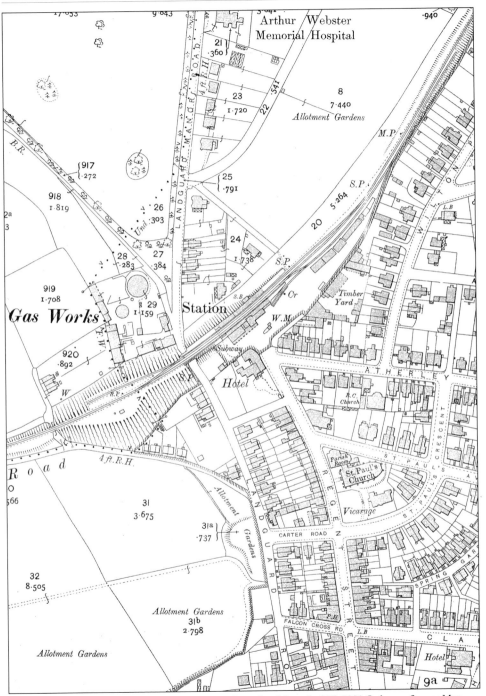

Shanklin station.

Reproduced from the 25", 1908 Ordnance Survey Map

An up train passes the home signal to enter the crossing loop at Shanklin on a rather misty day.
The Gas Company's siding can be seen on the right.   *K. Nunn Collection*

A typical IWR passenger train of the late Victorian era is seen heading for Ventnor through a
section of woodland near Shanklin.   *K. Nunn Collection*

Route	Summer Min.	Winter Min.	Time of Journey Min.
Ryde to Ventnor	20*	45	32
Brading to Bembridge	30	45	7 ¼

Naturally, the IWR had insufficient capital to fund the electrification of its system and, whilst supportive of the idea, neither the County Council nor other District Councils were prepared to put ratepayers' money into such a scheme. On 27th June, 1910 Henry Day reported to the IWR Directors that the County Council had decided to take no steps with further unification and electrification of the Island railways.

On 1st January, 1908 fresh agreements with the IWC for the use of Ryde and Sandown stations came into effect and were due to last seven years; in the event they continued until after the end of the Great War. The night goods train was still running as the IWR agreed to carry out any shunting of IWC goods traffic at Sandown.

The IWR did not have a happy year in 1911. Mr Tahourdin last sat in the Chairman's seat at a Board meeting on 28th February when the traditional signing of the dividend warrants was carried out. His absence from the next meetings through illness received a brief mention and he died on 23rd November- in addition to the IWR he had been a Director of a number of obscure companies. Percy Gilbert was elected Chairman by his fellow Directors and Gilbert Rollo his deputy; the election became a regular ritual, a noticeable change from Mr Tahourdin's regime. In January 1912 Mr Malby took the vacant seat on the Board; he had just retired from the position of goods manager to the LSWR. Henry Day acquired another job in December 1911 when the Board approved his appointment as Secretary to the Solway Junction Railway Company (Francis Slade was a Director) - it cannot have been an onerous task!

In the August 1911 the first national railway strike took place, principally over union recognition. Henry Day reported that employees 'remained loyal' and a grateful Board granted each person an additional day's pay; they also acceded to a request for payment of wages weekly instead of fortnightly, an arrangement that had existed since the opening of the railway in 1864. At the next monthly meeting the Board agreed to pay rises for signalmen, porters, guards and platelayers. In January 1912 a communication, said to have been written on behalf of the staff, asked that a Conciliation Scheme be established, a favourite method of railway unions who were trying to recruit members and negotiate improved pay and conditions on their behalf; the Board ordered the Secretary to send a suitably polite refusal.

In February 1911, following advice from the police, the Board instructed that notices be erected in station yards forbidding betting under the Street Betting Act of 1906 - not that this stopped them! A few employees incurred fines and reprimands from Mr Day for other offences.

H.P. worked as a 'heavy goods guard'; he was suspended five days and suffered a pay reduction for three months following an accident on 28th October, 1901 during shunting at Shanklin.

A.S. did the same job when he and E.C. were each suspended one week and had their wages reduced by 1s. per week, after an engine ran into a goods van during shunting at Brading on 19th October, 1904.

J.W. joined the IWR in December 1876 as a labourer but soon became a porter. In a lengthy career, his misdemeanours included fines of 2s. 6d. in October 1893 'for causing 'Collins' bag to go astray' and 1s. for causing delay to 'Roaches' flour. A further 1s. fine followed in May 1896 for 'omitting to post a Whitsuntide Bill on Board rented of W. Forteath'. In 1908 he received a one week suspension for drunkenness but retired in 1910 on an allowance of 5s. a week until age 70 when his old age pension began.

For many years the IWR purchased, as a matter of routine, a mix of Welsh and North Country coal of good quality. Having Percy Gilbert on the Board was most useful as, being a Director of at least two coal merchants, he understood the market. He scrupulously kept the business of the railway separate from that of his companies who were certainly not favoured by the Board in

* The Ryde to Ventnor line had to wait another 20 years before the Southern Railway provided such a service in summer months.

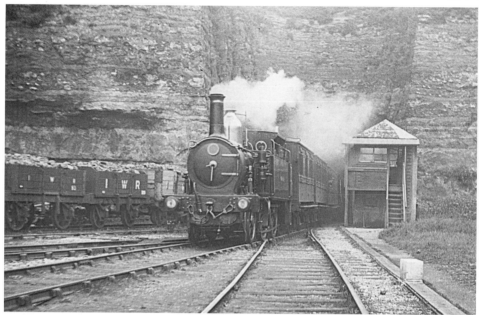

Ventnor was a popular location with photographers. A beautifully clean 2-4-0T bursts out of the tunnel with a down train past the signal box. Two IWR dumb-buffered wagons can be seen on the left with a third that is thought to be IWC.   *K. Nunn Collection*

Ventnor stands next to the water crane at Ventnor *c.* 1910. Note the weighing machine to the left. The building on the right was used by one of the coal merchants.   *Real Photographs*

their deliberations. Naturally coal purchases would be mentioned in the Minutes with monotonous regularity. Supplies were badly affected in the spring of 1912 when a national coal strike forced railway and shipping companies to reduce services. The IWR was no exception and Henry Day reported the introduction of a restricted train service and a cut in employees working hours. The railway resumed full time working from 22nd April, despite having a tiny stock of coal estimated to last only until about 26th May. Further supplies were secured although the price had risen noticeably. Hetton steam coal cost 16s. 9d. a ton in November 1910 but on 26th June, 1912 the Board thought themselves fortunate to secure a cargo of South Hetton Hartley at 18s. 3d., delivered into the company's wagons at St Helens - this price was cheap as a cargo of Penrykyber Welsh coal cost 24s. 9d. The award of a pay rise to miners led to similar demands by other groups of workers. In May the Board granted increases in pay to drivers and firemen in the company's employ. The greater numbers of drivers and firemen was a consequence of shorter working hours and the need to provide an increased train service.

	to be increased from		to		
	s.	d.	s.	d.	
The two eldest drivers	5	9	6	3	per day
Driver L.	5	9	6	0	per day
Driver R.	5	6	5	9	per day
Driver C.	5	3	5	6	per day
Four firemen	3	9	4	0	per day
Firemen when acting as Relief Drivers	5	0	5	0	per day

Employees who served with the company from its early days were reaching advanced ages and had to retire. In the absence of pensions under the age of 70, the Board frequently granted a small payment to provide the men with a modest income; two gangers who retired in December 1912 each received 5s. a week. Soon afterwards the Board appointed a Mr Stratton from the LSWR as foreman platelayer at 5s. 5d. per day, plus his removal costs to the Island. Within a month he reported that the line needed lifting and packing with more ballast in a good many places. This could not be done with the employees available, so a special gang of ten men had to be taken on for six to eight weeks to complete the task. Pay for Sunday working had been introduced several years previously, and from 2nd November, 1913 employees who were forced to work more than 12 hours in a day were paid overtime.

Changes also took place in the management of the railway. Henry Brent asked the Board in April 1908 to be relieved from some of his duties and recommended Horace D. Tahourdin as a suitable replacement. H.D. Tahourdin had 3½ years of experience in the locomotive, carriage and wagon departments for which he was said to have shown great aptitude. He was appointed assistant Engineer at a salary of £200 a year from 31st March, 1908. In April 1912, on Mr Brent's recommendation, H.D. Tahourdin was promoted to the position of Engineer and locomotive & carriage & wagon superintendent; his pay rose to £260 a year from 1st January, 1913. Henry Brent was retained as Consulting Engineer at a salary of £150. Mr Brent's duties were expected to occupy an average of three days a week and involved general supervision and inspection of plant, locomotives and rolling stock - he also covered for the absence of Mr Tahourdin during illness or holiday. Mr Tahourdin's status rose when he acquired a motor car; we know this because in December 1909 the Board authorised its storage at Ryde Works, no doubt it could be borrowed if there was a breakdown along the line!

Amongst matters occupying the minds of the Directors was a proposal to construct an aerial ropeway to carry coal to gas works belonging to the Sandown Gas Company. The Directors inspected the site in November 1912 during a visit to the Island but were evidently unimpressed. They asked the gas company to establish whether landowners would grant wayleaves over the route that the ropeway was intended to pass - evidently they refused as nothing more took place.

There were a number of schemes for ferries or tunnels connecting the Island with the mainland at this time. The *Isle of Wight County Press* discovered that the LSWR had bought land in the Lower Pennington Marshes, near Keyhaven, on which to build a dock and landing

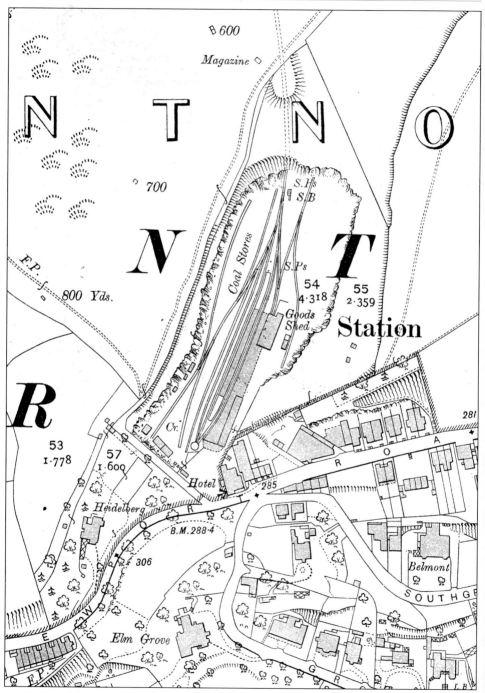

Ventnor station.

Reproduced from the 25", 1908 Ordnance Survey Map

stage for Transatlantic passengers travelling to London; it was rumoured that a train ferry would operate to the Island. There was a scheme for a four mile electric tube railway between Stokes Bay and Ryde at an estimated cost of £750,000; the Isle of Wight Chamber of Commerce felt a train ferry to be a more practical proposition. Finally, a correspondent reported to readers of the *Isle of Wight County Press* the present position concerning the Solent Tunnel scheme. In 1901 promoters secured an Act of Parliament for a railway between Lymington and Yarmouth but the undertaking had been unable to raise the necessary capital.

By 1913 relations between the IWR and IWC had become 'cordial' and tickets between Ryde and Ventnor could be had for travel by either company's route. When a vessel got stuck under the drawbridge at Newport the IWR helped out with the loan of some carriages and special trains worked through to Ashey on the occasion of the races on 23rd-24th April, a regular occurrence. The IWR had been granted running powers over the RNR in 1872 but they were invoked only on special occasions such as Ashey race days. The IWC, under the management of the Willmott family, standardised its fare structure and in response the IWR reduced fares on its own trains to 1½d. a mile first class and 1d. per mile second class. The summer train services on both companies lines began somewhat earlier than in previous years on 1st June. The IWR was advertising in the *Portsmouth Times* day excursion trips *from* Portsmouth and Southsea to IWR stations at 3s. 6d. first and 2s. 6d. third class. Groups of 20 or more could take advantage of a special third class rate of 2s. A seven day weekly season ticket cost 7s. 6d. first and 5s. 6d. third class, all Island seasons 20s. 6d. first and 15s. 6d. third whilst first class '250 mile' tickets could be had for £1 12s. or about 1½d. a mile. At a Board meeting on 25th March, 1914 the company's reluctance to embrace third class accommodation reached another milestone when the Board decided to introduce third class fares locally and discontinue cheap afternoon excursion tickets - the IWR persisted in retaining second class for through fares, despite numerous complaints and attempts by the mainland companies to secure a change of policy. IWR trains carried over one million passengers in 1913, a bumper year. Goods traffic was proving equally satisfactory; in the last few weeks of 1913 20 large vessels berthed at St Helens loaded with coal and an assortment of building materials.

Income was matched with some prudent expenditure. In 1912-1913 the company spent £80 on a southerly extension of the platform coverings at Shanklin; Sandown received a new goods and parcels office in June 1910 and some expenditure was incurred in preparation for an extension of the platforms in May 1914. All the running lines on the main line and the Bembridge branch were in chaired track, although recent purchases had been of second-hand LSWR track rather than new material. Sidings, however, remained in flat-bottom rails well into Southern Railway days. On 30th December, 1913 the Board authorised the conversion of the machinery in Ryde Works to electricity in place of steam.

The refreshment rooms at Sandown were in a separate building a few yards south of the main station building. It had a distinctly more ornate exterior than the company's other properties with fancy ridge tiles and embellishments. The lofty windows and high ceiling must have imported a light and airiness to the refreshment rooms of which there were two adjoining the platform, staff rooms occupied the other side of the building and a basement served as a store. Unfortunately the rooms were never particularly profitable and income had to be bolstered by a 'tap' room. In 1913 a local brewery ended their tenancy after the IWR failed to renew the drinks licence - a refreshment room at Ryde St Johns seems to have closed about 10 years previously. In January 1914 the Board instructed Henry Day to sell off the furniture and fittings and convert the accommodation into offices. Mr Day took over the southernmost room for his office, the clerks occupied the other rooms whilst the basement became a paper store. In September 1914 the Board authorised the conversion of the upstairs rooms in the station building at Sandown to a residence for the station master at a cost of £55 - presumably Simeon Lodge, the station master's house, was to be sold off.

Finally, mention should be made of a fire and its aftermath. In August 1911 £3 5s. 6d. was paid for 'services rendered by fire engine' but when and where the conflagration took place was not recorded. The fire had no apparent effect on the IWR's activities, but in November 1913 the Board authorised the purchase of 40 'Kylfyre' fire extinguishers at 5s. each 'for protection of company's property'.

Isle of Wight Railway
Train and Boat Services

The following REVISED SERVICES will be run on and from DECEMBER 1st and until further notice

All previous services being cancelled

WEEKDAYS

Mainland connections (down)

Victoria (dep)	6.15	8.55	11.25		1.42	
London Bridge "	6.35		11.20		1.50	
Waterloo "	5.15 / 8.10	6.20 / 9.45	9M10 / 11.30	9B25	11.20	1.15	3.45
Portsmouth "			11B40		1.50	2.50
Southsea (Clce Pr) (dep)		9.40 / 11.40	2.0		4.55	6.40

Island — Down (Ryde → Ventnor)

	Ryde Pier Head (dep)	Ryde Esplanade	Ryde St. Johns Rd.	Brading	Sandown	Shanklin	Wroxall	Ventnor (arr)
	8.20	8.24	8.28	8.36	8.42	8.52	9.0	9.5
	10.28	10.32	10.37	10.45	10.53	11.0	11.8	11.13
	12.15	12.19	12.23	12.32	12.38	12.45	12.53	12.58
	1.10	1.13	1.18	1.31	1.37	1.43	1.55	2.0
	2.45	2.49	2.53	3.1	3.7	3.14	3.29	3.34
	3.40	3.43	3.48	3.56	4.2	4.8	4.16	4.21
	4.40	4.43	4.48	4.56	5.3	5.9	5.17	5.22
	5.33	5.37	5.41	5.49	5.55	6.2	6.10	6.15
	7.15	7.19	7.23	7.31	7.36	7.42	7.50	7.55

Island — Up (Ventnor → Ryde)

	Ventnor (dep)	Wroxall	Shanklin	Sandown	Brading	Ryde St. Johns Rd.	Ryde Esplanade	Ryde Pier Head (arr)
	8.0	8.6	8.14	8.20	8.26	8.34	8.38	8.42
	9.20	9.25	9.33	9.39	9.44	9.52	9.56	9.59
	10.20	10.25	10.33	10.40	10.46	10.53	10.57	11.2
	12.8	12.13	12.21	12.27	12.32	12.40	12.44	12.48
	1.5	1.10	1.18	1.25	1.31	1.39	1.44	1.47
	2.8	2.13	2.19	2.25	2.30	2.38	2.42	2.45
	3.8	3.13	3.20	3.26	3.32	3.40	3.44	3.48
	4.35	4.40	4.46	4.51	4.56	5.4	5.8	5.12
	5.35	5.41	5.48	5.55	6.0	6.8	6.12	6.20
	6.50	6.55	7.2	7.7	7.12	7.20	7.24	7.27
	8.10	8.15	8.22	8.28	8.34	8.44		

Portsmouth Harbour (arr): 10.3 / 10.5 — Victoria (arr): 9.20, 11.52, 12.0 — London Bridge — Waterloo: 1.51, 1.45, 2.25, 5.10

SUNDAYS

Victoria (dep)	9.0	8.55	1.10	1.10
Waterloo "	8.40	12.10 / 12.20		

Island — Down (Sundays)

	Ryde Pier Head	Ryde Esplanade	Ryde St. Johns Rd.	Brading	Sandown	Shanklin	Wroxall	Ventnor
	8.35	8.38	8.42	8.50	8.57	9.3	9.12	9.17
	9.25	9.28	9.32	9.40	9.45	9.51	9.59	10.5
	10.15	10.20	10.27	10.33	10.38	10.45	10.49	10.53
(Southsea 6.20) 7.0	7.4	7.8	7.16	7.22	7.28	7.37	7.42

Island — Up (Sundays)

	Ventnor	Wroxall	Shanklin	Sandown	Brading	Ryde St. Johns Rd.	Ryde Esplanade	Ryde Pier Head
	2.15	2.20	2.27	2.32	2.37	2.45	2.49	2.52
	4.7	4.12	4.20	4.27	4.33	4.41	4.45	4.48
	8.40	8.45	8.52	8.57	9.3	9.10	9.14	9.18

Portsmouth Harbour (arr): 5.20, 9.50 — Victoria (arr): 8.2, 8.10 — Waterloo: 9.17 (3B35)

A - Arrives 4.51 p.m. on weekdays. B via Eastleigh. M - Mondays only. Through passengers travelling via Southsea Pier must make their own way between Portsmouth Town Station and Clarence Pier. Conveyances will be provided for Luggage. In consequence of the demands of the Military Authorities it may be found necessary to temporarily suspend and after certain of the Services advertised hereon.

BRADING HARBOUR BRANCH

WEEKDAYS

	Bembridge (dep)	St. Helens "	Brading (arr)	Brading (dep)	St. Helens "	Bembridge (arr)
	8.0	8.5	8.10	8.27	8.32	8.37
	9.16	9.24	9.29	9.45	9.50	9.55
	10.30	10.35	10.40	10.46	10.51	10.56
	1.15	1.20	1.25	1.32	1.37	1.42
	2.15	2.20	2.25	2S32	2.36	2.41
				3.2	3.7	3.12
	3.18	3.23	3.28	3.57	4.2	4.7
	4.42	4.47	4.52	4.57	5.2	5.7
	5.38	5.43	5.48	6.1	6.6	6.11
	7.0	7.5	7.10	7.32	7.37	7.42
	8.20	8.25	8.30	8.37	8.42	8.44

SUNDAYS

	Bembridge (dep)	St. Helens "	Brading (arr)	Brading (dep)	St. Helens "	Bembridge (arr)
	2.23	2.28	2.33	2.39	2.44	2.49
	3.10	3.15	3.20	3.25	3.30	3.35
	4.17	4.22	4.27	4.37	4.42	4.47
	8.35	8.40	8.45	9.5	9.10	9.15

S - Saturdays only

Sandown November 1915
HK Day General Manager

Timetable for November 1915.

Chapter Thirteen

The Great War and Afterwards

In August 1914 war broke out between Austria and Germany on one side and Serbia, Russia and France on the other. Within days Britain was drawn into the conflict when Germany invaded neutral Belgium, bound to Britain by treaty. The Government took control of the railways at midnight on 4th/5th August, 1914 using powers obtained in an 1871 Act; in practice management was delegated to a Railway Executive Committee composed of managers of the more important companies. The IWR officers and Board of Directors remained in being and continued to run the railway largely as before, but subject to directive from above. Compensation from the Government for loss of traffic was based on a comparison between actual net income with income in 1913 when, by good fortune, the IWR had a profitable year!

Almost immediately the military called up Directors and employees who were reservists. Capt. Waring joined his Yeomanry and soon went abroad. Six months later Mr Rollo went off on 'Active Service'. The Board in its depleted state continued to meet in London at monthly intervals. There were increasing difficulties in gaining a regular supply of coal at a reasonable price and a catalogue of other problems: buses plying between hotels and the station at Ventnor ceased running when the horses were requisitioned, there was a decline in income from advertising, a virtual cessation of business at St Boniface Stone Quarry, and requests for reductions or waiving rents paid by golf clubs, etc.

Within weeks of the start of war the REC issued the first of many circulars and instructions, most of little relevance to the Isle of Wight. Non-essential expenditure ceased, labour became scarce and materials that could be purchased rocketed in price. Locomotives and rolling stock were stored and routine maintenance reduced to a minimal level. The only significant expenditure was on rails, chairs and sleepers so that the programme of renewal of the permanent way could be maintained. When supplies of new materials became unavailable small amounts were bought second-hand, frequently from the LSWR; sleepers were of English oak supplied by a Winchester firm.

The REC removed one important area from the control of the Directors and Manager: staff wages and conditions. The railway trade unions negotiated a national agreement with the REC acting on behalf of the Government and there were several awards of war bonuses, pay rises funded by the Government that the IWR paid without comment. Individuals were not, however, any better off because there was a steep rise in the cost of living accompanied by a hefty rise in income tax.

Once the immediate effects of the outbreak of war had been overcome, tourists ventured back to the towns served by the railway. Only Ventnor seems to have suffered appreciably as it had been much favoured by foreign visitors including Germans who patronised the German-American liners to and from Southampton - they vanished when war broke out and with them went the town's prosperity.

Towards the end of 1914 heavy rain resulted in flooding of the LSWR/LBSCR Joint railway at Ryde, whilst a slip at Apse was made good 'with only 1 hour's delay to passenger services'. Goods traffic remained buoyant; an additional siding was put in at Ryde St Johns Road for the Central Railway in January 1915.

The national press continued to publicise the virtues of taking a holiday in the Island and one article went so far as to list the golf courses! In 1915 the IWR offered seven day season tickets at 7s. 6d. first or 5s. second class; all-Island tickets cost 14s. 6d. first and 10s. third. On the other hand, the usual mainland excursion trains were suspended and people were encouraged to spend their holidays at home. Many steamers had been requisitioned for war work, leading to a reduction in sailings between Portsmouth and Ryde to seven on weekdays and four on Sundays; in the opposite direction there were eight and three respectively.

Between Southsea and Ryde there were two trips a day, except on Sunday where there was just one each way. A year later just two of the normal complement of six steamers were available to work the Portsmouth to Ryde route.

The silting of the harbour at Bembridge continued to concern the Board. The Chairman, Secretary and solicitor (Mr Beale) attended a meeting with the Board of Trade Development Commission in an abortive attempt to gain grants or loans of £30,000 to dredge the harbour thoroughly. In the meantime Capt. Dennis of the Royal Engineers advised that, in an emergency, the military would flood the lowlands of Brading harbour and destroy the railway bridges between St Helens and Bembridge. Bridges had already been mined and two old carriages taken over for defence use at St Helens Quay. A seaplane base was built on the company's land near Bembridge point on the seaward side of the Spithead Hotel.

In 1915 a local newspaper reported the first death of an employee on active service. J. Jackson, who had worked on the railway since 1913 joined the army and was:

... killed whilst fighting with the 2nd Hants Regiment at the Dardenelles on the 30th Ult. [30th May, 1915]. His father is at Lucknow, India, with the 2nd Wessex Field Artillery. One son is in the Persian Gulf with the R. F. A., another is at Watford with the Territorials, and a third is on transport service, so the family are doing well for their King and country. Jackson was working as a porter on the I. W. Rly when war broke out. For a small railway, the company contributed a very fair contingent to the colours and this is the first fatality among them.

Members of the Board visited the Island on 14th May, 1915 when they inspected the railway and complimented staff on the clean and tidy stations. Some recently-purchased carriages, a new booking office at St Helens and toilets at Bembridge were pronounced satisfactory as were repairs to the earth slip at Apse. Sandown station required a thorough repaint whilst furniture in the first class waiting room at Shanklin needed to be upholstered and the floor recovered.

In January 1915 enginemen were granted pay rises to 5s. 9d. per day but were required to take turns working in the workshops for which they received a reduced rate of 5s. The head goods guard and his assistant were each granted an allowance of 3s. per week for coping without a third guard - this lasted until May 1916. Other changes affected station masters who lived in accommodation provided by the railway, i.e. at Shanklin, Sandown, St Helens, Bembridge and Brading; they were paid 30s. per week plus free housing but from 30th May, 1915 it was decided to increase their wages to 37s. but charge 5s. per week for rent, rates, taxes and water. The absence of a station master's house at Ventnor had been remarked upon as long ago as September 1898 when Henry Brent prepared plans for replacing three cottages near the station with a better class of house. Nothing was done at the time as a proposed funicular would have resulted in their demolition. In August 1915 the houses were inspected by the Directors during one of their periodic visits to the Island. This time they decided to give the two tenants notice to quit and all three dwellings (the third being empty) were converted into one house for the station master at a cost of £136. The Ventnor station master received a pay rise to £2 2s. per week from 10th April, 1916, plus an additional 5s. for superintending Wroxall station. Those persons who had free passes over the railway gained further when the Board sanctioned their retention for a second year because leather used for the covers was 'difficult to obtain'.

Compared with 1913, in 1915 the IWR spent an extra £307 on permanent way materials and £397 on the rolling stock. Some economies were made as the following letter from H. K. Day to the Board of Trade shows:

Isle of Wight Railway Company
Secretary and Traffic Manager's Office
Sandown, Isle of Wight
23rd December, 1915

Sir,

Mixed Trains

For the convenient working of Traffic and the saving of waste mileage, we desire to run the following Passenger Trains on our Brading Harbour Branch line between Bembridge and Brading Junction, as 'Mixed' in accordance with the conditions contained in the Orders made by the Board of Trade under the 'Regulation of Railways Act, 1889' and I shall be glad to receive the sanction of the Board of Trade to this proposal:
Four trains from Bembridge to Brading on Weekdays and one on Sundays
Four trains from Brading to Bembridge on Weekdays and one on Sundays
I enclose for your information a current Timetable showing bracketed in 'red' the trains we proposed to run as 'Mixed'. At present we do not run any 'Mixed' trains on the Railway.
The Brading Branch line is practically level throughout.
    I am Sir,
        Your Obedient Servant
        H. K. Day
            Secy & General Manager

The introduction of mixed trains avoided having to steam an additional engine for goods work. Services could be worked by one locomotive on the Bembridge branch with another on the Ventnor line and a third in the afternoon. There was a gap in the passenger service on the branch in mid-morning so it is likely the branch locomotive also worked goods trains on the main line. The timetable for November 1915 was typical of the service operated during the war.

Disruptions to services included an incident on the evening of 27th December, 1915 when a slip in Sandown cutting blocked the line until 8 pm the next day - in the meantime traffic was carried between Sandown and Brading by road. Three days later a labourer received fatal injuries at Wroxall, when struck by the step of a van on a passing passenger train whilst crossing the railway.

After an inspection in 1916 the IWR purchased Nunwell House and land adjoining the station at Sandown for £370, and within a few months had let it for £45 per annum. The reason for the purchase became clear, when the Board reserved the right to set back a wall adjoining an access road to permit a diversion of the road so that the up platform could be extended.

At the beginning of 1917 the Government effectively banned travel except for 'business and health purposes' by ordering the abolition of most reduced fares, a 50 per cent increase in ordinary fares and a reduction in train services. Such was the labour shortage that two apprentices were taken on in Ryde Works to replace those who had joined the Army. The effects of reduced maintenance began to show; on 21st January five sheep strayed on to the line at Wroxall through a gap in the hedge and were killed by a train; a claim for £25 compensation was agreed at £22 10s. less £4 7s. 6d. already received for the carcasses. In April H.D. Tahourdin asked to be released following his commission as a Second Lieutenant in the Railway Operating Corps. Mr Sweetman, the works foreman, took charge of the locomotive, carriage and wagon shops and Mr Stratton managed the permanent way. Alfred Malby was increasingly absent from Board meetings due to ill health. Given that Messrs Rollo and Waring were still away on active service the meetings became more problematic, so it was no surprise when Mr Malby resigned. Sir Charles J. Owens, a Director of the LSWR who had been that company's General Manager between 1898 and 1911, took his place. The financial position permitted some modest expenditure and in December 1917 the Board approved the substitution of electricity for gas in Ryde Works - work authorised in 1913 but never carried out.

At the February 1918 Board meeting, apart from the signing of dividend warrants, most discussion was about staff. Station masters asked to be paid for working Sundays but instead were given a pay rise of 5s. a week. They, together with the clerical staff, also wanted a scale of salaries

One of the oldest four 2-4-0Ts and a train of NLR four-wheel carriages potter towards St Helens with a train to Brading just after the Great War. Out of view to the left was the embankment road and harbour.   *G.W. Tripp/NRM*

This exterior view of Shanklin was taken after the construction of extensions to the station buildings and the addition of ornate matching ridge tiles. In the centre can be seen the original booking office and station master's house.   *Lens of Sutton*

63   SHANKLIN. — (Isle of Wight). — The Railway Station. — LL.

laid down, a superannuation fund set up and sick pay extended. The Board agreed to grant two months' full pay and two months at half pay during sickness. Henry Day discussed the other matters with the staff without success but the REC eventually imposed a national agreement. The REC ordered a further increase in pay for those working in workshops by adding a war bonus amounting to 12½ per cent of their total earnings, a reflection of the rise in the cost of living.

By then so many employees had volunteered for 'Kitchener's Army' or been called up that the railway was critically short of staff. True, the trains still ran but there were numerous other jobs that had to be done. The first female employee seems to have been a 'girl messenger' who started work on 12th March, 1917 at St Helens; despite being paid much less than her 'boy' counterparts she stuck at the job until May 1921. In 1918 four female clerks started work in the General Manager's office and two remained in the company's employ into Southern Railway days. Two of the ladies were quite young, as in 1919 they received the Ministry of Transport rate of 17s. 6d. per week for female clerks aged 16 and a year later the age 17 rate of £1 1s. 6d. Following the death of the station master at Sandown in 1918, his colleague at Wroxall was promoted and moved to the larger station. To fill the vacancy at Wroxall Miss D.J., who had worked briefly as a clerk a few months earlier, rejoined the company as a temporary station master on a wage of £1 per week including a lodging allowance. She resigned after three months probably because of the poor pay - her male replacement got £2 a week including the war wage.

In May 1918 Henry Brent advised the Board that Ventnor tunnel needed repairs. Although work began towards the end of the year a lack of labour led to delays and only the worst affected areas were repaired - the remainder to await better times.

The end of the war had no outward effect on the Isle of Wight Railway. The IWR remained under Government control and the Railway Executive Committee continued to issue instructions mainly in the area of staff wages and working conditions. On the other hand traffic began to pick up: excluding Naval and Military traffic, the IWR carried 894,472 passengers that year compared with 652,136 in 1917.

The Railway Executive Committee ordered another increase in wages; from 1st January, 1919 the working hours of workshop staff were reduced to 47 hours per week; from 1st February engineers, traffic staff (excluding inspectors and station masters), enginemen, firemen and cleaners were granted a 48 hour week. Within weeks most employees in the industry were given an eight hour working day, paid overtime, Sunday pay and annual holidays - IWR employees already received such benefits. During 1919 men returning from the forces were offered jobs - the result of a national agreement with the National Union of Railwaymen. Not all chose to return to the IWR but those that did were sufficient to swell the wages bill. This led to the dismissal of temporary staff for whom no such protection existed. A couple still managed to gain black marks.

E.B. worked as the Ryde signalman when suspended for one week on 18th September, 1922 for having left his box to enter a Public House whilst on duty two days previously. He delayed the 11.20 am up at Brading by eight minutes.

E.C. joined the railway in March 1879 as a cleaner and rose to the position of fireman and later engineman. He incurred fines for minor collisions during 1904 and was demoted to fireman on 6th August, 1914 'for running into Ventnor with the side rod of his engine fastened up with wire - split pin having come out and he had not a spare one to replace it.' Evidently a good worker, he was reinstated as an engineman the following December.

A timetable commencing 1st March, 1919 reflected the familiar winter pattern with nine trains each way between Ryde and Ventnor plus an additional train on Saturday evenings. Five trains gave through connections to and from London. On Sundays there were four trains each way, most of which connected with the Portsmouth steamers and London trains. The growth in the passenger traffic noted in 1918 continued during the 1919 summer season, as people took advantage of their first opportunity since the end of the war to get away for a holiday. However, neither railways nor ferries were capable of operating to pre-war schedules - many steamers had not returned to their owners and those working the Ryde to Portsmouth route were severely overcrowded.

On 1st March, 1919 Horace D. Tahourdin resumed his duties as Engineer and locomotive superintendent. On 4th June the Board agreed to a pay increase to £400 per annum plus war

Isle of Wight Railway

From 1st March, 1919 until further notice

WEEKDAYS

Down trains

Station											SO
Ryde Pier Head	Dep.		9.13	10.50	12.38	1.23	2.33	4.0	5.50	7.25	
Ryde Esplanade	Arr.		9.18	10.55	12.41	1.26	2.37	4.4	5.53	7.29	
Ryde St. Johns	Arr.		9.24	11.0	12.45	1.30	2.43	4.10	5.58	7.33	
Brading Junction	Arr.	8.10	9.33	11.9	12.55	1.40	2.52	4.18	6.7	7.41	8.40
Brading Junction	Dep.	8.20		11.10		1.53	2.53	4.20	6.7	7.42	8.48
St. Helens	Arr.	8.22		11.15		1.58	2.58	4.25	6.12	7.47	9.5
Bembridge	Arr.	8.27		11.20		2.3	3.3	4.30	6.17	7.52	9.15
Sandown Junction	Arr.	8.32	9.40	11.15	1.0	1.47	2.58	4.24	6.13	7.47	8.57
Shanklin	Arr.	8.33	9.46	11.23	1.6	1.53	3.7	4.30	6.19	7.53	9.2
Wroxall	Arr.	8.44	9.55	11.32	-	2.2	3.16	4.39	6.28	8.2	9.10
Ventnor	Arr.	8.47	10.0	11.37	1.18	2.8	3.21	4.44	6.33	8.7	9.15

Up trains

Station										SO	SO	SO
Ventnor	Dep.	7.55	9.20	10.20	11.50	1.28	2.55	4.50	5.43	7.15		
Wroxall	Dep.	8.1	9.25	10.25	11.55	1.33	3.0	4.55	5.48	7.21		
Shanklin	Dep.	8.8	9.33	10.33	12.2	1.41	3.7	5.2	5.55	7.29		
Sandown Junction	Dep.	8.14	9.39	10.39	12.8	1.47	3.13	5.8	6.0	7.35		
Bembridge	Dep.	8.5		10.30		1.28	3.5	4.55	5.52		8.35	7.20
St. Helens	Dep.	8.10		10.35		1.33	3.10	5.0	5.57		8.40	7.25
Brading Junction	Arr.	8.15		10.40		1.38	3.15	5.0	6.2		8.45	7.30
Brading Junction	Dep.	8.20	9.44	10.44	12.14	1.53	3.19	5.13	6.7	7.41		
Ryde St. Johns	Dep.	8.28	9.53	10.53	12.23	2.1	3.28	5.21	6.16	7.50	9.3	
Ryde Esplanade	Dep.	8.32	9.57	10.57	12.27	2.5	3.32	5.25	6.20		9.10	
Ryde Pier Head	Arr.	8.35	10.0	11.0	12.30	2.9	3.36	5.28	6.24		9.14	9.18

SO = Saturdays only

SUNDAYS

Down trains

Ryde Pier Head	Dep.	1.17		3.7			7.45		
Ryde Esplanade	Arr.	1.21		3.10			7.49		
Ryde St. Johns	Arr.	1.25		3.15			7.53		
Brading Junction	Arr.	1.33		3.23			8.2		9.5
Brading Junction	Dep.	1.33	2.39	3.25	4.37		8.3		9.10
St. Helens	Arr.		2.44	3.30	4.42		8.8		9.10
Bembridge	Arr.		2.49	3.35	4.47		8.13		9.15
Sandown Junction	Arr.	1.39		3.29			8.8		
Shanklin	Arr.	1.46		3.35			8.14		
Wroxall	Arr.	1.55		3.44			8.23		
Ventnor	Arr.	2.0		3.49			8.28		

Up trains

Ventnor	Dep.	2.15		4.7		8.40	
Wroxall	Dep.	2.20		4.12		8.45	
Shanklin	Dep.	2.27		4.20		8.52	
Sandown Junction	Dep.	2.32		4.27		8.57	
Bembridge	Dep.	2.23	3.10	4.17	7.50		8.48
St. Helens	Dep.	2.28	3.15	4.22	7.55		8.53
Brading Junction	Arr.	2.33	3.20	4.27	8.0		8.58
Brading Junction	Dep.	2.37		4.33			9.3
Ryde St. Johns	Dep.	2.45		4.41			9.10
Ryde Esplanade	Dep.	2.49		4.45			9.14
Ryde Pier Head	Arr.	2.52		4.48			9.18

bonus, to commence when he qualified as a member of the Institute of Civil Engineers. Henry Day's employment as Secretary and General Manager came up for discussion on 16th April, 1919. The solicitors drew up a contract covering the period from 30th June, 1919 until the date of his retirement three years later when he would receive an annuity of £300 per annum - in fact Mr Day deferred his retirement until the company ceased to exist at the end of 1922.

September 1919 was marked by the first railway strike to have a serious effect on the IWR. The seeds of the dispute had been sown before the war when railway unions sought representation for railwaymen throughout the industry; wages varied as did the level of union representation. During the war unions negotiated an additional war wage that by 1918 had risen to 33s. per week. In March 1919 there were increases in the basic wage for drivers, firemen and cleaners that in most cases exceeded their pre-war rates plus war wage. The unions wanted increases for other grades to bring each up to the highest pre-war wage paid in that grade on *any* railway, plus war wage and a minimum of £3 a week. The Government disagreed and a national railway strike began without warning on a Friday just as the summer season was ending. No trains ran in the Island for the next few days and most railway-owned ferries between Portsmouth and Ryde ceased to operate. For the IWR employees, the decision to strike followed a great deal of heart searching. As the *Isle of Wight County Press* reported, many had worked for the IWR for upwards of half a century and were torn between loyalty to the union and a sense of duty to the company and the public. The public, however, found they could perfectly well travel by road and enterprising individuals soon arranged road bus services not just within the Island but as far as London. Much relief was expressed at the way supplies of foodstuffs could be maintained using road transport, the risk of starvation being a real fear - sugar, butter, margarine and meat were all rationed. After a few days the IWR began a limited service between Ryde and Ventnor with connecting services on the Bembridge branch - soon afterwards the strike ended. Volunteers to help operate trains included a Commander Denness, formerly a Lieutenant Commander in the Royal Naval Volunteer Reserve, who was staying at Sandown, had served an apprenticeship on the Midland & South Western Junction Railway and had experience of the French railways during the war. Commander Denness drove some IWR trains assisted by H.D. Tahourdin as fireman; the chief clerk A.E. Woods and M. Buckett, the traffic inspector, acted as guards. Stations and signal boxes were looked after by station masters who remained at their posts. Season ticket holders and other regular travellers later presented Commander Denness with an inscribed silver salver paid for by subscription. The IWR Board chipped in with £10 and made special payments of up to £25 to each employee who worked through the strike.

The writing was on the wall for Britain's railways. Railway Regulation Acts had forced safety improvements and a tightening of controls over operation and management. However, the Railway Executive Committee demonstrated there could be efficiency savings following some form of unification of railway companies and they therefore remained under Government control beyond the end of the war. It was common knowledge that the railways had not been fully compensated for their efforts and would need an injection of capital - money that they could not generate. The Government favoured Nationalisation, but its attempts in 1919 merely created a Ministry of Transport to oversee a non-existent nationalised railway. Following formation of the Ministry in August 1919 the Railway Executive Committee was disbanded; it held its last meeting in December 1919 and railways were free of Government control.

The amount of compensation for loss of traffic paid to the IWR during the period of Government control totalled approximately £35,000. Of that, £5,507 6s. 6d. was received in respect of the five months ending 31st December, 1914 and most of the remainder accumulated during 1915-1917. From mid-1918 onwards so much traffic was being carried during the summer months that the IWR had to pay over £2,000 a month to the Government, only to recoup the money during the off-season. The compensation included small amounts on account of arrears of maintenance built up during the war; unlike other companies, there is no evidence that the IWR took advantage of the situation to charge capital expenditure to revenue, quite the reverse.

Financially, a moderately profitable little railway had slipped into difficulties that it was incapable of fully overcoming. Running costs formed the major part of expenditure and dwindling

Towards the end of the IWR's life *Ventnor* approaches Ryde Esplanade with a train of Metropolitan stock on a down working.   *K. Nunn Collection*

Wroxall station seen in 1920 still possesses a single platform but has gained a covering to the front of the station building.   *IWSR Collection*

A view of Ventnor station seen from the hillside in 1920. The 1876 goods shed is the prominent building on the left and to the right can be seen the coal sidings. The island platform has finally gained a covering. *R. Silsbury Collection*

The caves in the hillside were used by the coal merchants. A number of sidings were added to serve them over the years. *R. Silsbury Collection*

Summer fashions are much in evidence as *Wroxall* arrives at Brading with a Ventnor train. To the left was a goods store in the goods yard. The date is probably 1923 or 1924.
C.G. Woodnutt/ T. Cooper Collection

Wroxall approaches the station at Sandown on a down train past the far end of the down sidings, the date is 1923-1924.   *Real Photographs*

profits had to be devoted to pay a dividend to shareholders. The amount of capital, whether in stock or debentures, had not increased since the purchase of the Brading company in 1898 and although borrowing powers were not exhausted, income would not have funded additional interest that the issue of more capital required. The compensation from the Government proved quite inadequate in the face of the higher material and labour costs that had become prevalent, and all that could be afforded was the purchase of spare parts for locomotives, boilers for two steam cranes at St Helens and permanent way materials. These purchases were sufficient to keep the railway in operation but they were insignificant when compared with the level of capital expenditure that was so obviously necessary. The writer of an article in *Railway and Travel Monthly* noted how the stations badly needed modernisation and commented that the island platform at Ryde St Johns Road was quite inadequate for the traffic it handled; a complaint had been made in 1907 about overcrowding on the footbridge between the platforms. Clearly facilities for passengers had not kept pace with the increasing numbers using the railway during the summer months.

The Isle of Wight, however, continued to enjoy a boom in the numbers of visitors. Returns to the Board of Trade show that passenger traffic during summer months had not just recovered but increased over pre-war. By contrast, goods traffic fell after war began and continued to decline after it ended; traders no longer depended solely on the railways because of a plentiful supply of war-surplus lorries.

Year ending 31st Dec.	Passenger traffic Numbers carried			Season tickets	Goods traffic		Gross receipts* £	Total† expenses £
	First	Second	Third		Minerals tons	General tons		
1919	25,615	2,772	835,946	292	14,610	12,205	69,872	49,886
1920	17,674	2,483	912,404	340	14,208	11,287	91,028	70,040
1921	10,043	1,399	875,627	306	18,585	10,529	86,672	65,437
1922†	19,559	1,671	1,196,368	327	44,444	13,618	74,512	53,995

The figures for total expenses require some explanation. Inflation pushed up the cost of living during the war and continued to do so until 1920. This was reflected in regular wage increases for employees and in the price of coal. It took some time for fares to catch up, but from 15th January, 1920 the Ministry of Transport ordered a hefty rise - tickets were hurriedly stamped with the new price and the entry 'revised fare'. A refusal to issue third class through fares to mainland stations led to a re-emergence of innumerable complaints; the Board's attitude was that there should be no change unless the rate was upwards!

Isle of Wight Railway

Excursions from Shanklin from 18 July 1921 until further notice

To	Trains	Third return fare	Issued on
Ventnor	9.46, 11.00 am, 3.07 pm	1s.	each Weekday
Brading	10.33 am, 2.23 pm	9d.	each Weekday
St Helens	10.33 am, 2.23 pm	1s. 3d.	each Weekday
Bembridge	10.33 am, 2.23 pm	1s. 6d.	each Weekday
Ryde (St Johns Road)	10.33 am, 2.23 pm	1s. 9d.	each Weekday
Newport	9.33 am, 1.37 pm	2s. 3d.	Tuesday, Wednesday, Thursday
Cowes	10.33 am	3s. 3d.	Monday, Tuesday
Freshwater	10.33 am	4s.	Wednesday, Friday

A motor bus connects with Cowes floating bridge for Osborne House

---

* For comparison, we have set out figures for individual stations during 1923 in a separate table.

† excludes receipts from rents and fees for stock transfers

Traffic to and from IWR Stations in 1923

Station	Ryde St Johns	Brading	Sandown	Shanklin	Wroxall	Ventnor	St Helens	Bembridge
Annual receipts:								
Passengers	7,841.4.4½	2,062.8.6½	13,029.14.10	14,944.6.8	1,885.0.0	13,718.0.0	1,376.10.10	3,942.2.4
Parcels	333.14.0	133.5.5½	914.1.4	844.0.9	380.0.0	926.0.0	160.1.4	470.11.2
Goods	673.17.1	411.6.6	481.14.10	554.19.5	9.0.0	390.0.0	308.5.5	7.5.6
Various	177.12.5½	116.19.10	186.19.5	159.14.2	52.0.0	215.0.0	67.18.6	608.1.1
General goods tonnage (monthly):								
Forwarded	49	72	14	17	1	44	600	2t 5c
Received	250	8	117	137	7t 11c	138	300	12
Coal and coke tonnage (monthly):								
Forwarded	140	3	1	18	-	4	650	-
Received	3,190	176	750	900	75t 7c	480	50	155
Number of milk churns dealt with daily:								
Forwarded Summer	-	1	-	6	4	5	3	-
Winter	-	-	-	-	4	3	3	-
Transferred Summer	-	3	50	-	-	-	-	-
Winter	-	2	30	-	-	-	-	-
Received Summer	6	3	10	10	-	3	-	-
Winter	2	4	-	-	-	3	-	-
Number of regular season ticket holders:	4	4	34	15	12	4	9	7
Number of Summer	14	6 + 2 guards	12	14	2	10	2 stn. 4 quay	4
staff employed Winter	12	do	9	10	2	9	2 stn. 4 quay	3
Monthly number of passengers booked: (heaviest month in 1923)	24,486	8,744	28,151	36,704	11,387	26,056	4,533	8,234
Monthly number of tickets collected: (heaviest month in 1923)	36,652	10,829	70,016	72,025	15,459	55,900	5,877	12,466

Displaying virtually nothing of SR origin this photograph of *Wroxall* taking water at Ryde St Johns Road is dated after 1923. The large wooden goods shed behind the locomotive was demolished when the station was remodelled in the late 1920s. *R. Silsbury Collection*

The little boy shows great interest in *Wroxall* as it heads south with a Ryde to Ventnor working in early SR days. It was not long before both the locomotive and carriages would be no more. *Real Photographs*

This view taken at Sandown on 20th September, 1926 shows the signal box and island platform
in more detail; clearly it was not high season!   *K. Nunn Collection*

The only Southern Railway influence evident in the summer of 1924 is the newly arrived ex-
LSWR class '02' locomotive No. 22. It is hauling a train of IWR North London Railway carriages
up the incline out of Sandown bound for Ventnor.   *T. Cooper Collection*

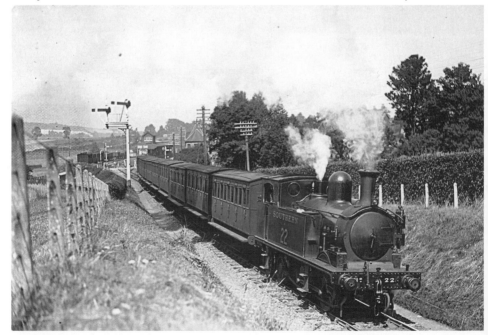

A timetable beginning on 9th May, 1920 showed 10 trains each way daily during the week with no extra Saturday trains. The Sunday service had deteriorated as there were only three trains each way in the afternoon and early evening, a consequence of higher wages and shorter working hours. The following summer service differed from the previous season only by the running of an additional train connecting with a new Waterloo fast train leaving Portsmouth at 10.0 am.

A national coal strike marred the 1921 season resulting in a reduction in train and ferry services in April. Local carriers and others sought to profit from the difficulties by publishing timetables of bus services. The road services multiplied and outlasted the strike to become precursors of a network of omnibus services throughout the Isle of Wight. In May the Brompton Motor Company began advertising the first air service - 10 minute pleasure flights from Seaview at a cost of 12s. 6d. Railways returned to normal in mid-July but as the following entry in the *Isle of Wight County Press* for 21st May shows, the damage had been done:

Probably not since the early days of railways have holidaymakers at Whitsuntide been deprived of the advantages and facilities offered by an augmented service of trains, as they were this year owing to the continuance of the suicidal coal trade dispute. Worse than this, there was a greatly restricted service of trains and steamboats, with the result that Island lodging house keepers and hotel proprietors were waiting in vain for the arrival from the mainland of hundreds of visitors who had provisionally booked accommodation in the vain hope that the coal miners would have been at work before the holiday!

Soon after the end of the strike, prices began to collapse as the country's economy entered a lengthy period of recession. This, coupled with uncertainties over the future of the company dissuaded the Board from embarking on any significant expenditure; an exception was the dredging of the approaches to the quays at St Helens. Although the company had expected some contribution towards the costs as part of Government compensation, the matter bounced around between the company and various Government departments without success. In desperation, the IWR lodged an objection to the Railways Bill in 1921 on the grounds that it had not been adequately recompensed for anticipated expenditure on the harbour. This led to a meeting with Sir Herbert Walker, General Manager of the LSWR, who agreed that the latter would credit the IWR with £16,000 as part of the sale of the railway to the LSWR in 1922 - the Board finally accepted a tender and work to dredge the harbour began soon afterwards.

Just as the creation of the Island railways had been instigated principally by people resident outside the Island, so the next stage in their evolution would be settled by men sitting in Parliament. The fate of the Isle of Wight Railway Company was sealed by the passing of the 1921 Railways Act. It sanctioned the creation of four regional railway companies and set out how a final payment of compensation would be divided. From a total payment of £60,000,000, the IWR eventually received £19,767; this permitted the continued payment of the interest to shareholders until Grouping in January 1923.

On 5th October Henry Day reported the retirement of engineman W.V. after 57 years' service at the age of 71 and W.L., a 74-year-old boilersmith who retired after 53 years with the company; each received a pension of 10s. a week. Another retired engineman had his pension increased from 7s. 6d. a week but died a few weeks later. One or two employees died before attaining pension age: A.E. Woods, the Chief Clerk and Cashier, died on 17th August, 1921; he was not replaced.

Following an inspection of the railway by Sir Herbert Walker, General Manager of the LSWR, and several officials in November 1921, negotiations began for the sale of the IWR to the LSWR. Terms were set out in a letter from the LSWR Secretary on 9th March, 1922 and discussed at the next Board meeting on 29 March. Although the Directors considered IWR debenture holders would be satisfactorily compensated, they expected shareholders to reject the offer in respect of ordinary stock. Mr Day penned a lengthy reply and the outcome was a meeting at Waterloo on 1st June of:

St Helens Quay photographed in 1920. Note the unusual signal on the left used for positioning wagons on the weighbridge; the wagon is standing in front of the weighbridge hut.

R. Silsbury Collection

A later view of the harbour taken during the 1930s shows the south quay on the left, several of Chaplin's containers next to the hand crane on the west quay, with *Ballaster* and two of Chaplin's barges tied up to the north quay to the right. St Helens gas works can be seen in the centre.

Real Photographs

For the LSWR -   Sir Herbert Walker - General Manager, Mr Knight - Secretary, Mr Bishop - solicitor and Mr Newhook - Accountant.

For the IWR -   Mr Gilbert - Chairman, Mr Rollo - Deputy Chairman, Mr Meares - solicitor and Mr Day - Secretary.

Speaking on behalf of the IWR, Percy Gilbert reminded the LSW that, as part of a larger organisation, the company and its successor expected to make significant savings in operating costs. Sir Herbert Walker replied by observing that economies would be necessary to balance the necessary reduction in fares, the IWR lacked any reserve fund to pay for renewals and South Western stock commanded a higher price than the stock it replaced. IWR Directors could expect compensation equal to four years' fees and staff 'would receive fair and liberal treatment'. At the next Board meeting on 7th June the Directors resolved to put amended terms to shareholders. The offer, contained in a circular issued to shareholders on 21st June, ensured they would receive a dividend from LSWR stock comparable to that they had received from the IWR. As shareholders actually exchanged their IWR stock for SR stock the settlement is best set out as follows:

Nominal value	For each £100 of IWR stock	Amount and class of LSW stock to be issued	Amount and class of SR stock actually issued
£177,000	Preferred Converted Ordinary Stock	£100 Preferred Converted Ordinary Stock	£80 Preferred Ordinary Stock
£177,000	Deferred Converted Ordinary Stock	{£7 5s. 8d. Preferred Converted {Ordinary Stock and {£10 5s. 8d. Deferred Converted {Ordinary Stock	£5 16s. 6d. Preferred Ordinary Stock and £101 9s. Deferred Ordinary Stock
£84,012	4% Preference Stock	£114 5s. 3½% Preference Stock	£79 19s. 6d. 5% Preference Stock
£200,750	4% Debenture Stock	£133 6s. 8d. 3% Debenture Stock	£100 4% Debenture Stock

At this point the Minute book leaves us high and dry. The discussions of 26th July, 1922 were the last recorded in the book and no record survives of the next scheduled meeting on 25th October or, for that matter, any subsequent meetings that may have taken place.

On 16th November, 1922 special meetings of shareholders and debenture stock holders took place at the Cannon Street Hotel, London. Percy Gilbert summarised the circumstances leading to the meeting and reminded those present that they had been 'called together in obedience to an Act of Parliament — the Railways Act, 1921 — passed after the war and period of Government control of the railways in the wisdom of Parliament'. He emphasised that amalgamation was compulsory 'whether the shareholders like it or not'. Details were given of the terms by which the company would be sold to the LSWR including the initial offer and improvements the Board had secured. In addition, shareholders would receive dividends at the same rate as those paid for 1921, i.e. preferred converted ordinary stock 4 per cent, deferred converted ordinary stock 2½ per cent and preference and debenture stock 4 per cent. Shareholders unanimously voted to accept the offer. Directors were voted £3,600, equivalent to four years' fees, out of IWR funds as compensation for loss of office. Sir Charles Owens, a Director of the LSWR, joined the SR Board where he remained until his retirement in 1930.

After the shareholders' meeting the Board met for a presentation to Henry Day marking his retirement after almost 55 years of service, one of several numbers of staff to retire at this time; he must have been thankful that he could retreat to his home at Brading without a thought as to future events. Horace D. Tahourdin and roughly 190 IWR employees transferred to the new company.

At a meeting held at Waterloo on 17th November, LSWR shareholders sanctioned the amalgamation of their railway with its neighbours. The terms were approved by the Railway Amalgamation Tribunal and sealed on 23rd December, 1922.

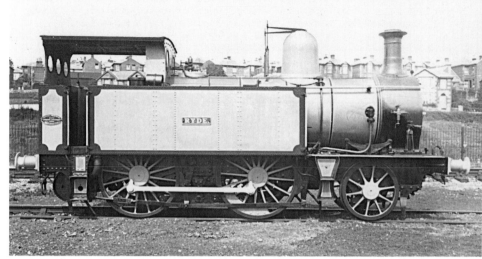

Ryde was cosmetically restored in the vain hope that it might be preserved. Painted in works grey but lined out in IWR style it waits at Ryde for its final journey to the mainland in 1933.
A.B. MacLeod/R. Silsbury Collection

Although taken in BR days, this photograph shows the impressive three-arch bridge between Shanklin and Wroxall. '02' class No. 29 *Alverstone* is hauling a down train in the summer of 1965.
T. Cooper

On 1st January, 1923 the Southern Railway Company came into being. It was formed by an amalgamation of the London & South Western, London, Brighton & South Coast, South Eastern & Chatham railway companies. By arrangement they had absorbed several smaller lines including those in the Isle of Wight. No longer would Ryde St John's Road station be a 'frontier' station where IWR and IWC trains passed on to the metals of the LSWR and LBSCR Joint Committee, nor would IWC trains be accepted on sufferance at Sandown. The creation of the Southern Railway welded the Island railways into one system - even if some old loyalties remained.

Thus faded from existence one of Britain's smaller railway companies. Apart from its early life, it is fair to say that the IWR's history was not particularly eventful. Despite the opinions of its critics, the railway went about its business of serving visitors and the local populace quietly and without fuss for some 60 years. The survival of the railway between Ryde and Shanklin is surely a testament to its success.

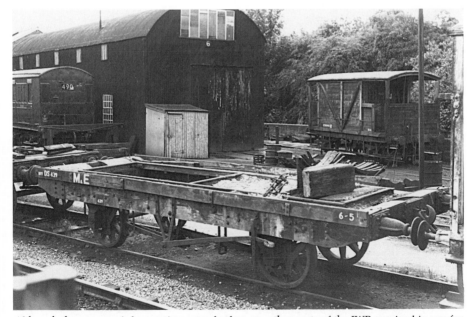

Although the company's locomotives were broken up, other parts of the IWR survived in use for many years. This photograph of Ryde Works yard shows the corrugated iron workshop erected in 1876 and the IWR boiler truck 439s; the boiler truck was broken up in October 1966.

R. Silsbury Collection

Chapter Fourteen

Ventnor's Piers, Tramways and Railways

The climate throughout the Island can vary considerably in the course of a single day. A visitor to the western part of the Isle of Wight could encounter fog, it might be raining in Sandown Bay, whilst Ventnor basked in brilliant sunshine. Ventnor's attraction as a resort was based principally on its mild winter climate with the surrounding downs forming a screen from cold winds; in summer sea breezes tend to keep the maximum temperature within comfortable limits. These qualities were recognised as long ago as 1676 when it was written 'the air is commended both for health and delight'.

Until comparatively recently, tuberculosis of the lung, commonly known as consumption, was a scourge that afflicted many. Doctors could only prescribe rest, fresh air and good food in the hope that the body's own defences would arrest the disease. Invalids were encouraged to travel to Ventnor where the climate was said to be helpful to their recovery. The influx of visitors soon created a shortage of accommodation and this led to a boom in the construction of villas. Even so, in 1830 it was little bigger than its neighbour Bonchurch and had no shops, roads nor postal deliveries. That year Ventnor was visited by a distinguished doctor, Sir James Clarke, who, impressed by the climate, added his voice to those who had already discovered its health-giving benefits; his book called *The Sanative Influence of Climate on Diseases* published in 1846 merely added to the stampede. In 1831 an estimated 76,848 passengers were carried by coach and omnibus to and from Ryde - they kept on coming.

The town was so popular that by 1851 the population had reached 3,500. An 1859 gazetteer reported the town possessed four first rate hotels, several good inns, neat marine villas and lodging houses - over 40 people ran businesses affording accommodation for visitors. Other facilities included 'commodious baths, belonging to Mr Wm Bull'. So many building speculators had been attracted that land prices had risen from £100 an acre in 1830 to upwards of £800 to £1,000. In 1867 the Royal National Hospital for Diseases of the Chest opened; it was extended several times and received visits from members of the royal family including Queen Victoria.

Henry James thought the town rather unattractive and wrote in 1870:

There is too much brick and mortar; there are too many smoking chimneys and shops and public-houses; there are no woods nor brooks nor lonely headlands; there is none of the virginal stillness of Nature. Instead of these things there is an esplanade mostly paved with asphalt, bordered with benches and little shops and provided with a German band. To be just to Ventnor, however, I must hasten to add that once you get away from the asphalt there is a great deal of vegetation.

James mentioned the existence of an Esplanade. In 1844 an Act authorised creation of Improvement Commissioners who subsequently spent over £3,000 on lighting, paving, drainage and other works. Three years later £850 was expended on a 450 yds-long Esplanade - a feature that any well-to-do Victorian society would demand. Its seems a primitive pier was also built to serve steamers which brought travellers from the mainland; previously row-boats had been used to land passengers on the open beach. The pier was soon wrecked by the sea.

The promotion of the IWES in 1859 and 1860 held out the prospect of a more comfortable, speedy and reliable journey to Ventnor. But the railway had some competition. In November 1861 the Ventnor Pier and Harbour Company published a Prospectus in which it proposed to raise £15,000 for construction of a harbour, pier and quay. It was planned to construct two breakwaters with a western arm running south and thence south-east for 600 ft, whilst the

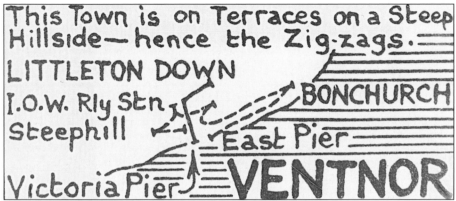

This Town is on Terraces on a Steep Hillside—hence the Zig-zags.
LITTLETON DOWN
I.O.W. Rly Stn
Steephill
BONCHURCH
East Pier
Victoria Pier
VENTNOR

Map of early tramway schemes at Ventnor.

other spur would run 700 ft to the east and south-west for 300 ft. The Esplanade would be widened to give ample room for the landing of passengers and goods. The Chairman was Thomas Willis Fleming who, having broken with the IWES, saw a direct ferry route from Stokes Bay as a viable alternative to the railway; the other Directors were local men and included Francis Atherley, Deputy Chairman of the IWES.

The Ventnor Harbour Company obtained Parliamentary approval in 1862 to raise £20,000 and under the management of the Engineer, Richard Saunders, construction of the western breakwater began in April 1863. Two parallel rows of wooden piles were erected, lined with timber and filled with stone and soil carried by narrow gauge railway from Collins Point, a natural groyne. By June the breakwater, then described as a pier, reached 100 yards out to sea. Steamers first used the pier on Coronation Day, 29th June, but within days it was the scene of the wreck of the steamer *Chancellor* belonging to the Isle of Wight Ferry Company. *Chancellor's* departure from Stokes Bay had been delayed and by the time it reached Ventnor the tide had turned. A Director of the harbour company encouraged the captain to go alongside the pier but the falling tide left the vessel grounded on rocks and holed. Weather conditions deteriorated soon afterwards and the ensuing storm threw *Chancellor* broadside onto the beach; the vessel broke in two and was later declared a total loss. Such bad publicity did nothing for the fortunes of the harbour company, but the pier was nevertheless extended during the next winter and by the end of March 1864 a substantial pier head had been added. A converted tug operated to Littlehampton for connection with the London trains but, to the discomfort of her passengers, often returned with a cargo of 10 tons of coal for sale at prices undercutting local merchants! Work on the eastern breakwater had begun, but in October 1864 storms resulted in its virtual destruction, along with much of the western pier and part of the Esplanade. As a result the company was forced to return to Parliament in 1865 for powers to extend the time for completion and raise more money. The elements contrived to wreak more damage during the winter of 1865-1866 and in the face of this the company was wound up. The remains of the breakwaters were auctioned by Francis Pittis in May 1867 when they fetched just £533 10s.

The site of the railway station adjoining Newport Road (renamed Mitchell Avenue in 1926) could not be more inconvenient. Whilst distances were not significant, the steep gradients were a considerable disincentive, especially on the uphill journey to the station! In 1863 Richard Saunders formed the Ventnor Tramway Company, and within 12 months plans had crystallised into a comprehensive network of tramways with the title Ventnor and Bonchurch Tramways. In 1865 a Bill went before Parliament applying for powers to issue £30,000 in £10 shares and raise £10,000 in loans, to finance construction of 2 miles 5 chains of standard gauge steam-powered street tramways. They would have connected the railway station with the town, Bonchurch and the works of the Ventnor Harbour Company by means of several changes in direction and gradient. Parliament received petitions from a number of residents in opposition and threw out the Bill on 9th May, 1865.

Other railways had designs on Ventnor. The CNR and its successors repeatedly supported schemes that would have taken the railway closer to the town, including the Yarmouth and Ventnor Railway, Tramway and Pier Co. It gained an Act of Parliament in 1871 for a 19 mile railway from the IWR at Ventnor along the back of the Island to Freshwater and Yarmouth, where a tramway to a pier was planned. The IWNJ obtained powers for a connection to the line from its Sandown to Newport line with the intention of running through trains from the Southampton steamers at Cowes to Ventnor. The Parliamentary powers lapsed.

Despite the failure of tramway proposals in the 1860s, many hoped for a rail link connecting the railway with town. In 1880 some IWR Directors got together to form a second Ventnor Tramway Company; the prime mover seems to have been the IWR Chairman Joseph Bravo, but when he died a year later the company faded away having achieved nothing.

The inconvenient location of the station did not concern the wealthy as they would be met by their own horse-drawn transport. Several hotel proprietors operated horse buses to carry visitors to and from their establishments and paid the IWR a modest rent for the privilege of using the station yard - similar arrangements existed at Shanklin and presumably at Sandown. On at least one occasion complaints were made that the drivers were making a nuisance of themselves as they touted for custom. The IWR Board instructed that 'Drivers must not shout out and run after people getting out of the trains'. Margaret Huish, widow of Capt. Huish, organised a local subscription in 1887 to pay for a cabmen's shelter. That year the Royal Marine, Crab & Lobster and Queen's Hotels each paid £20 for the use of the station yard whilst Henry Brown, who contracted to carry passengers and parcels to and from the town, paid £30.

In 1870 the Ventnor Pier & Esplanade Company was formed to build an iron pier. Its Act of Incorporation authorised a share capital of £30,000 and borrowings of £10,000. Construction began in November 1871 but *ten* years passed before steamers could land at the pier! Storms destroyed much of it during the following winter and the local authority was forced to buy the remains. Reconstruction began in 1885 with T. R. Saunders as resident Engineer. The Royal Victoria Pier was formally opened two years later by the Attorney General, Sir Richard Webster QC, MP, son of the late Thomas Webster. This time the pier survived the elements and sundry alterations and additions. Steamers to the mainland operated regular services in the summer months, but they ended with the Great War and only excursion steamers called at the pier thereafter. A section was demolished as a wartime measure in 1940 and, although the pier was rebuilt and reopened in 1955, it closed in 1971 and has since been demolished.

In 1884 proposals appeared for another railway. The Shanklin and Chale Railway gained its Act of Incorporation in 1885, but when a second Bill was placed before Parliament in the following session for an extension to Freshwater it was thrown out. The Directors then fell in with the Isle of Wight Central Railway and, following two more Acts, changed its name to the Newport, Godshill & St Lawrence Railway. In 1896 fresh proposals were put before Parliament for an extension to a terminus near Ventnor Park, on the same level but some distance from the town. In a belated attempt to stop the interloper, Horace Tahourdin, the IWR Chairman, offered running powers over the IWR, but supporters of the Bill convinced Parliament that the line would generate some healthy competition. Worked by the IWC, the railway from Merstone to St Lawrence opened in 1897 and in 1900 an extension to Ventnor came into use. It never prospered as fares and goods rates were no cheaper than those of the

IWR, and few passengers could be prevailed upon to use the Southampton and Cowes route in preference to that via Portsmouth. The IWC purchased the line in 1913.

If the Newport, Godshill & St Lawrence Railway made no money for its owners, it did no appreciable harm to the IWR. Horace Tahourdin summed up the situation, if rather pompously, at a shareholders' meeting:

> . . . There has been another railway opened to Ventnor which is perhaps a little shorter from Cowes than our line, but the communications and connexions that the new railway has with the mainland companies are such that I do not think it is likely to do the Isle of Wight Railway Company very much harm. Still, there it is, and we may lose a little of the traffic into Ventnor. Still, I feel the gradual growth of things in the Island will soon compensate for that . . .

The IWR introduced some combined railway and ferry fares to Cowes and Southampton via Ryde but otherwise matters remained very much as they were. This was much to the frustration of local residents who had accused the IWR of discouraging traffic by levying high fares and goods rates - an eagerly looked-for price war between the IWR and IWC never came about.

Within Ventnor itself, proposals appeared in 1889 for a funicular railway called the 'Ventnor Lift' between the station and Esplanade Hotel. Powered by an oil-fired steam engine working an endless belt, tramcars would have picked up or dropped the belt when required. Two routes were suggested: one would have been 1,552 ft long on a mean slope of 1 in 5.8 entirely in a tunnel with an intermediate station; the other would have been 1,718 ft long on a mean slope of 1 in 6.05 with two intermediate stations, about 200 ft of the line being above ground. In 1891 John H. Blakeley, an Engineer, put before the Town Board proposals for a 'Ventnor Incline' from the shore to the station at a cost estimated at £10,000. The IWR agreed to contribute up to £100 towards Parliamentary costs and subsidise its operation to the tune of £200 a year. It seems the local authority favoured an extension to the top of St Boniface Down on land owned by Mrs Caroline Evans, a local dignitary, but when they met a negative response the scheme faded away.

In 1897 Mrs Evans made it known that she was minded to give the Down to the town. Soon afterwards the Ventnor Inclined (Light) Railway Company Limited was formed and, encouraged by the Urban District Council and IWR, made application to the Board of Trade for a Light Railway Order. The Directors included Dr John G. Sinclair Coghill, senior physician at the chest hospital, Godfrey Baring JP and Ernest Wetherick, an auctioneer and Chairman of the Urban District Council. Three 5 ft 9 in. gauge railways were proposed:

1. Railway No. 1 beginning in the garden of a house on the Esplanade opposite the pier and running due north in a straight line through a tunnel under Hamborough Road, various properties and Church Street before emerging at a 'Central Station', a length of 518 ft rising 80½ ft. The estimated cost was £4,215 10s. 6d. for a single line with a passing track in the centre.

2. Railway No. 2 would have continued variously on a viaduct, underground or in a cutting before burrowing under Newport Road to emerge in the station yard, a length of 1,156 ft. rising 175 ft. This section would have cost £7,215 14s. 2d. for a single line with a passing loop. A 50 ft covered foot way connected railways 1 and 2.

3. Railway No. 3 would have begun at right angles to railway 2 rising to the top of St Boniface Down, a length of 870 ft with a climb of 342 ft. It would have cost a further £2,444 8s.

Capital would have been raised by the issue of £10,000 in ordinary shares, £10,000 preference shares and £6,000 debentures. The most favoured tender received was for £20,920, considerably more than the Engineer's estimate of £13,876, whilst the third line would have added more. At a meeting on 23rd March, 1898 at the Westminster Palace Hotel, Victoria Street, Westminster, the IWR Board met a deputation of promoters when the proposals were discussed in some detail. The IWR agreed to subscribe £5,000 towards construction costs and another £1,000 if the

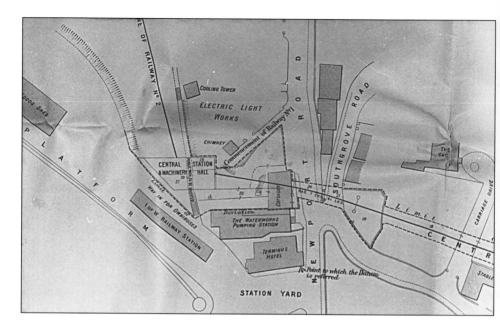

Route plan of the Ventnor Funicular Railway of 1898.

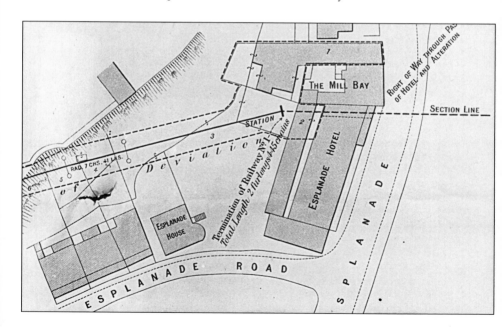

third line was built; this was on condition that promoters raised the remaining capital by a set date and adhered to estimated costs. The Light Railway put two seats on the Board at the disposal of the IWR and the latter obtained authority to subscribe to the undertaking in its 1898 Act. In 1899 the Board of Trade approved an application for a Light Railway Order for railways 1 and 2 - an application for railway 3 was not granted as Mrs Evans had not agreed terms with the local authority. Plans to use water power had been abandoned in favour of electricity bought from the 'Central Station of the Isle of Wight Electric Power Company' - it was said there was an insufficient supply of water but a more likely reason for the change was the appointment of a power company Director to the Board of the light railway. Although seemingly well thought through, the scheme faded away; the powers lapsed on 10th March, 1903 when just £7 capital had been subscribed! In 1905 a resurrection of the idea for a lift from the Esplanade to Hamborough Road met with a similar fate when the local authority declined to make any contribution to its cost.

In 1907 380,000 people arrived at Ventnor by train and another 15,000 by steamer. Thoughts of a funicular railway were not forgotten and on 21st October, 1908 Ventnor Urban District Council decided to promote its construction. The Council commissioned Fritz Behr, an Engineer who lived in Ventnor, to prepare plans at a cost of £250; he was described as 'the inventor of the monorail' and had built the Listowel and Ballybunion Railway in Ireland on the Lartigue system, a peculiar line with trains running on a single rail supported by trestles. He proposed a system for Ventnor similar to that used on another of his undertakings, a cliff railway at Treport, consisting of a metre gauge (39⅜ in.) single line in two portions:

1. Railway No. 1 from the railway station to Esplanade would have been 540 yards long descending at 1 in 4.54 and 1 in 6.25 under two roads to a station to the north of Grove Road. It would then have passed under Grove Road before the gradient eased to 1 in 10.53 under Church Street to a second station. The final section descended to the Esplanade where it terminated behind Esplanade Hotel, a right of way passing through the hotel; the estimated cost totalled £14,340 5s.
2. Railway 2 running to the downs would have run for just under ¾ mile along a footpath, through a shallow cutting at a gradient of 1 in 4.25, then on an embankment at 1 in 2.7; near the summit the gradient would have eased to 1 in 4 through a short cutting to a terminus 640 feet above sea level. This line added £5,498 13s. to the bill.

Worked by electricity on an endless belt system, each car had a capacity for 46 passengers in four compartments and the journey over the whole railway would take 15 minutes at fares of 4d. on the lower section and 3d. to the downs. A half-hourly service would operate up the downs but more frequently over the main section.

In November 1908 Henry Day met a committee of the Council and subsequently recommended the IWR support the scheme by providing some land and contributing to any loss in working, subject to certain conditions. Three cottages near the station belonging to the IWR were to be demolished for an access road to a 'Machinery Hall'. At a public meeting at the Town Hall on 7th December a vote was passed in favour of the scheme, despite some dissent over the costs that would fall on ratepayers. In July 1909 the council asked for a postponement of a hearing before the Light Railway Commissioners whilst it discussed terms with landowners. Talks broke down and an amended plan had to be considered; in April 1910 Henry Day informed the IWR Board that the undertaking had been abandoned. Meanwhile, the local population had been venting its feelings in letters to the local newspapers. One correspondent propounded the Esplanade to Hamborough Road scheme, another wanted electric trams along the streets, even an escalator was suggested.

Henry Day 'mentioned' to the IWR Board numerous proposals for railways or tramways in the years leading up to 1914. Those emerging in 1910 included an electric street tramway zigzagging from the Esplanade via High Street and railway station to Lowtherville (Upper Ventnor).

In 1912 Theodore R. Saunders and Mr Wetherick, proposed an electric railway in a tunnel from the Esplanade to Church Street - it would not have gone to the railway station as councillors believed the IWR should build that section. Costing an estimated £8,891 10s., two cars each with a capacity of 15 persons would have taken a minute for the journey at fares of 2d. up and 1d. down. On 9th November, 1912 the IWR Board met a deputation from the Council, when one councillor expressed the view that if the town was to recover its prosperity a lift must be built from shore to town, railway station and to the top of the Down. Percy Gilbert indicated that the IWR would renew its offer made in 1909 to give up three cottages adjoining the station, said to be worth £500, a site in the station yard for a machinery shed and pay something towards any loss in running costs. All concerned parted amicably, but at a Board meeting on 31st December a letter from the clerk to the UDC was read suggesting the IWR promote and work the 'New Funicular Railway' aided by the local authority - the exact opposite of what had been discussed a few weeks before! Naturally the IWR Board would not be drawn into such a commitment and a month later Henry Day reported the council had put off considering the matter - that was the end of it.

In February 1913 the Ventnor Road Car Company Limited was formed to operate motor buses connecting the Esplanade, railway stations, golf links and Bonchurch. It persuaded a considerable number of local residents to invest in the firm, purchased a vehicle with spares for £865 15s. 5d. and wrote to the IWR asking if land could be made available near the station for storing 'three cars'. The IWR offered a site near Chaplin & Co.'s stables for £6 per annum, tenants being expected to pay the cost of clearance, estimated at £156, and erect a garage - it was politely refused. The Ventnor Road Car Company seems to have been relatively successful until 1914; within a year the car had been sold for £600 and shortly afterwards the company was wound up.

Ventnor's prosperity suffered badly following the outbreak of the Great War when several of the best hotels and boarding houses closed for the duration. As late as 1919 a writer commented that 'the pretty little town is sadly neglected' and added that Ventnor was the only south coast resort to claim Government aid. Within a year or two Ventnor revived as visitors returned to the Isle of Wight; perhaps not as wealthy as before but at least they came. There was talk of building a lift as a war memorial, but the thought of making money out of it was condemned by some as inappropriate, a more conventional memorial was eventually erected. Following the death of Mrs Evans in 1922, 221 acres of St Boniface Down was presented to the National Trust on condition that nothing was done to interfere with the site's natural beauty; apart from the construction of a World War II radar station her wishes have been respected.

Although strictly beyond the scope of this book, mention should be made of an inclined railway proposed by the Southern Railway. It was H.D. Tahourdin who convinced SR management of the virtues of the project during a visit of inspection. Existing plans were brought up to date and in 1925 the SR Act authorised compulsory purchase of land between the station and a terminus near the Beach Hotel, a length of 2 furlongs 3.68 chains. The route would have begun in the south-west corner of the station goods yard, passed under Newport Road, then descended to the west of Grove Road to The Grove where it was planned to divert Marlborough Road. From there onwards it followed the 1909 scheme. There were no covered sections except where the line passed under Newport Road, descending at 1 in 5.25, then at 1 in 6.25 through The Grove before easing to 1 in 8.1 for the final section. Numerous properties were purchased along the intended route for quite hefty sums but they were never needed. The scheme fell from favour following Mr Tahourdin's retirement in 1926 but it was not until 24th November, 1927 that the SR Board officially decided to abandon the funicular, ostensibly because a motor omnibus had been put on between the railway station and the town. Thus died the last serious attempt to build a cliff railway at Ventnor.

Chapter Fifteen

Locomotives

Construction of the railway was carried out with the assistance of two steam locomotives named *Stuart* and *Grafton*. *Stuart* had quite an eventful life even before its arrival in the Isle of Wight. At a meeting of the Board of the Glasgow, Paisley, Kilmarnock & Ayre Railway on 21st August, 1840, James Kennedy, works foreman of Edward Bury & Company, promised delivery of two four-wheeled locomotives within two months at a cost of £1,480 each. Delivered in January 1841 as Nos. 18 *Stuart* and 19 *Bute*, they were standard Bury products, with 13 in. cylinders, bar frames and a large spherical topped copper firebox shell appreciably higher than the boiler barrel, known as a 'haystack' or 'haycock' pattern. Bury locomotives were amongst the best of the period but such was the pace of locomotive development that by the end of the decade they were obsolete. The company's successor, the Glasgow and South Western Railway, rebuilt *Stuart* in July 1853 to a tank engine but it was one of four old engines sold by auction on 20th June, 1860 to unknown buyers. *Stuart* then disappeared from sight until early 1863 when it arrived at Brading for use in the construction of the Isle of Wight Railway. In an advert for the sale of contractor's plant at Wroxall on 19th April, 1866 a footnote stated that an engine, presumably *Stuart*, would run from Shanklin to Wroxall in connection with the 10 am train from Ryde. *Stuart* passed into the ownership of Warrant Finance Company and Mr Dorrell used it working spoil trains between Shanklin and Ventnor, a menial duty for which it seemed well suited. The IWR bought the locomotive with other plant in December 1867 and renamed it *Brading*.

Grafton is said to have arrived in May 1862 but as the contractor did not sign the construction contract until December 1862 this date is clearly wrong - a year later would be more likely. The locomotive was offered for sale with some of Henry Bond's plant and described in the *Isle of Wight Times* of 11th April, 1866 as '. . . a four-wheel locomotive with cylinders 18-inch stroke by Hawthorn & Company, Leith'. In reality, it is thought to have been rebuilt by Hawthorn's from a much older locomotive. Frederick Furniss purchased *Grafton* for £465 and took it to Hayling Island to assist in the construction and operation of the line to Havant. After the LBSCR took over the working of the railway from Furniss in 1872, he sold the locomotive to I. W. Boulton of Ashton-Under-Lyne, a well-known dealer in second-hand railway equipment. Known to Boulton as *Brighton*, he described it as an 0-4-2 box-type saddle tank with a haycock firebox; the wheels measured 3 ft 6 in. and cylinders were 11 in. by 18 in. After being hired out for various tasks, Boulton sold the locomotive to Brunner, Mond & Co. in about 1876 for use at their chemical works at Northwich, Cheshire where it ended its days.

The purchase of motive power for working the railway was first mentioned, not in a meeting of the IWR Board, but in a letter from Charles Beyer of the firm Beyer, Peacock & Co. on 21st January, 1863, when he wrote that his partner, Charles Peacock '. . . was in London last week and settled with Mr Fowler about 4 Tank Engines for the Isle of Wight, to be the same as Llangollen, but we have not received the official order . . .'

The absence of an order was hardly surprising as the IWR Minutes did not record any formal discussion of the matter until 16th June. The Board asked John Fowler, the Engineer, to seek tenders for five locomotives. At the following meeting on 23rd June tenders for their delivery on 1st March and 1st October, 1864 were read out, but the Directors deferred a decision whilst they busied themselves with more urgent matters. A month later the Board accepted a tender from Beyer, Peacock & Company, Gorton Foundry, Manchester for five locomotives at £2,250 each, subject to John Fowler's approval of the design. Formed in May 1854, Beyer, Peacock & Co. of Gorton, Manchester were a reputable supplier of locomotives to railways in Britain and throughout the world. The locomotives were to one of the firm's standard designs that had first originated in 1861 with an order from the West Midland Railway. They were neat little 2-4-0 side tanks with inside cylinders and tiny weatherboards over the firebox. The locomotives presented a clean and well balanced appearance when compared with 4-4-0Ts supplied by the

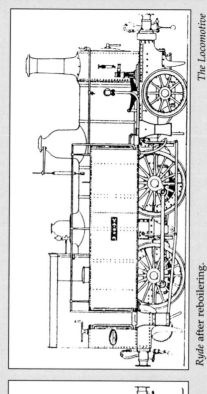

Sandown after receiving a cab and handrails along the tank sides.

The Locomotive

Ryde after reboilering.

The Locomotive

same makers to another of John Fowler's lines, the Metropolitan Railway. According to the late D.L. Bradley,* the 2-4-0Ts were painted in a dark chocolate with vermilion and gold lining; certainly they carried standard Beyer, Peacock embellishments including tall copper-capped chimneys, brass domes with safety valves over the firebox, beading to the splashers, brass name plates attached to the side of boilers and maker's plates on the tank sides. Beyer, Peacock allocated works progress numbers and duly constructed five locomotives. Before the IWR was ready to accept delivery it was clear that not all could be afforded, a reduction in the order to three was negotiated and Beyer, Peacock found other buyers for the surplus locomotives. One was sold to a Signor A. Albani of Leghorn, North Italy for £2,250 whilst the fifth went for £2,150 to the Great Western Railway for use on its Ordsall branch. The five 2-4-0Ts were:

Progress No.	Tried in steam	Delivered	Notes†
400	28th April, 1864	17th June, 1864	*Ryde*
401	5th May, 1864	21st June, 1864	*Sandown*
402	6th May, 1864	22th June, 1864	originally to be *Shanklin* but sold to A. Albani
403	12th May, 1864	28th June, 1864	originally to be *Brading* but delivered as *Shanklin*
404	21st May, 1864	26th January, 1865	sold to GWR as their No. 343

(The delivery dates used in this chapter were taken from Beyer, Peacock records and seem to have been the dates of dispatch from Manchester.) Shipped from Portsmouth, the locomotives were landed at the quay at Brading on 20th July, 1864. All three seem to have been quite satisfactory in use and Beyer, Peacock's records contain few references to requests for spare parts, one dated 4th November, 1867 being for 12 extra piston rings 'Piston rings to be 15⅛ in. diameter instead of 15 in. . . . Wanted immediately.'

The locomotives were subject to a period of approval and 12 months elapsed before Beyer, Peacock asked for £3,587 16s. due to them. The Board considered the matter at a meeting on 29th August, 1865 and instructed the Secretary to offer preference shares until such time that instalments could begin. Beyer, Peacock were subsequently given 100 £10 ordinary paid-up shares and £2,730 in second preference shares as security for the debt.

At a Board meeting on 27th June, 1867 Joseph Bourne submitted a list of plant lying at Wroxall that would be useful to the railway; it included a quantity of permanent way materials, one locomotive (*Stuart*) and some wagons. The Board clearly appreciated their value and offered £1,100 in preference shares. The finance company accepted the offer but retained a lien upon the locomotive and trucks for £600 until 1870 when the IWR cleared the outstanding debt. Carrying the name *Brading*, the locomotive entered service on permanent way and freight trains, a continuation of its previous task of hauling stone and spoil - Ventnor stone was used in many buildings in towns along the line so *Brading* must have earned her keep. Board of Trade returns described it as a 2-4-0 well tank with 4 ft 6 in. coupled wheels, 14 in. x 18 in. cylinders and weighing 18½ tons.

The three Beyer, Peacock 2-4-0Ts were sufficient whilst the line ran only as far as Shanklin but once the section opened to Ventnor the railway experienced a shortage of motive power. On 21st August, 1867 Joseph Bourne expressed a need for an additional locomotive as part of a package of improvements. The Board deferred a decision and when he raised the subject again on 5th December, the Board asked Mr Bourne whether 'with the addition of the Engine purchased of the Warrant Finance Company, he could not manage to carry on the Winter traffic'. A further request at the following meeting on the 19th met with the response that 'the Directors hope that the Warrant Finance Company's engine may be repaired more rapidly than a new one could be built'! On 17th February, 1868 Joseph Bourne finally convinced the Board that it could delay no longer. Although Beyer, Peacock quoted £2,250 or a list of materials for £1,900, the whole amount could not be paid at once. Beyer, Peacock requested

---

* *A Locomotive History of the Railways on the Isle of Wight* by D.L. Bradley (the Railway Correspondence and Travel Society 1972).

† Dimensions, etc. mainly taken from Beyer, Peacock records are summarised separately; they differ in a few respects to other sources, mainly in relation to weights.

Staff seen with *Sandown* at Ryde. During the 1880s the four older 2-4-0Ts received cabs and handrails along the tops of the tanks, taller chimneys had been fitted some years earlier. *Sandown* has yet to receive metal brake blocks or a new boiler.   *T. Cooper Collection*

Sandown waits to leave Ventnor with an up train at about the turn of the century. Note that the dome has been repositioned to the centre ring of the boiler. A good supply of coal is piled high in the bunker.   *Real Photographs*

payment in three equal annual instalments carrying interest on the balance of 5 per cent per annum but after negotiation they waived the interest. *Ventnor* was identical to the 1864 trio except for minor changes, probably to ease maintenance, including the addition of a rear weatherboard. Beyer, Peacock records state it was delivered on 19th October, 1868.

During the early 1870s the Minutes recorded purchases of boiler plate and numerous spares as the level of heavy repairs rose. In May 1868 the IWR Board agreed to buy crucible cast-steel tyres to replace iron tyres used on the existing locomotives. Joseph Bourne quoted a price of £43 per ton from the Monkbridge Iron Company instead of iron tyres then costing £31 per ton. The Board promptly informed him that they could be bought more cheaply from the Patent Shaft Company or Messrs Lloyds Foster & Co. - information clearly gleaned from those Directors who sat on the Boards of other railways! The benefits of using steel tyres and rails cannot be over emphasised as they reduced wear and significantly increased adhesion, allowing locomotives to haul heavier loads.

On 27th December, 1870 Joseph Bourne wrote to the Board stating a requirement for a fifth 2-4-0T financed partly by the sale of 'the old contractor's locomotive' *Brading* that he estimated would fetch £500. The IWR vainly offered Beyer, Peacock £500 on delivery and instalments of £25 per month thereafter. In a fit of pique the Board resolved to take its custom elsewhere and asked Joseph Bourne to make enquiries of other manufacturers. They were evidently unsatisfactory, as on 5th October he put forward fresh terms from Beyer, Peacock agreeing to accept £150 cash before dispatch from the works and £40 per month beginning one month after delivery. Beyer, Peacock added the proviso that any unpaid instalment would carry an interest charge of 10 per cent per annum; naturally the IWR took care to avoid incurring this penalty, and arranged for Messrs Bravo and De Pass to guarantee payments for which they received an allotment of 'B' debenture stock as security. The Board signed a contract on 14th December, 1871 for the purchase of *Wroxall* at a total cost of £2,400, delivery was on 16th April, 1872. *Wroxall* differed slightly from previous deliveries: the dome and Salter balance safety valves were placed in the middle of the boiler barrel, it had a short chimney, nameplates on the tank sides and a square cab with three round windows enclosing the bunker. Although Beyer, Peacock's records made no mention of a change in specifications, the late D. L. Bradley stated that *Wroxall's* arrival followed a change in the locomotive livery to Furness red with black bands and gold lining. Photographs show that the lining on the sides of tanks was in the form of three panels with reversed curving at corners and a centre panel little wider than the maker's plate; later repaints had the tanks lined out as a single panel. As before, brass and copper work were brightly burnished.

On 12th February, 1872 Joseph Bravo, IWR Chairman, reported to the Board that the contractor's locomotive *Brading* had been sold. That month it was working for the contractor building the IWNJ where it remained until at least June 1872; according to George Young, the IWNJ were the purchasers. Who actually paid the £400 purchase price of the locomotive is unclear, as on 29th August, 1872 it was reported that a Mr Wright, who was said to be the buyer, had asked the IWR to carry out certain repairs; the IWR Board ordered that the locomotive be retained until he paid for them. *Brading* then passed out of sight until 1875 when it was being employed on construction of the Ryde & Newport Railway with the name *Dorothy*. When the RNR opened in December 1875 *Dorothy* handled passenger services and remained on the line until the following June, when the Joint Committee of the CNR and RNR took over. *Dorothy* seems to have made a brief return visit to the Sandown to Newport line before migrating to St Helens to help in construction there.

Joseph Bourne wrote to the Board on 14th March, 1876 proposing the purchase of a 'locomotive required for Goods Traffic, one third more power than those in present use'. He enclosed a quote from Beyer, Peacock for £2,150 cash, or £2,525 if payment was by an initial £150 and instalments of £40 per month for five years. On 16th May, 1876 the IWR placed an order for (a new) *Brading*; it was delivered on 22nd December, 1876. *Brading* had larger tanks, firebox and cylinders, spring balance safety valves and square windows to the front and back of the cab. The improved financial position permitted the dispatch of a cheque to Beyer, Peacock on 28th March, 1878 for over £2,500 to clear the amounts owing for the locomotives supplied before *Brading*; payments for *Brading* continued until November 1881.

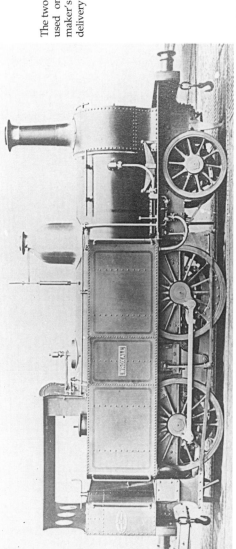

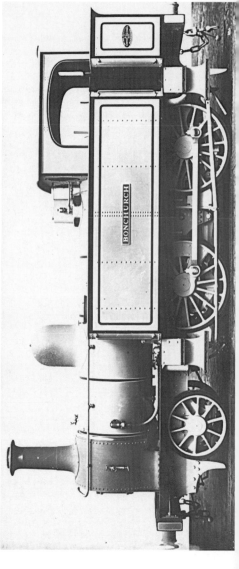

The two basic types of Beyer, Peacock 2-4-0Ts used on the IWR is epitomised in these maker's photographs of *Wroxall* before delivery in 1872 and *Bonchurch* in 1883.

A.B. MacLeod/IWSR Collection

On 16th October, 1882 the Board placed an order for *Bonchurch* from Beyer, Peacock for £2,100 cash, delivery to be made by the second week of March; in fact Beyer's delivery date was not until 18th April, 1883 but, as the *Isle of Wight Times* recounted, it did not go according to plan:

On Monday last [26th April, 1883] as an engine belonging to the Isle of Wight Railway Company was being conveyed from Southampton to St Helens, a serious and very untoward accident occurred. Owing to a squall of wind, the engine got loose and fell into the water, dragging the barge down with it . . .
The engine *Bonchurch* which sunk in a barge about 1½ miles off St Helens last week was successfully raised and landed on shore on Monday afternoon [30th April]. Two dockyard 'lumps' raised the locomotive at high water, and she was afterwards taken to low water mark, and from thence hoisted onto the quay. The *Bonchurch* is said to be worth over £2,000, so that the raising of her may be considered a very fortunate thing.

The newspaper told only part of the story. The regular steamer was unavailable and a replacement tug *Mizpah* lost control of the lighter *Nancy* carrying the locomotive during a squall. *Bonchurch* received little damage apart from an unwelcome covering of sand and after a visit to Ryde Works entered service on 1st June. Nominally the same size as *Brading*, *Bonchurch* looked more modern in appearance. It had a larger external coal bunker, a more roomy cab with two square windows to the front and back, a plain dome and Ramsbottom safety valves over the firebox. *Bonchurch* also differed by having beading around the tank tops and filler covers at the front of the tanks instead of adjacent to the footplate as on the other IWR locomotives; it later received new filler holes sealed by wooden bungs - primitive but effective. The IWR dispatched a cheque on 1st February, 1883 for £2,300, presumably including a £200 delivery charge.
    Mention was made in Chapter Eleven of the use of a locomotive *Stanley* during construction of the BHIR. A Manning, Wardle & Co. class 'M' 0-6-0 saddle tank, it was sold in March 1875 to Scott & Edwards of Stratford-upon-Avon for use on construction of the Alcester to Beardley line for the Great Western Railway. The firm then secured the Brading company's contract and *Stanley* was sent to the Island to assist in construction work. There, it was joined by the elderly locomotive *Stuart*, alias *Brading* and *Dorothy*. During 1879 one of the pair passed into the ownership of the BHIR, followed within the next 12 months by the other. At some date the Manning, Wardle gained a change of name to *Bembridge* whilst *Dorothy* metamorphosed into *St Helens*. When the line to Bembridge opened in 1882 *Bembridge* handled most of the work and *St Helens* rarely emerged from the locomotive shed at St Helens Quay, except to visit Ryde Works for overhaul. In September 1893 the Brading company sold *St Helens* for £650 to Charles Westwood, the contractor building the Newport, Godshill & St Lawrence Railway between Merstone and Ventnor; renamed *St Lawrence* the locomotive lasted until 1898 when it was broken up for scrap at Whitwell. *Bembridge* appears in the IWR's returns to the Board of Trade from 1885 although it remained BHIR property until 2nd August, 1898.
    During the 1880s the older locomotives received heavy repairs. *Ventnor* burst a cylinder in July 1883 and received a new set; replacements for the 1864 engines followed shortly afterwards. During routine repairs the older locomotives had received front and rear weatherboards but they were later replaced by cabs similar to that carried by *Wroxall*. The nameplates were moved to the tank sides and maker's plates to the side sheets at the rear of the footplate entrance. They also received lengthy handrails along the top of the tanks so the unfortunate fireman could clamber to the front of the engine whilst in motion to sand the rails; the handrails were removed following the passing of safety legislation in 1900. Handrails apart, the 2-4-0Ts presented a most attractive appearance with the red paint set off by polished copper-capped chimneys, brass bell-mouthed domes and a profusion of brass fittings. Purchases of spares in 1885-1886 included three crank axles, several sets of cylinders and four locomotive tube plates; such was the level of expenditure that it is likely the boilers were also heavily repaired at this time.
    Prior to 1892 the ability to stop a train depended on the combined skill of the crew in working the locomotive hand brake and the guard applying his brake. This changed when the

Shanklin, seen at Shanklin on 12th May, 1920, has long since lost her tank handrails, the dome has been painted over or replaced, whilst the chimney is a shorter local creation. *H.C. Casserley*

Ventnor receives water on the turntable at Ventnor. The cylinder below the cab is the air reservoir for the Westinghouse brake.   *G.W. Tripp/NRM*

Regulation of Railways Act became law in 1889, obliging companies to fit automatic continuous brakes to locomotives and rolling stock used in passenger trains. The matter was mentioned in IWR Minutes for 24th February, 1892 when a tender was accepted for the supply of fittings for the Westinghouse air brake; fitting the brake was carried out at Ryde Works. Drawings in the custody of the National Railway Museum show the proposed arrangement of brake fittings on the locomotive *Bembridge* and one passenger guard's van. A manuscript entry alongside the van drawing listed components that the makers would supply and other fittings to be manufactured by local firms. By the end of 1892 eight locomotives and 57 carriages, passenger vans, covered goods vans, horse boxes and carriage trucks had been equipped with the Westinghouse brake at a cost of £2,112 13s. 7d. Although not receiving the same publicity, the effectiveness of the locomotive hand brakes must have improved following the replacement of wooden brake blocks by cast-iron ones; it was said that the wooden brake blocks visibly smouldered on each downhill journey from Ventnor and it became practice to place buckets of water at the ends of platforms just in case!

On 14th February, 1894 the Board accepted a tender for the supply of the first of a series of replacement boilers. The Minute book recorded the following orders:

Ordered	For	From	Cost of each
14th February, 1894	*Sandown, Shanklin* and *Ventnor*	J.S. White	£609
1st September, 1898	*Ryde* and *Wroxall*	J.S. White	£704
28th December, 1900	*Brading*	Beyer, Peacock & Co.	£600

The boilers had steel fireboxes but were otherwise little different from their predecessors. A replacement steel firebox had been ordered from J.S. White on 25th March, 1895 for *Brading*, the sale of the old copper box being offset against its purchase; after the purchase of a replacement, its existing boiler was transferred to *Bonchurch*. Numerous cheques for spares issued on 26th April, 1899 included:

J.S. White	for cylinder liners	£17 17s. 10d.
Beyer, Peacock & Co.	safety valves	£24 10s.
Wheeler & Hurst	locomotive castings	£13 19s. 6d.

Some insight into the manner in which the locomotives were operated can be gained from two letters from Henry Day to Henry Brent:

Dear Sir,
Burial of the Queen. Enclosed notice

Will you please arrange for a third Engine to be on the Main Line on Friday at 7.45 am to take light train to Ventnor at 8.12 or 8.20 as the case may be.
This Engine will work the 9.32 Special to Ryde St John's Road and pass thence to Whippingham. I have asked the Central Co. to provide a Fireman from St John's Road.
We will not want a fourth Engine as the thro train is taken off and only two Engines will be required on Saturday for the same reason.
Yours Truly
    H.K. Day

Easter Traffic

I should be glad if you would arrange for me to have engines as under for the Easter Holidays and oblige.

Wednesday, Thursday and Saturday }	3rd engine by 12.0 noon
April 3rd, 4th & 6th }	4th engine at 1.45 pm
Good Friday & Easter Sunday	2nd engine by 12.30 pm
Easter Monday	3rd engine by 9.0 am

Ryde, photographed at Shanklin on 3rd June, 1921, has undergone the same changes evident on *Shanklin*.   *H.C. Casserley*

Wroxall differed in a number of minor ways from its older brethren. Seen at Ryde Esplanade with a NLR carriage, the brass tank handrails complement its polished dome and copper-capped chimney.   *R. Silsbury Collection*

The next two views show an occasion when *Wroxall* ran into the allotments whilst shunting on the IWC side at Sandown. *R. Silsbury Collection*

Wroxall has not moved since the last photograph but some reinforcements have arrived. The bowler hatted gentleman might be Henry Brent; he would have been relieved that the hole in the bunker was not more serious. *R. Silsbury Collection*

Brading was a somewhat larger beast, having been bought mainly for goods work. It is seen leading an IWR luggage van on an up working at Shanklin on 13th May, 1920.   *H.C. Casserley*

The pride of the line *Bonchurch* puts on a display at Ventnor not long after its delivery. Although no larger than *Brading*, its exterior bunker, beading to the tanks and different cab gives it a much more modern appearance. An excellent example of Beyer, Peacock workmanship.

IWSR Collection

| Easter Monday | 4th engine by 3.0 pm. If traffic not heavy I may be able to dispense with this engine in which case I will wire you by one o'clock |
| Easter Tuesday, April 9th | 1st engine to be out in time to leave Ryde St John's Road at 7.30 am to work 8.10 am up. |

Although included in Board of Trade returns from 1885, *Bembridge* did not pass into IWR ownership until 1898; at one time it was painted green but when it gained a repaint in IWR red livery is not known. On 4th June, 1903 the IWR received a letter from Petroleum Products Limited offering a trial of their fuel system for two weeks. Coal delivered to St Helens cost about 2s. 8d. a ton and as this was 1s. 2d. more than that charged to the LSWR the IWR was eager to explore any means of making savings. The equipment was tested on steam plant at St Helens during August and, when it proved successful, on *Bembridge*. Although the company saved £5 6s. 7½d. per week, the cost of conversion and installation of oil tanks at St Helens made the system uneconomic. The IWC borrowed the engine for its own trials after which *Bembridge* reverted to coal burning. In March 1908 replacement cylinders were ordered from Manning, Wardle and fitted the following month. The locomotive underwent extensive repairs in June 1911 when Ryde Works fitted a replacement copper firebox, removed the safety valve cover, fitted a stove pipe chimney and made some rather ugly additions to the cab side sheets to give the crew more protection.

Routine purchases of spare parts included 12 sets of steel tyres from Societe Anonyme Des Acieries d'Angleur in July 1908, because their tender of £10 10s. per ton delivered to Ryde Works was appreciably less than quotations from British firms. Although Beyer, Peacock quoted £2 more than the French firm for a replacement crank axle for *Sandown*, the IWR accepted the former's price of £69, 'they being the makers of the Engine'. Minor mishaps included the breaking of a connecting rod on *Shanklin* on 2nd September, 1910, and when others were examined most of those on the smaller engines were found to be faulty. Replacements were provided of the same weight but with 50 per cent greater strength. Beyer, Peacock supplied various spares for *Bonchurch*: cylinders in October 1903, a crank axle in March 1908 and a copper firebox in June 1910, fitted the following November.

Activity in the workshops slackened following the onset of war; men joined up and reduced services permitted a scaling down of locomotive and rolling stock overhauls. On 16th April, 1916 Henry Day reported the receipt of a circular from the War Office asking if the company had any four- or six-coupled locomotives available for disposal. After discussion the Board offered *Bembridge* at a price of £750. An Admiralty barge collected *Bembridge* from Ryde Pier on 27th July, 1916 - the asking price being paid without question. It worked at Bulford in 1917 and remained in War Department service until sold or broken up in 1920; a writer to *The Locomotive* magazine in 1920 claimed *Bembridge* had been seen in Mesopotamia but it is thought never to have left Britain. One of the 2-4-0s replaced *Bembridge* on the Bembridge branch - only *Bonchurch* with its larger external bunker did not take its turn. Each carried a flexible steam pipe for connecting with a stationary engine at the south end of the Brading station which pumped water from the river into the adjacent water tank - a task performed by the locomotive working the branch.

In July 1917 the REC sent a further circular asking for locomotives for service overseas; this time the Secretary wrote that one locomotive had already been sent and two awaited repairs, leaving five in use. In mid-1917 *Brading* underwent an overhaul when the copper and brass was either painted over or removed; shortly afterwards a cast-iron tapered chimney from the Newport firm of Wheeler & Hurst replaced the Beyer, Peacock original. The other locomotives similarly lost their finery when passing through workshops. Following the Armistice the IWR placed a steady stream of orders with Beyer Peacock for spare parts:

	£	s.	d.
March 1919 - whistles, chimneys and smokebox doors	101	5	0
September 1919 - copper fireboxes for *Ryde* and *Shanklin*	280	0	0

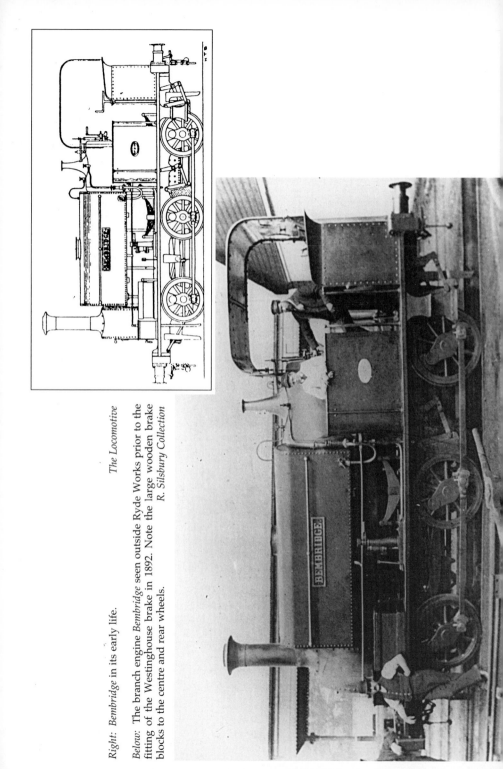

Right: Bembridge in its early life.

The Locomotive

Below: The branch engine *Bembridge* seen outside Ryde Works prior to the fitting of the Westinghouse brake in 1892. Note the large wooden brake blocks to the centre and rear wheels.

R. Silsbury Collection

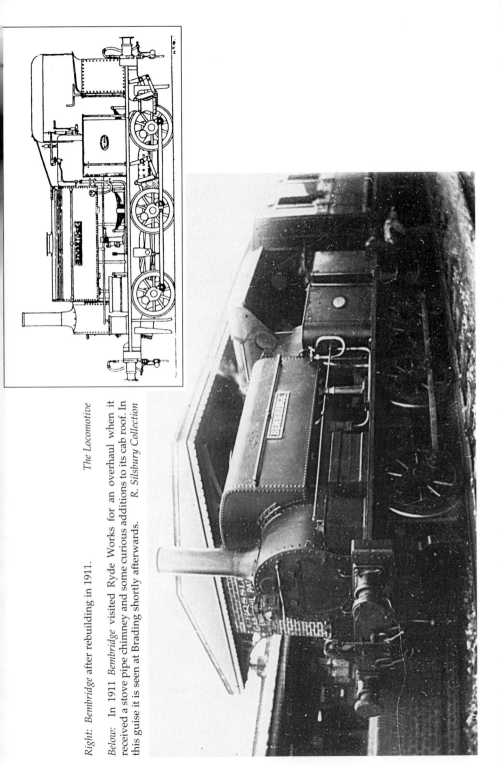

Right: Bembridge after rebuilding in 1911.

The Locomotive

Below: In 1911 *Bembridge* visited Ryde Works for an overhaul when it received a stove pipe chimney and some curious additions to its cab roof. In this guise it is seen at Brading shortly afterwards. *R. Silsbury Collection*

Bonchurch with the inevitable luggage van in tow, leaves Shanklin on an up train on 12th May, 1920.   *H.C. Casserley*

An IWR train on the LSWR/LBSC Joint Railway. In 1919 *Bonchurch* passes under Rink Road bridge, Ryde with a down train consisting of a NLR carriage and examples of most of the older Oldbury carriages.   *Lens of Sutton*

			£	s.	d.
October 1919 -	for *Bonchurch* -	steel boiler & copper firebox	1,560	0	0
		cast-iron blast pipe & cap	6	12	6
		two valve spindles	8	15	0
		cylinder cover, lubricator	5	15	0
December 1919 -	a crank axle for *Brading*		180	0	0
April 1920 -	a pair of side tanks for *Shanklin*		297	0	0
	various motion parts for *Bonchurch*		188	0	0
June 1920 -	cylinders, firebox and other parts for *Ventnor*		564	0	0

SR locomotive and boiler registers recorded the following details of boilers carried by the company's motive power:

	Boiler fitted	Firebox fitted	Boiler pressure	Cylinders
Ryde*	December 1900	December 1900	125 lb.	15 in. x 20 in.
Shanklin*	December 1895	December 1895	125 lb.	15 in. x 20 in.
Ventnor	no details recorded			
Wroxall	December 1900	1920	125 lb.	16 in. x 20 in.
Brading	December 1902	not recorded	125 lb.	16 in. x 24 in.
Bonchurch	December 1921	December 1921	160 lb.	16 in. x 24 in.

Descriptions of the locomotive livery varied somewhat over the years but, given the way in which hues could change and the fickle nature of memories, this was not surprising. The boiler, tank and bunkers continued to be lined although by the turn of the century it was less elaborate than hitherto. Lining failed to show on many photographs, but this was a consequence of the photographic process rather than a conscious change in policy. By the end of the war locomotives were running in a rich, dark Midland Railway red, separated by thin yellow lining from a black edging to tanks and bunkers.

In July 1919 Mr Tahourdin submitted a report on the condition of the existing locomotive stock and, following discussion, the Board agreed to approach the Railway Executive Committee for the loan of a locomotive, nominally to replace *Bembridge*. They had only large tender engines available and in September J. F. Wake of Darlington offered a Beyer, Peacock 2-4-0T similar to *Bonchurch* built in 1885 for the Midland & South Western Railway. Unfortunately the locomotive's condition coupled with an asking price of £3,225 led to its rejection; an offer in April 1920 from the same firm of two other locomotives was similarly refused. In June 1920 two Great Northern Railway locomotives were also rejected after inspection. The Board also had to refuse an offer of a locomotive from the Metropolitan Railway in January 1921, after the Ministry of Transport refused to pay the difference between the £750 paid for *Bembridge* and £2,200 asked for the Metropolitan engine.

There were few purchases of spares during 1921, and the only order of note followed an incident on 10th October when a connecting rod broke on *Brading* whilst shunting a train at Ryde Pier Head; a replacement from Beyer, Peacock cost £127 10s. With the exception of *Sandown*, the locomotives were reasonably sound but all suffered from cracked frames - a long-standing problem. *Sandown* was banished to the Bembridge branch where its poor condition could be lived with, at least for a time. It would travel down from Ryde to Brading each morning with a goods train and make its return journey in the same manner at the end of the day - the shed at St Helens having closed. In July 1922 the IWR Board considered a request from Mr Tahourdin to place an order for spares and a replacement boiler, apparently for *Sandown* - the matter was referred to the LSWR. *Sandown* received no repairs although Eastleigh did prepare drawings and presumably manufactured components for other IWR engines in late 1922 and early 1923.

Of the seven locomotives inherited by the Southern Railway from the Isle of Wight Railway, Mr Urie reported to the Locomotive and Carriage Committee (LSWR Section) on 3rd May, 1923:

* the boilers for these locomotives were apparently exchanged in 1921.

The Isle of Wight and Plymouth, Devonport and South Western Junction Railway locomotives . . . which number 19 are in fairly good condition except the locomotive *Sandown* belonging to the Isle of Wight Railway, which it is recommended be sold as scrap or broken up. Arrangements have been made to send two LSW tank engines of 177 (0-4-4) tank class to the Island and for these to be equipped with the Westinghouse brake.

The Island companies' locomotives were allocated running numbers in a separate 'w' series. Two from the FYN were allocated numbers 1-2, nine from the IWC 4-12 and the IWR locomotives 13-18. *Sandown* never carried a number and was shipped back to the mainland in May 1923 for breaking up later that year. The departure of *Sandown* was matched by the arrival of two LSWR class 'O2' 0-4-4Ts of comparable power to *Bonchurch* for the Ryde to Ventnor line. Ryde Works scampered to fit locomotives with LSWR-style lamp irons as shortly afterwards *Ventnor* and *Brading* were transferred to Newport and *Shanklin* to the Bembridge branch. *Shanklin* left the rails at Bembridge on 5th June due to a defective rail flange and the worn state of the turnout; a fitter responsible for the engine was 'suitably admonished'. For the 1924 summer season two more 'O2s' arrived, IWC 4-4-0T No. 6 transferred from Newport for use on the Ventnor line and 2-4-0T No. 5 saw service on the Bembridge branch. *Wroxall* remained on the main line until early 1925 when it was restricted to goods duties. *Bonchurch* replaced *Brading* at Newport where it worked goods trains or acted as yard and station pilot. All except *Sandown* were eventually repainted in SR green livery. At the end of the 1925 season *Ventnor* was laid aside, followed by *Brading* in April 1926 and several IWC locomotives.

Shanklin remained in intermittent use on the Bembridge branch until condemned in November 1927. *Bonchurch* followed in May 1928 as its retention could not be justified when there was a plentiful supply of class 'O2' 0-4-4Ts. Apart from *Sandown* broken up at Eastleigh, the 2-4-0Ts were sold locally giving the Island scrap merchants a field day. *Ventnor* went to Mr Ball at Ryde and *Brading* to a Mr Hunt. Messrs Jolliffe of Cowes bought *Bonchurch* in August 1928 and later resold the boiler to a Portsmouth laundry.

By 1929 the only IWR locomotives in service were *Ryde* and *Wroxall*. They took turns on the Bembridge branch services and goods duties at Ryde. The driver of *Ryde* received a reprimand after it rolled off the turntable at Bembridge on the evening of 18th May. Apparently the brakes were defective and the engine moved unexpectedly whilst being turned on the turntable; fortunately services returned to normal after two hours. Similar incidents occurred on 9th September and 18th August, 1930, although by then LBSC class 'A1X' 0-6-0Ts had taken over branch duties. *Ryde* received a general overhaul at Ryde Works and when returned to traffic in October 1929 had a modified cab, Drummond chimney, polished steel buffers and SR-style nameplates. After running in on the Bembridge branch it went to Newport in April 1930 for service on the Freshwater line. *Wroxall* followed *Ryde* into workshops and received a new cab salvaged from IWC No. 8, a Beyer, Peacock 2-4-0T withdrawn at the end of 1929, second-hand cylinders, a Drummond chimney, replacement tank side sheets without visible rivet heads, and standard SR nameplates. It spent a short period on the Bembridge branch before joining *Ryde* on Freshwater line services.

On 2nd July, 1932 *Ryde* was taken out of service after a day spent deputising for 'O2' No. 21 between Newport and Cowes. Although officially withdrawn on 9th July, the locomotive eventually entered Ryde Works to receive a replacement cab in the original style, a Beyer, Peacock chimney and a repaint in works grey with black and white lining in the IWR style. In June 1934, after being extensively photographed, *Ryde* was hauled to Medina Wharf and shipped to the mainland where it joined a number of other locomotives and relics stored in the paint shop at Eastleigh. Plans to create a Southern Railway museum were foiled by the outbreak of World War II. On 8th April, 1940 the locomotive was taken to the dump and broken up a few days later.

Wroxall remained in service until just before the arrival of a fourth 'E1' 0-6-0T and was shipped back to the mainland on the return journey of the floating crane on 23rd June, 1933. It was broken up at Eastleigh soon afterwards.

Chapter Sixteen

Passenger and Goods Rolling Stock

On 16th June, 1863 the IWR Board asked John Fowler, the Engineer, to seek tenders for the following items of rolling stock (the term 'rolling stock' is attributed to Capt. Huish who first used this description in the early 1850s):

4	First Class Carriages
12	Composites (4 with 'Break' compartments)
8	Second Class
20	Wagons

The Board returned to the matter on 23rd July, 1863 when they accepted a tender and specification from the 'Oldbury Wagon Company', actually the Railway Carriage Company Limited of Oldbury, near Birmingham. Commonly called Oldbury, the firm had been formed in the 1850s by Richard W. Johnson and was one of several suppliers of rolling stock to railways at the time. Frederick Twynam, an IWR Director, was a Director for many years.

On 1st June, 1864 the IWR Board concluded an agreement with the Railway Carriage Company to pay for their purchases by instalments. 'Oldbury Carriage and Wagon Company' also expressed a willingness to take up 100 shares if it could tender for any future requirements. Whilst welcoming the investment, the Board made it clear that any tender would have to quote a fair market price and the rolling stock offered needed to be acceptable to the Engineer.

The rolling stock was to a standard design built by the firm for a number of railways in the 1860s. Differences in buffer heights, couplings, axleboxes, wheels and springing that plagued the operation of Britain's early railways had been largely eliminated and the IWR benefited by purchasing locomotives and stock from just two manufacturers. The four-wheel carriages had hardwood bodies with very shallow arc roofs, rectangular mouldings at waist level, and blue glass toplights to all compartments. Saloon composites had a single first class saloon flanked by small second class compartments whilst other carriages had three or four compartments of equal width. Bench seats backed onto each compartment division but saloons also contained two roomy armchairs that on occasions could be replaced by a table. Doors were hinged on the right (apparently an Oldbury practice) and were of different widths, doors to first class compartments being wider than the rest. Brake seconds had a single brake wheel working on tyres of that carriage. One oil lamp served each compartment; none of the carriages had heating of any kind. The significant amount of first class accommodation and the small number of goods vehicles showed clearly where the company expected its income to come from. The goods stock were conventional wooden three-plank open wagons with a carrying capacity of approximately 6 tons and drop doors midway along each side; they had sprung buffers but apparently lacked brakes. The rolling stock had the following running numbers:

Passenger stock:	1-4	three-compartment brake seconds
	5-8	four-compartment seconds
	9-20	three-compartment saloon first/second composites
	21-24	three-compartment firsts
Goods stock:	1-20	open wagons

The carriages and wagons were shipped from Southampton to Ryde, landed at the Isle of Wight Ferry Company's quay and hauled through the streets to the railway station. Passenger services began on 23rd August; goods traffic did not begin until about December. On 5th October the Board authorised Capt. Huish to buy two 'break' vans for the goods traffic and on 20th January, 1865 to accept tenders for six ballast wagons and 10 coal wagons - the ballast

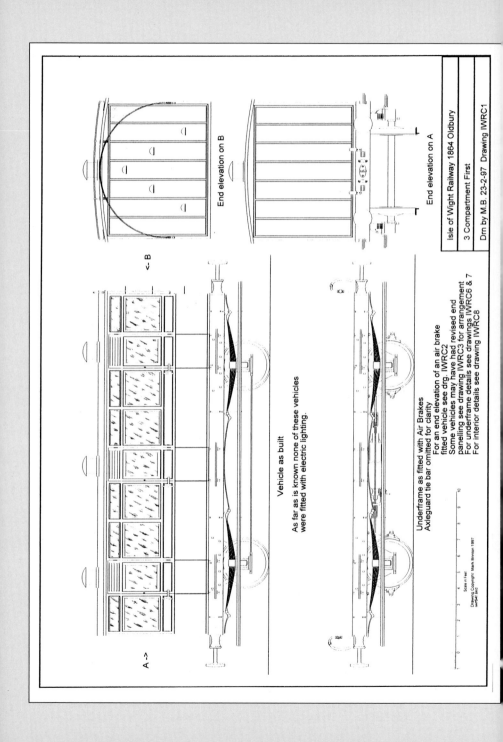

End elevation on B

<- B

End elevation on A

A ->

Vehicle as built

As far as is known none of these vehicles
were fitted with electric lighting.

Underframe as fitted with Air Brakes
Axleguard tie bar omitted for clarity

For an end elevation of an air brake
fitted vehicle see drg. IWRC2
Some vehicles may have had revised end
panelling see drawing IWRC3 for arrangement
For underframe details see drawings IWRC6 & 7
For interior details see drawing IWRC8

Scale in Feet

Drawing Copyright Mark Brinton 1997
iwrfirst.skd

Isle of Wight Railway 1864 Oldbury

3 Compartment First

Drn by M.B. 23-2-97   Drawing IWRC1

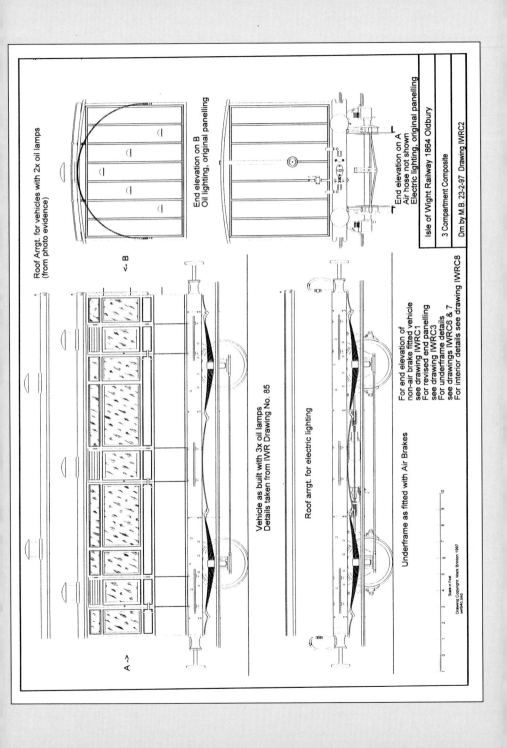

Roof Arrgt. for vehicles with 2x oil lamps
(from photo evidence)

End elevation on B
Oil lighting, original panelling

<- B

End elevation on A
Air hose not shown
Electric lighting, original panelling

A ->

Vehicle as built with 3x oil lamps
Details taken from IWR Drawing No. 85

Roof arrgt. for electric lighting

Underframe as fitted with Air Brakes

For end elevation of
non-air brake fitted vehicle
see drawing IWRC1
For revised end panelling
see drawing IWRC3
For underframe details
see drawings IWRC6 & 7
For interior details see drawing IWRC8

Isle of Wight Railway 1864 Oldbury

3 Compartment Composite

Dm by M.B. 23-2-97 Drawing IWRC2

Scale in Feet
0 1 2 3 4 5 6 7 8 9 10

Drawing Copyright Mark Brinton 1997
iwrbf45.skd

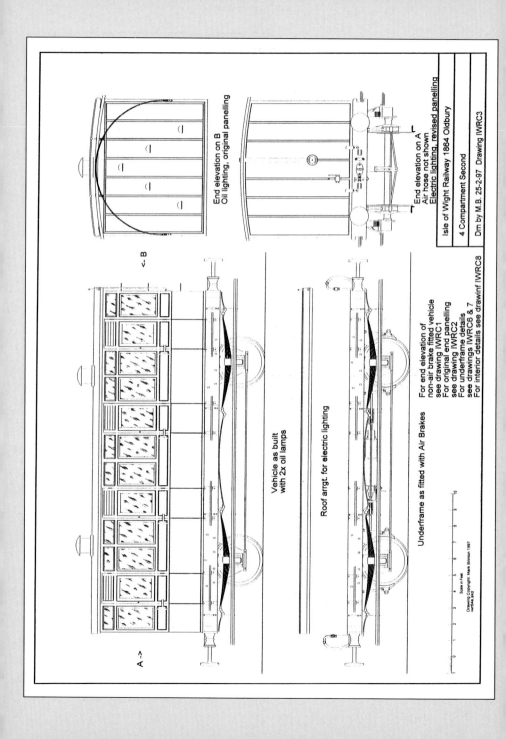

End elevation on B
Oil lighting, original panelling

<- B

A ->

End elevation on A
Air hose not shown
Electric lighting, revised panelling

Isle of Wight Railway 1864 Oldbury

4 Compartment Second

Dm by M.B. 25-2-97 Drawing IWRC3

Vehicle as built
with 2x oil lamps

Roof arrgt. for electric lighting

Underframe as fitted with Air Brakes

For end elevation of
non-air brake fitted vehicle
see drawing IWRC1
For original end panelling
see drawing IWRC2
For underframe details
see drawings IWRC6 & 7
For interior details see drawinf IWRC8

Scale in Feet

0 1 2 3 4 5 6 7 8 9 10

Drawing Copyright: Mark Brinton 1997
iwrb4a.skd

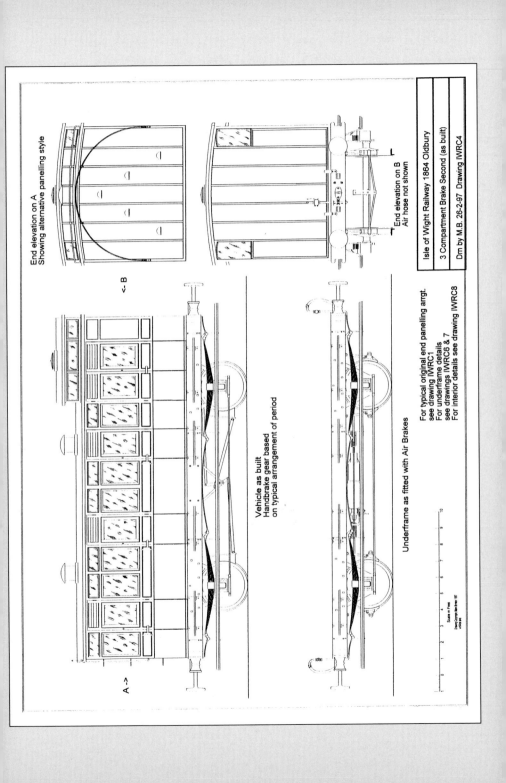

End elevation on A
Showing alternative panelling style

<- B

End elevation on B
Air hose not shown

Isle of Wight Railway 1864 Oldbury

3 Compartment Brake Second (as built)

Dm by M.B. 26-2-97 Drawing IWRC4

Vehicle as built
Handbrake gear based
on typical arrangement of period

Underframe as fitted with Air Brakes

For typical original end panelling arrgt.
see drawing IWRC1
For underframe details
see drawings IWRC6 & 7
For interior details see drawing IWRC8

A ->

Scale in Feet

Drawing Copyright Martin Brown 1997
IWRC04.MAC

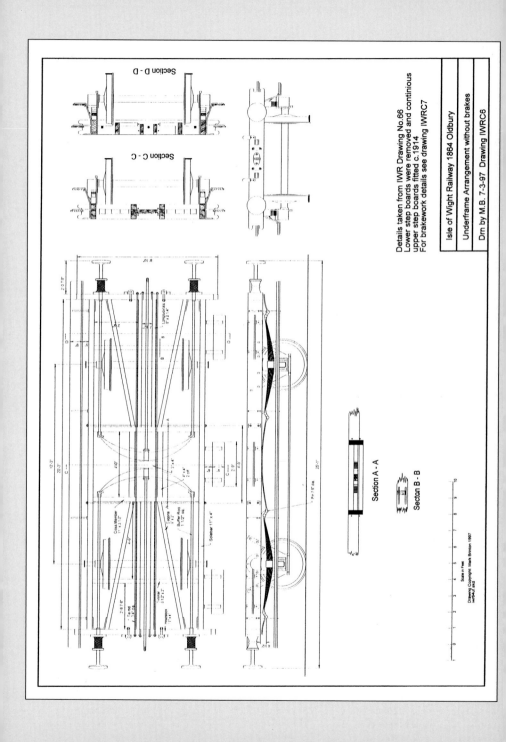

Section D - D

Section C - C

Section A - A

Section B - B

Details taken from IWR Drawing No.66
Lower step boards were removed and continious
upper step boards fitted c.1914
For brakework details see drawing IWRC7

Isle of Wight Railway 1864 Oldbury

Underframe Arrangement without brakes

Dm by M.B. 7-3-97 Drawing IWRC6

Scale in Feet

wagons seem not to have been purchased. Ten wagons were ordered on 1st August, 1865 to be paid for by quarterly instalments lasting seven years at a rate of £14 10s. per wagon per annum. The Minute book also mentioned the offer of a small mobile hand crane from Kirkstall Forge Company for £100. However, the railway could not pay anything off the bill until May 1874, by which time the debt had risen to £237 13s. 4d. including costs and interest claimed at 5 per cent; the IWR Board refused to pay more than 4 per cent and ordered the issue of £227 of 'B' debenture stock!

By the end of 1864 the company possessed 30 goods wagons and a year later numbers had risen to 40 wagons and three other vehicles, including two timber trucks and a brake van; all had come from Oldbury. The 40 wagons then in stock consisted of 30 coal wagons with sprung buffers and 10 with dumb buffers. Returns to the Board of Trade for 1864 showed that the IWR ran mixed trains, but this was short-lived and separate goods trains began operating following delivery of the brake van. The Minute book naturally failed to mention any locomotive or rolling stock liveries. The carriages would have been varnished but the colour of the wagons is not known; slate grey would seem to be the most likely. Photographs show widely spaced letters *IWR* the height of a single plank but with a running number the height of two planks thus: *No 21*; another wagon had small lettering throughout.

Along with the locomotive *Stuart*, the IWR purchased a number of dropside wagons from the finance company in 1867. The Minutes failed to mention the number of wagons bought, but there were probably at least 12 as Board of Trade returns show this number added to stock in 1867; a further eight wagons were added during the next two years. The contractor building the railway from Sandown to Newport made use of some and a few may have ended up in the ownership of the IWNJ. By the end of 1867 the IWR had 54 goods vehicles plus the brake van.

Whilst the IWR possessed a sufficient number of carriages, there was a distinct shortage of other stock. The railway, for example, lacked horse boxes or carriage trucks with which to carry horse-drawn carriages. Suitable wagons were also required 'to carry furniture vans' - large containers used to convey a family's possessions to and from the Island. This was put right between 1868 and 1872 when the following purchases were made from Oldbury:

in 1868 two carriage trucks.
in 1869 six covered vans and four timber trucks. A coal truck was rebuilt into the company's first cattle wagon.
in April 1870 one horse box and 10 coal wagons.
in April 1872 12 'mineral' wagons, two covered vans, four timber trucks. Another coal wagon was converted to a carriage truck.

As an indication of their costs, the 1869 deliveries cost £1,254 whilst the horse box and wagons supplied in 1870 amounted to £255 10s. and £112 each respectively, paid by instalments; Mr E. Pritchard charged £155 for shipping them to the Island. The covered vans came in for comment when Joseph Bourne reported in March 1869 that two had left the rails at Sandown blocking the line for two hours; he attributed the derailment to 'the horn-plates being imperfectly fixed'.

The opening of the tramway through the streets of Ryde in 1871 created a need for additional accommodation for passengers' luggage. Two carriages bought from the Ryde Pier Company in 1865 were converted to vans and in 1871 an additional luggage van was added to stock. One of these was probably the subject of a drawing in the care of the National Railway Museum showing a rather primitive vehicle with open balconies at each end, a hand brake, double doors to each side and simple plain wood mouldings. In September 1872 Joseph Bourne approached the IWR Board with a proposal to purchase an additional 12 carriages. After asking him to justify his request, on 23rd January, 1873 the Board reluctantly ordered five five-compartment third class carriages from Oldbury at £460 each, payment to be £46 each per year spread over 10 years. They followed this up on 18th March, 1875 with an order for three second class carriages at £460 each and ten wagons at £12 each; five more 8 ton

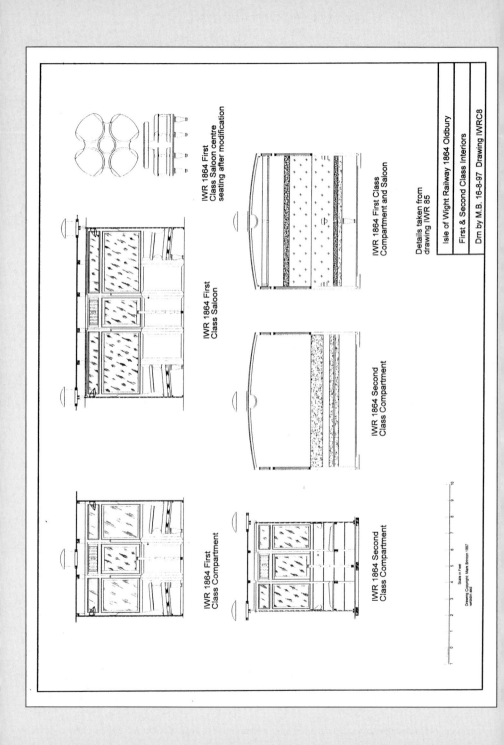

IWR 1864 First Class Saloon centre seating after modification

IWR 1864 First Class Saloon

IWR 1864 First Class Compartment and Saloon

IWR 1864 Second Class Compartment

IWR 1864 First Class Compartment

IWR 1864 Second Class Compartment

Details taken from drawing IWR 85

Isle of Wight Railway 1864 Oldbury

First & Second Class Interiors

Drn by M.B. 16-8-97 Drawing IWRC8

Scale in Feet

Drawing Copyright: Mark Brinton 1997

wagons were ordered in July and one wagon was converted to a cattle wagon. A month later, the Board approved orders for two sets of locomotive tyres, eight sets of carriage and wagon tyres and various other fittings.

In April 1876 the company ordered a 10 ton travelling crane for £637 10s. from J. Taylor & Co. and from Oldbury one luggage van, a horse box, three covered goods wagons and two cattle trucks. A further 10 wagons ordered in November were delivered the following year, followed in 1879 by a second goods brake van. Brake van No. 1 had a low closed compartment and open balconies at each end, but No. 2 looked much more modern with a roof covering the whole length of the van. The railway then had sufficient goods stock and no further additions were made until 1892. The debt for the rolling stock was paid off in June 1885.

In March 1882 the Board authorised the seeking of tenders for four additional carriages. A tender was read out on 17th April from the Railway Carriage Company quoting £352 each for first/second composites and £350 for seconds. Two composites and four seconds were ordered - the last new carriages bought. Slightly longer than earlier carriages, they had a higher arc-shape roof and no toplights. Composites had the same seating arrangement as those of 1864, i.e. a single first class saloon flanked by second class compartments. Seconds had four equal sized compartments. Naturally the IWR did not employ this stock on the BHIR and in July the Board authorised the modification of carriage 35 and van 25 at a cost of £261 12s. 11d. for service on the line. Four-compartment second No. 35 became a composite with a first saloon in place of two end compartments; the compartment at the opposite end was later downgraded to third class. The van received little more than a brake wheel. This was followed in June 1884 by a decision to convert three second class carriages into brake carriages; this may have been when brake seconds 1-4 were rebuilt as passenger guard's vans. IWR No. 2 received a higher roof profile to match the 1882 stock.

The varnished teak livery applied to passenger stock was said to have been somewhat redder than on other lines. Mouldings were picked out in red and white lining; compartments were identified by gilt shaded lettering applied to each door at waist level. The arrival of additional carriages during the 1880s coincided with the application of an elaborate garter device carrying the words Isle of Wight Railway Company. Supplied by Tearne & Sons Ltd,* the body of the garter was medium blue, the remainder gilt whilst the ornamentation was shaded brown and the lettering blue; a larger version without ornamentation was supplied in 1885. Each carriage generally carried a garter centrally placed below waist level with the running number inside, although the exact position and number of garters varied.

The original 1864 stock had been split into three nominal sets. The third class carriages were initially kept together in their own train but other purchases joined the sets or acted as spares. By the 1880s the normal formation seems to have been eight assorted carriages with one luggage van and a brake van at the Ryde end. This was by no means a settled arrangement as photographs show that much longer trains were operated on occasions.

In 1884 and 1885 the IWR was, somewhat unusually, offered more rolling stock. On 7th April, 1884 some carriages from the LSWR were politely refused - we can only speculate why the offer was made but it probably related to proposals for the sale or lease of the Island railways to the mainland companies. At a Board meeting on 19th August, 1885 Mr Connor reported that Oldbury had approached the IWR with the offer of three carriages supplied in 1881 to the Golden Valley Railway which had been returned due to a lack of money. James Connor was authorised to go ahead with the purchase if Oldbury would sell them for no more than £500; they were not added to stock until 1887 so there must have been some further haggling.

Two of the Golden Valley Railway carriages were six-wheel saloons; one seated first class and the other second class passengers. They had open balconies at each end surrounded by ironwork bearing the initials 'G. V.', lower body panels had six panels of mouldings, one panel being larger than the others. The centre set of wheels were suspended from the outside of the solebars to give extra sideplay. The third vehicle was a guard's van with a balcony, side doors and lookouts. The three became a regular sight on the Bembridge branch where they worked

---

* Details of the transfers were given in *Railway Heraldry* by G. Dow (David & Charles, 1973).

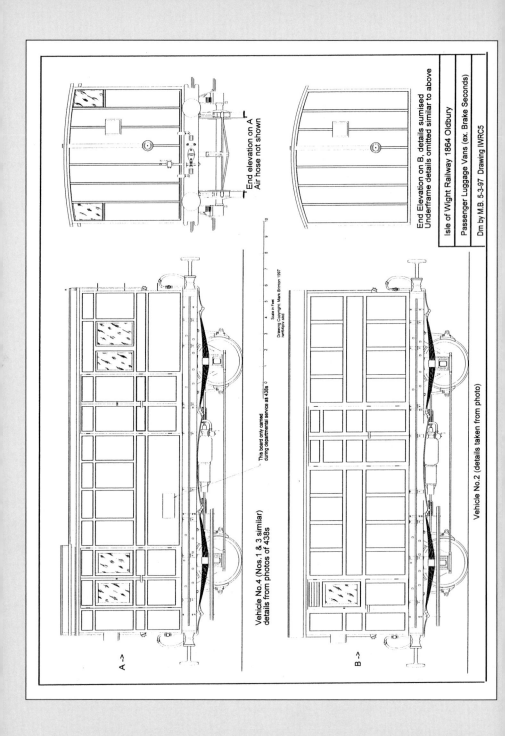

End elevation on A
Air hose not shown

End Elevation on B, details surmised
Underframe details omitted similar to above

Isle of Wight Railway 1864 Oldbury

Passenger Luggage Vans (ex. Brake Seconds)

Dm by M.B. 5-3-97 Drawing IWRC5

Vehicle No.4 (Nos.1 & 3 similar)
details from photos of 438s

This board only carried
during departmental service as 438s

Scale in Feet
Drawing Copyright Mark Brinton 1997
Iwr54pix skid

Vehicle No.2 (details taken from photo)

A ->

B ->

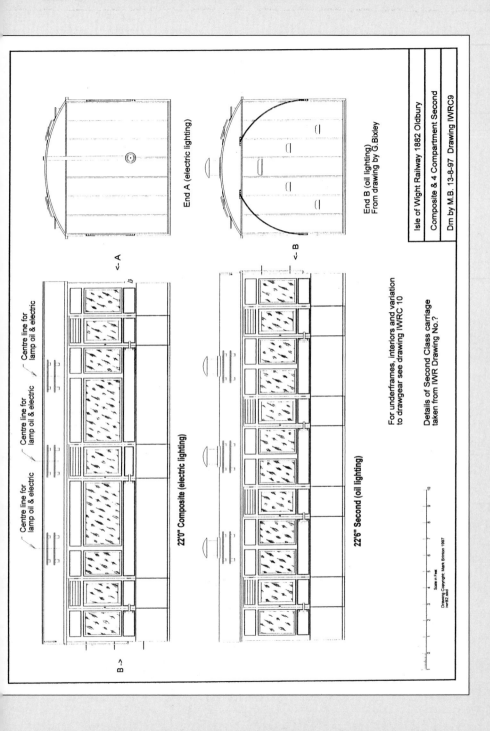

End A (electric lighting)

End B (oil lighting)
From drawing by G.Bixley

Centre line for
lamp oil & electric

Centre line for
lamp oil & electric

Centre line for
lamp oil & electric

22'0" Composite (electric lighting)

22'6" Second (oil lighting)

For underframes, interiors and variation
to drawgear see drawing IWRC 10

Details of Second Class carriage
taken from IWR Drawing No.?

Scale in Feet

Drawing Copyright: Mark Brinton 1997
iwrl2.skd

Isle of Wight Railway 1882 Oldbury

Composite & 4 Compartment Second

Drn by M.B. 13-8-97 Drawing IWRC9

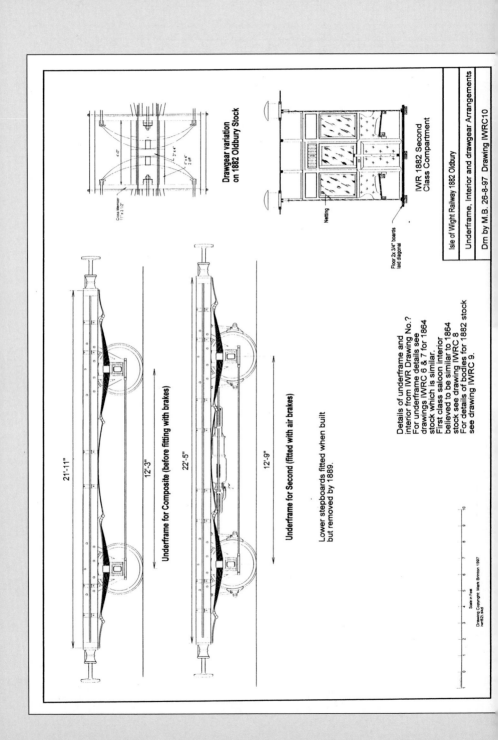

Drawgear variation on 1882 Oldbury Stock

Cross Member 1½" x 3" x 1½"

IWR 1882 Second Class Compartment

Netting

Floor 2x 3/4" boards laid diagonal

Underframe for Composite (before fitting with brakes)

21'-11"

12'-3"

Underframe for Second (fitted with air brakes)

22'-5"

12'-9"

Lower stepboards fitted when built but removed by 1889.

Details of underframe and interior from IWR Drawing No.?
For underframe details see drawings IWRC 6 & 7 for 1864 stock which is similar.
First class saloon interior believed to be similar to 1864 stock see drawing IWRC 8
For details of bodies for 1882 stock see drawing IWRC 9.

Scale in Feet

0 1 2 3 4 5 6 7 8 9 10

Drawing Copyright Mark Brinton 1997
iwr82c.fmd

Isle of Wight Railway 1882 Oldbury

Underframe, Interior and drawgear Arrangements

Drn by M.B. 26-8-97 Drawing IWRC10

Few photographs exist to show the IWR carriages in service. Older Oldbury carriages had attractive blue glass toplights shown to perfection in this close up of a grounded body - the curtains are later additions! *R. Silsbury Collection*

An Oldbury five-compartment second seen in the final days of its life as a grounded body. Note the single quarterlight between doors. *R. Silsbury Collection*

Sometimes described as the royal saloon as it is once said to have conveyed Queen Victoria on a journey to Ventnor, the body of IWR No. 38 photographed at Freshwater in 1949, many years after its withdrawal from traffic.   *R. Silsbury Collection*

The Metropolitan carriages can best be illustrated by this photograph of a six-compartment third at the end of its life in March 1929. The location is Ryde St Johns Road.   *H.F. Wheeler*

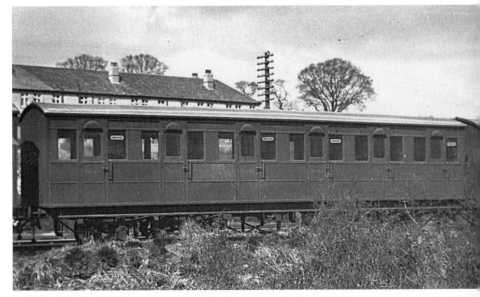

passenger services for many years. Oldbury carriage No. 35 or an Oldbury five-compartment third often ran with the set, presumably to provide additional and third class accommodation.

The fitting of the Westinghouse air brake to carriage stock was only one of several safety improvements carried out at during the 1890s. In a return to the Board of Trade the IWR reported that as at 30th June, 1889 all 137 wagons carried a primitive form of coupling with hooks, shackles and links. These couplings had been declared dangerous and a different form of three-link coupling was favoured; a batch of 25 new wagons bought on 12th January, 1893 for £1,052 10s. probably carried the more modern couplings when delivered. Ryde Works began replacing the old couplings; they were outlawed after 31st December, 1905 by which date all the wagons supposedly had the newer type. During the 1890s wagons began appearing with the letters *IWR* in large lettering, probably an introduction of Henry Brent. Standardisation in this area seems not to have been the company's forte as some wagons survived with smaller lettering for many years.

In 1897 and 1898 the IWR purchased 10 North London Railway four-wheel carriages. There were six four-compartment firsts and four five-compartment seconds. The firsts entered service on the IWR one as a first, one a first/second composite and four as seconds. Of the five-compartment vehicles, three became thirds whilst the remaining carriage and two Oldbury seconds were rebuilt at Ryde to passenger guard's vans. By then there existed a fourth short set for the daily fast train. A proposal to fit carriages with acetylene lighting was deferred by the Board on 22nd November, 1901 when the cost was found to be £475 - instead porcelain reflectors for the oil lamps was ordered. Similarly communication cords were never provided - a letter from Henry Day to the Board of Trade on the subject read:

. . . Directors are carefully watching the various experiments being tried by the larger railway Companies with a view to determining the most satisfactory means of communication.

Not a single occasion has arisen on this railway where any communication would have been used had it been in existence. The shortness of the trains allowing the whole train to be well under the observation of both enginemen and guard, both of whom have the most powerful brake yet brought out, and ready for immediate action.

The interiors of carriages received a mention in March 1901 when Henry Day wrote to Henry Brent:

Please receive herewith 110 2nd class Advertisements of Holliers Hotel to take the place of the Queen's Hotel Ventnor now in carriages. Please arrange for them to be placed in carriages as soon as possible and oblige.

In December 1903 Henry Brent reported that additional coal wagons would be required to cope with revised working arrangements at St Helens Quay (*see Chapter Eleven*). Twenty-five wagons had been bought in 1901, but they were not sufficient, and in February 1904 the Board authorised the purchase of a second-hand wagon from Messrs Fraser & Son of North Shields. It cost £25 delivered to Southampton with an option to buy more if satisfactory; two months later a further 19 wagons were bought. The whole 20 cost only £604 9s. 8d. but were the last purchases of goods stock. Staff at Ryde Works were perfectly able to 'rebuild' a wagon and when more were required they merely duplicated earlier designs, albeit somewhat longer and with an increased carrying capacity. Some effort was made to group particular types of vehicle, but of the remainder Ryde merely allocated the next blank running number to a new wagon or rebuild when it left shops in place of another withdrawn for similar treatment. Over the years, virtually the whole of the goods stock was rebuilt with new woodwork and only the use of second-hand wheels and ironwork betrayed their origins. In 1906 two tar tanks, Nos. 202-203, were constructed along with a small number of 15 ton open wagons; they proved rather large so later construction had a capacity of 12 tons or smaller. The tar tanks and a coal wagon cost £261 6s. - the tanks themselves being bought in for £111. Many of these wagons retained dumb buffers or thriftily possessed dumb buffers at one end and sprung at

WILLIAM JONES, 154, UPPER THAMES STREET, LONDON, E.C.

FOR SALE.

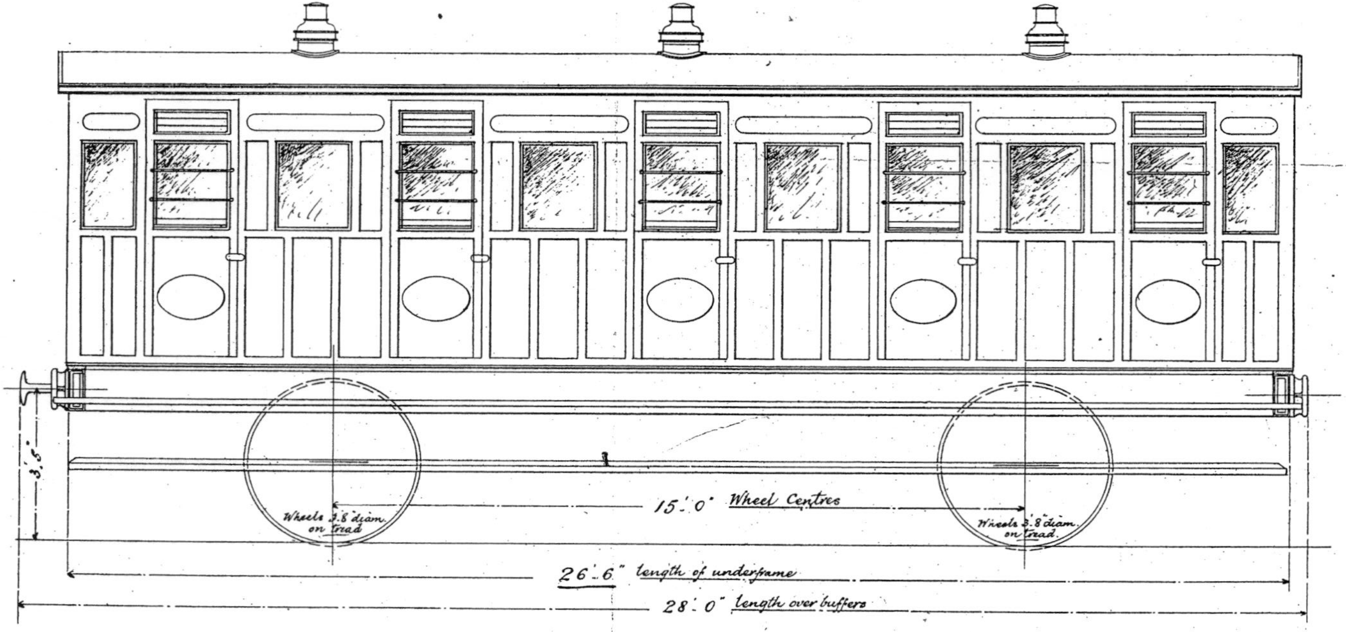

Wheels 3'6" diam. on tread

15'.0" Wheel Centres

26'.6" length of underframe

28'.0" length over buffers

Wheels 3'6" diam. on tread

3'.6"

Diagram of 3rd Class Carriages on Sale.

½" Scale

Drawings from William Jones' advertisement for the sale of North London Railway carriages as purchased by the IWR, 1897.

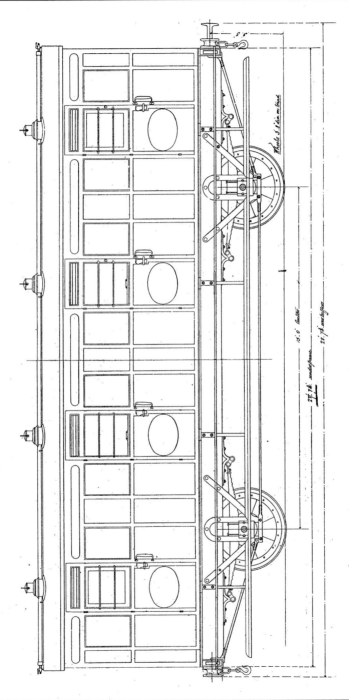

Built of teak throughout; mounted on four Mansell wheels. Close coupled; fitted for gas, and vacuum brake. All in thorough working order.

An assortment of wagons occupy the sidings at Shanklin as a train enters the crossing loop from
Ryde. The sign to the right of the locomotive belongs to one of the local coal merchants.
K. Nunn Collection

Shanklin draws into Ryde Esplanade station with an IWR train in early SR days. The first vehicle
is thought to be one of the Golden Valley carriages seen after rebuilding as a passenger guard's
van.   *R. Silsbury Collection*

the other. It was common for Wheeler Bros, a Ryde firm of builders, to supply a kit of timber components for the IWR to assemble. None of the company's documents recorded when goods stock began to be painted brown with black ironwork; possibly the change followed the appointment of H. D. Tahourdin as Engineer in 1908.

In December 1910 a letter of complaint was received via the Board of Trade about the absence of lights in the carriages whilst passing through Ventnor tunnel - it seems they were not always provided. The Board of Trade recommended that better lighting be provided, electricity being favoured in preference to gas because of the fire risk. After repeated discussions, the IWR Board accepted a tender from Messrs Leitner on 21st February, 1912 for the supply of electric light fittings for £1,191 and spares at £31 3s. During 1912 passenger brake vans were equipped with a charging unit and battery, power being carried along the roof and through connections between carriages - not all carriages were equipped and towards the end of the year the search began for more second-hand vehicles.

On 7th November, 1911 the Board of Trade issued an order that required the fitting of either-side brakes to the wagon fleet within 10 years. Although some progress was made, many wagons with single brakes remained when the SR took charge. A slightly better situation existed as regards wagons with dumb buffers; their use was outlawed in 1913 but 10 years later six with dumb buffers remained in use. To give an indication of the costs involved, £51 15s. was spent on the fitting of sprung buffers to nine wagons in January 1912. Ten new wagons were built in 1913 - this was despite a decline in the quantity of goods carried due to competition from road transport.

On 20th November, 1912 Henry Brent reported a visit to Eastleigh to inspect carriages the LSWR had for sale but he was evidently unimpressed. Further visits were made to see more LBSCR and LSWR stock without success. Enquiries continued intermittently until 25th March, 1914 when the Board authorised the purchase of 'a small train of about 6 coaches if suitable stock offers itself'. Two months later the Minutes noted the purchase of six carriages from the Metropolitan Railway at Neasden for £50 each. The LSWR hauled the carriages to Southampton, Mr Plascott shipped them to the Island and Ryde Works carried out renovations and fitted the Westinghouse brake. The carriages were still in workshops on 22nd July and probably did not enter service before war broke out at the beginning of August. On 19th August the Board accepted an offer of a further 12 carriages at £22 10s. each; they were shipped across from Southampton to St Helens later that year. The expense of renovating the first six carriages was charged to the capital account, but the second batch were regarded as replacements with their repairs financed out of revenue. When inspected by the Directors on 14th May, 1915 they were pronounced smooth and comfortable to ride in, also that the reupholstering and decorating had been satisfactorily carried out. Writers commented on the excellent condition of the IWR carriages. The first class compartments were deeply upholstered with cushioned seating, drop down seat arms, monogrammed white antimacassars and carpets. Even second class compartments had seat divisions and antimacassars. Although accommodation was provided for all three classes, no record has survived showing how the seating in each carriage was allocated - the IWR retained second class for mainland passengers until 1923.

The arrival of the Metropolitan Railway carriages prompted the purchase of a further batch of garter transfers. A more orthodox garter supplied in 1915 had black shading and a green garter enclosing a running number in the centre that was gilt with red and white highlights. Another version had the body colour in Oxford Blue.

The additional carriages permitted the withdrawal of 22 Oldbury vehicles including the three Golden Valley vehicles. By February 1916 £58 had been received from the sale of old carriages. One of the Golden Valley saloons was in workshops undergoing conversion to a passenger guard's van; £85 15s. 9d. had already been spent in stores for the work that was intended to turn out a vehicle with mouldings that matched the Metropolitan vehicles. The Metropolitan Railway carriages proved most satisfactory for the Ryde to Ventnor line services although the long wheelbase did not agree with some of the sharp curves. North London

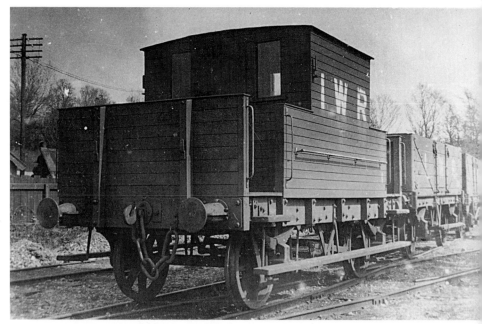

The IWR had two goods brake vans; this is No. 1 seen in late IWR days. Although odd to today's eyes, it was typical of goods brake vans built for a number of railways in the 1860s. *R.C. Riley*

The other brake van seen in SR livery had a much more modern appearance.
R. Silsbury Collection

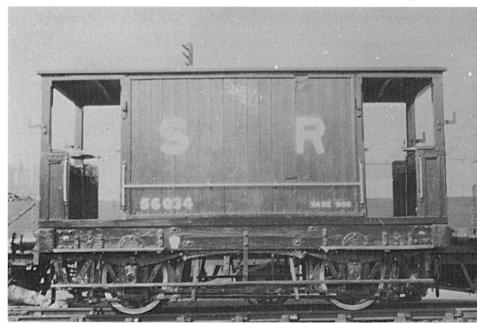

Amongst the wastes of Carpenters siding in about 1936 the body of the Golden Valley passenger guard's van slowly disintegrates. *G. Woodnutt/R. Silsbury Collection*

One of the Oldbury brake carriages stands at Ryde in its final guise as tool van 438s. It retained the remains of its birdcage roof observatory to the end. *R. Silsbury Collection*

IWR flat wagon No. 1 seen outside Ryde Works soon after the end of World War II. A.B. MacLeod had one side painted in IWR livery, traces of which it retains.

R. Silsbury Collection

Carriage truck No. 76 was modified in order to carry locomotive boilers between Ryde and St Helens quay. Here it sits in sidings at St Helens with an '02' boiler, behind can be seen the gasworks buildings .   *R. Silsbury Collection*

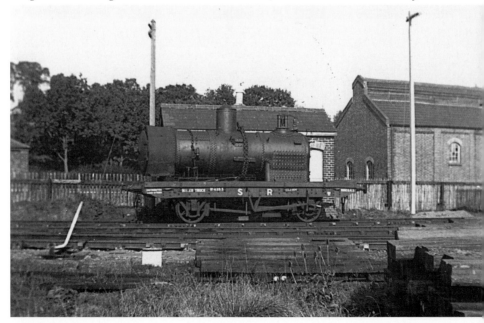

Railway (NLR) carriages replaced the Golden Valley vehicles on the Bembridge branch. Apart from those running as luggage and passenger guard's vans, six older Oldbury vehicles were retained, all of the three-compartment saloon type. Two were withdrawn in 1920 but the remaining four lasted until 1923. Of the remainder, Ryde Works took the opportunity to re-use the underframes in 'rebuilt' two plank open wagons, open carriage trucks, flat wagons and covered vans between 1913 and 1921.

In January 1917 a circular from the War Office was read out to the Board asking if the IWR possessed any goods stock that could be purchased. One hundred coal wagons were offered, a surprisingly large number that must have included all the oldest small capacity wagons. Nothing more was heard from the War Office so they must have secured their needs elsewhere.

From the Isle of Wight Railway, the Southern Railway inherited 59 coaching and 221 goods vehicles. Carriages had their second class compartments downgraded to third but otherwise there were few immediate changes. Some of the Oldburys and the Metropolitan carriages subsequently received repaints in lined green livery. Whilst in good condition they were non-standard and as soon as the opportunity arose replacements were transferred from the mainland.

By the start of the 1925 summer season, the IWR carriages had been collected together into five sets for Ryde to Ventnor line services - three of Metropolitan carriages, a set of NLR coaches and one of Oldbury high roofed stock. The older Oldbury carriages were used as extra accommodation during the summer months. In 1925 two sets of SECR bogie carriages arrived and entered service on the Bembridge branch; they were followed in 1926 by the first of a large number of LCDR four-wheel carriages for the main line. They replaced the older Oldbury and the NLR vehicles; a year later the remaining Oldbury carriages were taken out of service. As in IWR days, many bodies were sold locally and a few travelled as far as Hayling Island where their owners built them into holiday bungalows.

The last IWR passenger carriages in traffic were the Metropolitans withdrawn in 1928-1929; 12 bodies went to St Helens Duver where most became bathing huts; the remaining six ended up scattered in various places elsewhere in the Island. LSWR vehicles replaced most of the IWR passenger guard's and luggage vans between 1924 and 1926. An Oldbury passenger

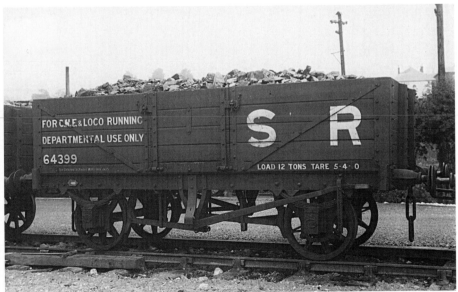

A typical IWR wagon is illustrated by this 12 ton wagon in use for locomotive coal during the 1930s.
A.B. MacLeod

guard's van and a NLR carriage were converted to tool vans, one of which lasted as the Ryde breakdown van until 1938. The horse box was replaced by a LBSCR vehicle in 1924 and most of the seven carriage trucks went in 1927-1928 when some LSWR and LBSCR machinery wagons arrived. A carriage truck was adapted to carry boilers between Ryde and St Helens for shipment to and from the mainland; it survived until October 1966.

Of the open wagons, those with non-standard 5, 6, 9 and 15 ton capacities were withdrawn first. Twelve 12 ton and a few 10 ton wagons were retained for the carriage of locomotive coal and ash; they lasted until 1959. The most long-lived open wagons in normal service were IWR Nos. 156 and 213, taken out of traffic on 27th January, 1934 and long since repainted in SR livery. The cattle wagons and covered vans went in 1927 when LBSCR replacements arrived. Most of the rail, timber and flat wagons lasted rather longer as they were used by the Engineers in an extensive programme of track renewals throughout the Island system; their end came in 1930 when the work ended. Two tar tank wagons were rebuilt on LSWR underframes sent from the mainland and lasted until 1947, along with the second brake van used on the weed-killer train. The 1864 mobile crane remained at Ryde Works where it assisted in dismantling locomotives undergoing overhauls; during a lengthy life it received Oldbury buffers but retained the old form of shackle coupling when saved for preservation by its makers Kirkstall Forge Co. The 1876 crane was paired with a match truck rebuilt from an IWR open wagon; they usually rested at or near St Helens Quay and during SR days were allocated to the Traffic department for 50 per cent of the time and to the CME as a breakdown crane for the remainder; the pair were broken up in 1969. St Helens Quay possessed no less that five assorted steam cranes for unloading coal and aggregate when the SR took charge (the dredger *Ballaster* contained a sixth); one soon transferred to Medina Wharf and most of the others disappeared during the 1930s.

An interesting survivor was the tiny works crane seen in March 1967 shortly before it was rescued for preservation by its builders.   *T. Hastings*

Chapter Seventeen

The Isle of Wight Railway Today

A few relics of the IWR can be seen during a trip over the line from Ryde to Shanklin and by walking parts of the closed railways to Ventnor and Bembridge.

Starting from Ryde, at St Johns Road alterations carried out during the 1920s enhanced rather than spoiled the character of the station. Up trains call at the original platform whilst a rebuilt island platform serves Shanklin-bound trains. The station buildings are still there as is the connecting footbridge and some platform canopies with a distinctive IWR monogram cast in the supports, a style repeated at Brading and Shanklin. The loop platform road on the down side became a siding, most of the signals have gone but a replacement signal box provided by the SR has taken over control of the whole line. Looking towards the workshops, the tube cars are maintained in a carriage shed that replaced the IWR buildings in 1938; the 1864 locomotive shed is used as a machine shop, the stone erecting shop is a bare shell and the corrugated iron carriage and wagon shop in the yard has long gone. The sites of the locomotive shed and goods yard on the up side of the line have been swept away. Monkton Mead Brook continues to flood the station although the existence of the live rail results in an immediate suspension of services. Recently the line's management returned to Ryde after a spell in residence at Sandown.

Double track exists as far the junction with the Newport and Cowes line at Smallbrook. Here the line becomes single just before it passes a wooden platform served, albeit at different heights, on one side by electric trains and on the other by steam trains working the Isle of Wight Steam Railway. No connections exist between the two railways even though they are but yards apart.

Brading is the best surviving example of an IWR station as it is largely unchanged since the alterations made in 1882. The line to Bembridge was lifted during the 1950s and little more than a grassy area remains; more recently the signals and second track to Sandown were removed leaving a single track through the former up platform, since relaid in modern flat bottom rail. The station building is disused as are the footbridge, signal box, island platform and its waiting room - surprisingly most of the platform coverings survive. The nearby station master's house is in private ownership.

At Sandown, history has gone full circle for it is the only crossing point south of Smallbrook. On the down platform the covering has been shortened whilst modern windows and doors have somewhat changed the appearance of the station building. The subway leads to an up platform completely devoid of buildings save for a glorified bus shelter. A track alongside but fenced off from the platform gives access to two engineer's sidings, the sole remaining part of the IWNJ line to Newport. On the down side, the site of the goods yard is a housing estate.

Just beyond Sandown station the railway crosses Lake Hill on a steel overbridge, a 1971 replacement for a structure made famous for its faded legend 'Too Low For High Bridge Buses'; the road was lowered soon afterwards making such a warning unnecessary. Just beyond the bridge on the down side is a wooden halt built in 1987 at a cost of £80,000 and regarded as a very good investment - it serves a sizeable population in the neighbourhood and passengers have only a short walk to the beach.

Shanklin is now the terminus of the line - another repeat of history. The down platform and station building have recently received some much needed repairs, most of the coverings remain but the site of the up platform is a flower bed whilst the goods yard has become a car park. The line ends in a substantial buffer stop as the bridge across Landguard Manor Road was demolished in October 1979. The platform road had always been on a slight gradient in the Sandown direction, but following an incident on 12th January, 1991 when a train departed without a driver or guard, the platform had to be rebuilt to create a level section!

Contractors removed the track from Shanklin to Ventnor in the spring of 1970 and the land was subsequently sold to the County Council. The first section towards Wroxall became a bridle way and forms part of the Worsley Trail. Quite apart from being good exercise, this stretch of line is worth walking by anyone with an interest in the IWR. Here, it is possible to experience

Who would have thought the IWR had ever ceased to exist? The Bembridge platform and signal box at Brading seen in early BR days remained virtually unchanged from the opening of the branch in 1882 until closure in 1953. *OPC Collection*

A hint of the future. This three-compartment Oldbury carriage body is one of several that reside at Havenstreet in the care of the Isle of Wight Steam Railway awaiting restoration. *R. Silsbury Collection*

the 1 in 70 gradient at first hand whilst appreciating the substantial earthworks and bridges that Henry Bond's men had to create in order to get the railway through to Ventnor.

The walk begins on the south side of Landguard Manor Road and for the first quarter of a mile follows an access road to a leisure park. Where the road veers to the right the trackbed continues straight on into a wooded cutting. The original bridges remain apart from that carrying the Newport to Shanklin road across the line rebuilt in 1992. Three Arch bridge marks the end of the climb, although the full benefits of the view across the Island can only be glimpsed through luxuriant vegetation clothing each side of the path. Upon approaching the outskirts of Wroxall, the walker will encounter a ribbon of housing, the gardens of which have encroached leaving only a narrow way. The footpath then diverts around the factory building and an industrial estate on the site of the goods yard before emerging onto a road overbridge.

Wroxall station is an odd mixture of old and new. The hotel and the road overbridge remain, but the latter is no longer connected to the road network as a road has been driven across the site of the station to a housing estate straddling the trackbed to Ventnor. The railway can no longer be walked along but the overgrown trackbed can be glimpsed as it passes below Manor Bridge road shortly before approaching the sealed entrance to Ventnor tunnel. The tunnel passed into the ownership of Southern Water and continues to supply water to the town of Ventnor - the ventilation shafts and spoil heaps can still be discerned by those sufficiently energetic to climb to the top of the down! The station yard at Ventnor was cleared in January 1972 and the closed-off entrance to the tunnel now emerges into yet another industrial estate. The eagle-eyed can discern coal merchants' cliff stores hidden behind buildings, but the only other indication that a railway existed is the station hotel.

Some of the Bembridge line has returned to nature but it is possible to walk parts of it. Near Brading station a public footpath crosses the Ryde to Shanklin railway to join the trackbed as it curves away towards Brading Quay. Apart from two minor deviations around the local sewage works, the path remains on the tracked most of the way to St Helens. Near the site of the cement works the crossing keeper's house looks across Brading harbour as it guards the site of Brading Quay. The path follows the old sea wall as far as the remains of the brick works at Carpenters siding. The remaining section to St Helens has reverted to farmland. The derelict station building at St Helens was sold in 1961 for use as a private house and has since been restored and extended. To seaward, the quays have been buried under modern housing that has also swamped the nearby gas works site; a hand crane on one of the quays that had been added during IWR days survived closure of the railway and the construction of housing only to succumb quite recently (1996) - it seems not to have fitted in with the ambience! The diligent might find a brick wall that had formed part of the locomotive shed on the north quay, but there is otherwise little to be seen. The nearby Duver is worth a visit to see the Metropolitan Railway carriage bodies in use as changing huts. Throughout the harbour other reminders of the past can be seen in the shape of the sea defences made using old railway materials. The embankment road between St Helens and Bembridge was sold to the County Council in 1971 who then abolished the toll. Beside the road can be seen a farm track occupying the trackbed for a short distance towards Bembridge. There, the station building survived until 1970 when it was flattened to make way for some yachtsmen's cottages. Across the road the memorial to Reverend J. Nelson Palmer presides over the site of the Spithead Hotel demolished soon after the station - it has a rather desolate appearance with little more than wind blown sand covering a pile of rubble to mark the spot.

The Isle of Wight Steam Railway at Havenstreet has a display of relics from the Island railways, including a few that belonged to the IWR. None of the company's locomotives escaped the breakers' torch but a unique collection of carriage bodies sold off by the IWR and its successor have been rescued for preservation. NLR carriage No. 46 was returned to service in 1986 and can be seen in regular use on the railway. Others awaiting restoration include Oldbury composite No. 10, first No. 21 and an unidentified second, all dating from 1864, 1875-built composite No. 35 and 1882 composite No. 38.

Appendix One

List of Directors and Chief Officers

The Isle of Wight Railway Company

Chairmen		
	James Simpson	1859 - 1868
	Alexander Beattie MD	1868 - 1875
	Joseph Bravo	1875 - 1881 *
	William McAndrew	1881 - 1884
	Horace F. Tahourdin	1884 - 1911 *
	Percy W. Gilbert	1911 - 1922

Deputy Chairmen		
	Francis H. Atherley	1859 - 1866
	Capt. Mark Huish	1866 - 1867 *
	Joseph Bravo	1869 - 1875 (post not filled 1875 to 1912)
	Hon. Gilbert Rollo	1912-1922

Directors		
	James Simpson	1859 - 1869 *
	Francis H. Atherley	1859 - 1867, 1875 - 1884
	Thomas Willis Fleming	1859 - 1861
	Alexander More	1859 - 1867
	Thomas Norton	1859 - 1860, 1867 - 1875 *
	Frederick Twynam	1860 - 1867
	Thomas Webster QC	1859 - 1861, 1866 - 1868 (Western Lines)
	Capt. Mark Huish	1861 - 1867 *
	George Young	1861 - 1884
	Joseph Bravo	1866 (Central Lines), 1867 - 1881 *
	William McAndrew	1866 (Central Lines), 1875 - 1884
	John Bailey Denton	1866 - 1868 (Western Lines), 1881 - 1884
	Alexander Beattie MD	1867 - 1875
	Abraham D. De Pass	1867 - 1897 *
	Albert Ricardo	1870 - 1874
	John M. Stobart	1884 - 1902 *
	Horace F. Tahourdin	1884 - 1911 *
	Capt. Henry F. Twynam	1884 - 1903 *
	Francis W. Slade	1884 - 1908
	Alfred F. Slade	1903 - 1906 *
	Hon Gilbert Rollo	1903 - 1922
	Percy W. Gilbert	1904 - 1922
	Charles F. Slade	1908 - 1922
	Percy Mortimer JP	1910 - 1922
	Capt. Walter Waring MP	1910 - 1922
	Alfred Malby	1912 - 1917
	Sir Charles J. Owens CB	1917 - 1922

* died in office.

The IWES Act of 1860 authorised up to six Directors (including the Chairman), a quorum to be three. By two subsequent Acts in 1863 and 1865, a further two Directors were authorised each for the Central Lines and for the Western Lines. These powers lapsed when authority was obtained to abandon the extension lines.

Secretaries	Charles Morrison	1860 - 1861
	Charles E. Reed	1861 - 1863
	Robert Hicks	1863 - 1893
	Henry K. Day	1893 - 1922
Solicitors	C.F. Fisher	1860 - 1865
	George T. Porter	1860 - 1869
	Messrs Porter and Twynam	1869 - 1882
	Beale & Marigold & Co.	1882 - 1922
Engineers	Hamilton H. Fulton	1859 - 1861
	John Fowler	1861 - not known
	Joseph Bourne	by November 1870 - 1884
	James Connor	1884 - 1888
	Henry Brent *	1888 - 1912
	Horace D. Tahourdin *	1912 - 1922
Managers	W. R. Page	May 1864 (appointment cancelled)
	Joseph Bourne	1864 - 1884
	James Connor	1884 - 1888
	Henry K. Day	1888 - 1922

* Engineer, Locomotive, Carriage and Wagon Superintendent

The Brading Harbour Improvement and Railway Company

In the absence of Minute books and other documents it has not been possible to compile a list of Directors. The Brading Harbour Improvement Railway & Works Act 1874 listed the first Directors as William Harris Saunders (a solicitor) and William Axon Mansell. The Act authorised three Directors and a quorum was two. The few surviving documents mentioned that Jabez S. Balfour became Chairman and Henry S. Freeman his deputy and manager. Mr Freeman later became Receiver and Manager.

The company's Act of 1896 changed the name to The Brading Harbour Improvement and Railway Company, altered the number of Directors to four and required the holding of a meeting within two months to elect fresh Directors. No records have been found of that or subsequent meetings, nor of the names of Directors appointed before the company ceased to exist.

Appendix Two

A Chronology of relevant Isle of Wight railway Acts of Parliament etc.

This summary contains the name of the Act, a brief description and the Parliamentary reference.

The Isle of Wight Eastern Section Railway Act 1860.
Incorporation of the 'Isle of Wight (Eastern Section) Railway Company' with powers to build a railway from Ryde to Ventnor etc.
23 & 24 Vict. Ch. 162. Date of incorporation 23rd July, 1860.

Isle of Wight Railways (Extensions) Act 1863.
Change of name to 'Isle of Wight Railway Company', powers to build the Central lines from Ryde to Newport and Wroxall.
26 & 27 Vict. Ch. 232. Date of incorporation 18th July, 1863.

The Bembridge Railway, Tramway and Pier Act 1864.
Incorporation, powers to construct railways.
27 & 28 Vict. Ch. 327. Date of incorporation 29th July, 1864.

Isle of Wight Railways (Steamers) Act 1865.
Powers to operate steam vessels etc.
28 & 29 Vict. Ch. 157. Date of incorporation 29th June, 1865.

Isle of Wight Railways (Extensions) Act 1865.
Powers to build the Western lines from Newport to Yarmouth and Freshwater.
28 & 29 Vict. Ch. 224. Date of incorporation 5th July, 1865.

Isle of Wight Railways Act 1867.
Additional Capital &c.
30 & 31 Vict. Ch. 174. Date of incorporation 12th August, 1867.

The Brading Harbour Improvement Railway and Works Act 1874.
Incorporation of the 'Brading Harbour Improvement and Railway Company', powers to build various works and a railway from Brading Quay to Bembridge.
37 & 38 Vict. Ch. 195. Date of incorporation 7th August, 1874.

Isle of Wight (Additional Capital) 1876.
Board of Trade Certificate granted under the Railway Companies Powers Act (27-28 Vict. Ch. 120) 1864.

South-Western and Brighton Railway Companies (Isle of Wight and Ryde Pier Railway) Act 1877.
Powers to build a railway from a junction with the IWR to a new pier at Ryde etc.
40 & 41 Vict. Ch. 107. Date of incorporation 23rd July, 1877.

The South Western and Brighton Joint Steam Vessels Act 1879
Authority for the LSW and LBSC to each raise £50,000 for the purpose of operating a ferry service.
42 & 43 Vict. Ch. 30. Date of incorporation 23rd May, 1879.

Brading Harbour Improvement Railway and Works (Additional Powers) Act 1881.
Extension of time for completion of railway, additional capital etc.
44 & 45 Vict. Ch. 24. Date of incorporation 3rd June, 1881.

Isle of Wight Railway Act 1890.
Purchase of additional land, additional capital etc.
53 & 54 Vict. Ch. 137. Date of incorporation 25th July, 1890.

Railway Rates and Charges No. 9 (Isle of Wight Railway, etc.) Order Confirmation Act 1892.
Revised rates and charges.
55 & 56 Vict. Ch. 47. Date of incorporation 20th June, 1892.
Board of Trade Certificate - IWR 1893
Certificate for additional capital authorised under the Regulation of Railways Act 1889.

The Brading Harbour & Railway Act 1896.
Additional powers and capital, change of name to 'The Brading Harbour & Railway Company'.
59 & 60 Vict. Ch. 243. Date of incorporation 14th August, 1896.

Order of the Light Railway Commissioners under the Light Railways Act 1896. Ventnor Inclined Light Railway.
Date of order 10th March, 1898.

Isle of Wight Railway (Brading Harbour and Railway) Act 1898.
Dissolution of the Brading Harbour & Railway Co. Purchase of railway by IWR.
61 & 62 Vict. Ch. 198. Date of incorporation 2nd August, 1898.

The Railways Act 1921.
Reorganisation and further regulation of railways. Creation of the Southern Railway Company.
11 & 12 Geo. 5 Ch. 55. Date of incorporation 19th August, 1921.

Appendix Three
Signal Diagrams

The 1871 Regulation of Railways Act obliged the Board of Trade to order an inspection of new railways and locations where alterations were being carried out. It became the custom for a company's Engineer to submit drawings showing the proposed layout of track and signalling prior to inspection. Although contemporary diagrams for most of the IWR stations have survived, none exist for Brading or the Bembridge branch. However, the signalling remained largely unchanged until the early years of the Southern Railway so we have included diagrams* based on a series prepared by C.N. Anderson when he worked in the Island at that time. The originals were not suitable for reproduction so have been redrawn in a standard format.

The signal diagram for the IWR signal box at St Johns Road station, Ryde, as drawn by Messrs Saxby & Farmer in 1892, shows the signalling as it existed following the opening of railways to Newport and Ryde Pier. When the latter opened, the LSW and LBSC built a second signal box north of the road overbridge. The north box controlled the connections at that end of the station and certain levers in both boxes were 'slotted' to prevent conflicting movements; they are shown in the diagram by means of a second arm at 45 degrees to the main signal arm. The IWR box became known as the south box. It was originally planned to work the sidings at the Brading and Ashey end of the station using the spare levers but when the IWR signal box was built in 1875 the Board of Trade insisted on the provision of ground frames 'A' and 'B' because of the distance of the connections from the box. In 1895 inner home signals for each line were added worked by levers 25, 26 (shunt signals), 29 and 30. Apart from fixing distant signals 34 and 35 at danger, there were no other significant changes until SR days.

Although dated 1924 the diagram of Brading is probably identical to the arrangements that came into use during 1882. Along with Sandown and Shanklin, the signalling remained virtually unchanged until 1923.

The earliest known IWR signal diagram that contained numbered points and signals was one produced for the alterations at Ventnor in 1877; it makes an interesting comparison with the 1892 plan. Photographs show that the gantry supporting signals 12, 13 and 14 was of the 'gallows' type in an attempt to make them more visible, but even so the arms were repeated as disc signals situated just inside the tunnel; this was before the days of colour light signals. Although disc No. 15 was worked as a distant signal its location halfway along the tunnel seems far from satisfactory; a replacement distant signal was subsequently provided beyond the tunnel mouth.

Of the signalling at Brading Quay, it should be mentioned that signal No. 7 occupied the same post as Brading distant No. 27. Similarly, at St Helens we see that Nos. 3 and 9 were on the same post albeit facing in opposite directions, the purpose of shunting signal No. 8 is not known. By 1924 the distant signal at Bembridge was unworked but in the past had probably been connected to lever 10.

---

* Certain diagrams omitted sidings whose connections were not worked from the signal box.

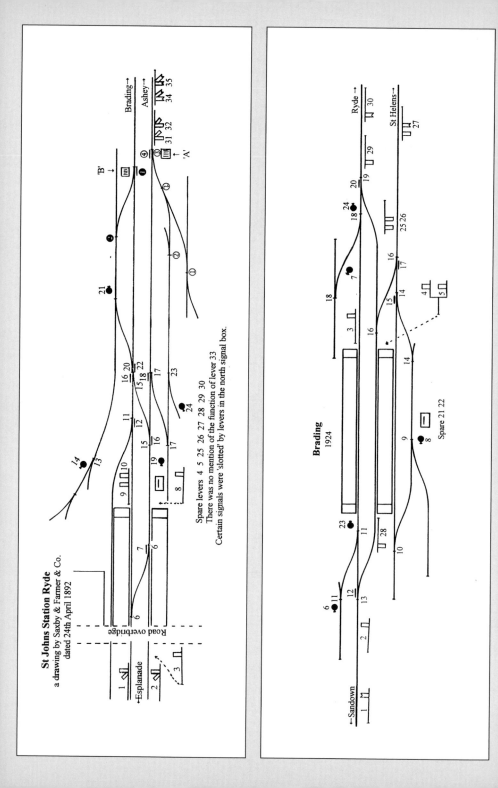

St Johns Station Ryde
a drawing by Saxby & Farmer & Co.
dated 24th April 1892

Spare levers 4 5 25 26 27 28 29 30
There was no mention of the function of lever 33
Certain signals were 'slotted' by levers in the north signal box.

Brading
1924

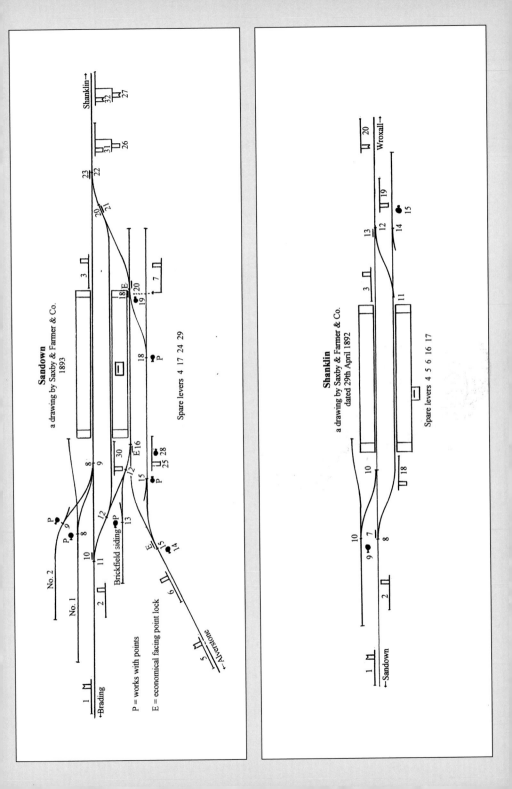

Sandown

a drawing by Saxby & Farmer & Co.
1893

Spare levers 4 17 24 29

P = works with points

E = economical facing point lock

←Brading

No. 1
No. 2

←Averstone

Brickfield siding

Shanklin→

Shanklin

a drawing by Saxby & Farmer & Co.
dated 29th April 1892

Spare levers 4 5 6 16 17

←Sandown

Wroxall→

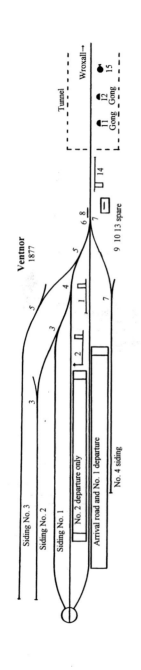

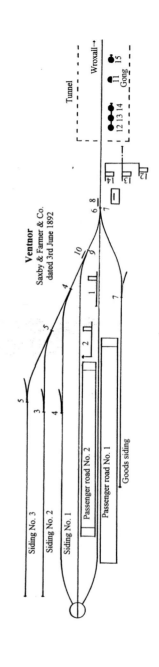

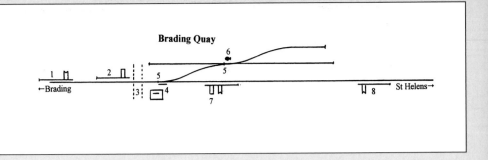

Brading Quay

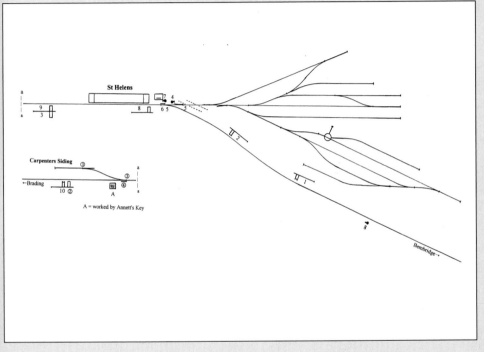

St Helens

Carpenters Siding

←Brading

A = worked by Annett's Key

Bembridge→

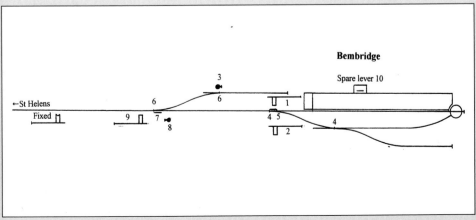

Bembridge

Spare lever 10

←St Helens

Fixed

Appendix Four

Summary of Locomotives owned by the Isle of Wight Railway

	Ryde Sandown&Shanklin	*Brading(I)/St Helens*	*Ventnor*	*Wroxall*	*Brading (II)*	*Bonchurch*	*Bembridge*
Maker	Beyer, Peacock	Bury	Beyer, Peacock	Beyer, Peacock	Beyer, Peacock	Beyer, Peacock	Manning, Wardle
Order number	S767		S2259	S2802	S3450	S6344	class 'M'
Works number(s)	400, 401 & 403		848	1141	1638	2376	517
Date built	1864	1841	1868	1872	1876	1883	1875
Type	2-4-0T	2-4-0WT	2-4-0T	2-4-0T	2-4-0T	2-4-0T	0-6-0T
Cost to IWR	£2,250 each	*circa* £600	£2,250	£2,390	£2,525	£2,100	£450
Cylinders	15 in. x 20 in.	14 in. x 18 in.	15 in. x 20 in.	15 in. x 20 in.	16 in. x 24 in.	17 in. x 24 in.	13 in. x 18 in.
Leading wheels	3 ft 6 in.		3 ft 6 in.	3 ft 6½ in.	3 ft 6½ in.	3 ft 6½ in.	
Coupled wheels	5 ft 0 in.	4 ft 6 in.	5 ft 0 in.	5 ft 0½ in.	5 ft 0½ in.	5 ft 0½ in.	3 ft 0 in.
Wheelbase	13 ft 9 in.		13 ft 9 in.	13 ft 9 in.	14 ft 6 in.	14 ft 6½ in.	11 ft 6 in.
Boiler diameter	3 ft 11¼ in.		3 ft 11¼ in.	3 ft 11¼ in.	3 ft 11¼ in.	4 ft 0 in.	3 ft 4 in.
Boiler length	9 ft 6 in.		9 ft 6 in.	9 ft 6 in.	9 ft 6 in.	9 ft 10 in.	8 ft 4 in.
Firebox length	4 ft 4 in.		4 ft 4 in.	4 ft 4 in.	4 ft. 4 in.	4 ft 4 in.	3 ft 3½ in.
Heating surfaces:							
Tubes	861.3 sq. ft		861.3 sq. ft	861½ sq. ft	890.6 sq. ft	889 sq. ft	500 sq. ft
Firebox	71 sq. ft		71 sq. ft	65¾ sq. ft	70.2 sq. ft	70½ sq. in.	50 sq. ft
Total	932.3 sq. ft		932.3 sq. ft	927¼ sq. ft	960.8 sq. ft	950½ sq. ft	550 sq. ft
Working pressure (psi)	120 lb.		120 lb.	120 lb.	120 lb.	160 lb.	120 lb.
Grate area	13.1 sq. ft		13.1 sq. ft	13.1 sq. ft	13.1 sq. ft	14.9 sq. ft	8 sq. ft
Tank capacity	820 galls		820 galls	820 galls	1,000 galls	1,000 galls	500 galls
Bunker capacity	1¼ tons (47½ cu. ft.)		1¼ tons (47½ cu. ft.)	1½ tons	24 c.	1 t. 19 c.	46 cu. ft
Weight in working order							
Leading wheels	7 t. 9½ c.		7 t. 9½ c.	7 t. 7 c.	8 t. 5 c.	7 t. 6 c.	
Leading coupled wheels	11 t. 13¾ c.		11 t. 13¾ c.	12 t. 0 c.	13 t. .7½ c.	15t. 2¼ c.	
Trailing coupled wheels	11 t. 5¼ c.		11 t. 5¼ c.	12 t. 0 c.	12 t. 15½ c.	13 t. 6¼ c.	
Total	30 t. 8½ c.	18½ tons	30 t. 8½ c.	31 t. 14 c.	34 t. 8 c.	35 t. 14½ c.	22½ tons

	Ryde	*Sandown*	*Shanklin*	*Ventnor*	*Wroxall*	*Brading*	*Bonchurch*
Date repainted in SR livery	by 6.1924	not	by 3.1925	*c.* 4.1924	not known	by 2.1925	by 5.1925
SR number	w13	none	w14	w15	w16	w17	w18
Withdrawn	9.7.1932	5.1923	11.1927	9.1925	23.6.1933	4.1926	5.1928
Cut up	*14.8.1940	1923	1927	1925	7/1933	1926	1928
Final mileage	1,502,638	1,374,751	1,492,121	1,348,548	1,350,574	1,212,753	1,326,067

* Official date. *Brading (I)* sold 1872, owned by BHIR under name *St Helens c.* 1879 to 1893. Bembridge sold 1916.

Appendix Five

Summary of Isle of Wight Railway Rolling Stock

Oldbury Stock

Nos.	Original type	Bought	SR No.	Renumbered	Withdrawn
	3 compt brake second	1864	980	not	26/9/25
2	3 compt brake second	1864	981	not	5/3/27
3	3 compt brake second	1864	982	not	26/9/25
4	3 compt brake second	1864	983	31/1/24	30/10/26
5-8	4 compt second	1864			1914
9	3 compt 1/2 saloon composite	1864			1914
10	3 compt 1/2 saloon composite	1864			1920
11	3 compt 1/2 saloon composite	1864	6338	30/4/24	5/3/27
12	3compt 1/2 saloon composite	1864			1920
13	3 compt 1/2 saloon composite	1864	6330	not	1923
14-17	3 compt 1/2 saloon composite	1864			1914
18	3 compt 1/2 saloon composite	1864	6331	not	27/2/26
19	3 compt 1/2 saloon composite	1864	6332	not	27/2/26
20	3 compt 1/2 saloon composite	1864	6333	not	1923
21-24	3 compt first	1864			1914
27	luggage van	1872			c. 1914
28-32	5 compt third	1873			1914
33	4 compt second	1875	2231	not	26/9/25
34	4 compt second	1875	987	not	26/9/25
35	4 compt second	1875			1914
36	luggage van	1876			1914
37	3 compt composite	1882	6344	31/10/24	5/3/27
38	3 compt composite	1882	6345	31/10/24	5/3/27
39	4 compt second	1882	2421	31/10/24	5/3/27
40	4 compt second	1882	2422	6/9/24	5/3/27
41	4 compt second	1882	2423	10/24	5/3/27
42	4 compt second	1882	2424	31/10/24	5/3/27

1-36 originally had a shallow curve to the roof, 37-42 had a more elliptical shape.

1-4 were rebuilt as brake/luggage vans.

1 and 3 were built with birdcage lookouts to the guard's compartment.

2 was rebuilt with a higher roof profile to match the 1882 stock. Latterly it had no windows.

4 was converted in October 1926 to tool van 438s for use by the Engineer's Bridge Department. It was condemned on 4th October, 1930.

33 & 34 were rebuilt as passenger luggage vans c. 1899, 33 was numbered by the SR as a 6 ton passenger luggage van. No. 34 was numbered as a passenger guard's van.

All second class compartments were latterly third class.

No. 11 was sold to a Mr Edney in May 1927.

No. 37 was sold to Mr Hall March 1927. Apparently it was taken by rail to Freshwater and then by road to its final resting place near Freshwater Church. The frame was broken up in August 1927.

Dimensions of the Oldbury vehicles can be scaled off the drawings in this book.

Ryde Pier Company stock

No.	Original Type	Bought	SR No.	Renumbered	Withdrawn
25	saloon first	1865	984	not	5/3/27
26	saloon second	1865	985	not	5/3/27

Dimensions:

25   26 ft 10 in. long, 8 ft 6 in. wide, 7 ft 3 in. high.
26   26 ft 9 in. long, 8 ft 6 in. wide, 7 ft 4 in. high.

Golden Valley Railway stock

No.	Original Type	Bought	SR. No.	Renumbered	Withdrawn
43 later 24	saloon first	1885	988	30/5/25	5/3/27
44 later 28	saloon second	1885	989	31/10/24	5/3/27
45	brake van	1885			1914

Dimensions:

43-44   31 ft 4 in. long, 8 ft 2 in. wide, 7 ft 6 in. high, both were six wheel vehicles.
45   not known.

North London Railway stock

No.	Original IWR Type	Bought	SR No.	Renumbered	Withdrawn
46	4 compt first	1897	6336	not	27/2/26
47	4 compt composite	1897	6337	not	27/2/26
48	4 compt third	1897	2428	not	27/2/26
49	4 compt third	1897	2429	not	27/2/26
50	4 compt third	1897	2430	not	27/2/26
51	4 compt third	1897	2431	not	27/2/26
52 later 27	brake/luggage	1897	986	not	29/8/25
53 later 43	5 compt third	1898	2425	not	27/2/26
54 later 44	5 compt third	1898	2426	not	27/2/26
55 later 45	5 compt third	1898	2427	not	27/2/26

Dimensions:

46-51   27 ft long, 8 ft wide, 7 ft high, 15 ft wheelbase.
52-55   26 ft 6 in. long, 8 ft wide, 7 ft high.

No. 44 was renumbered 444s and used as a mess and tool van by the CME Departmen, Ryde. It was condemned on 14th December, 1938.

Metropolitan Railway stock

IWR No.	No. compts	SR No.	Date ren.	Withdrawn	Final compts.	Final seating
5	8	2432	1/8/25	20/4/29		80 third
6	8	2433	7/2/25	20/4/29		80 third
7	8	2434	31/5/25	23/6/28		80 third
8	8	2435	29/5/26	23/6/28		80 third
9	8	6338	30/4/24	23/6/28	13333333	4 first 70 third
14	6	6339	30/6/24	20/4/29	113333	16 first 40 third
15	6	6340	31/3/24	23/6/28	113333	16 first 40 third
16	6	6341	30/5/25	20/4/29	113333	16 first 40 third
17	6	6342	7/2/25	20/4/29	111333	24 first 30 third
21	7	6343	23/8/24	23/6/28	3311333	16 first 50 third
22	7	6344	30/1/26	20/4/29	3311333	16 first 50 third
23	7	2430	9/1/26	23/6/28		70 third (ex composite)
29	6	2437	13/2/26	23/6/28		60 third
30	6	2438	7/2/25	23/6/28		60 third
31	6	2439	3/4/26	20/4/29		60 third
32	6	2440	2/5/25	20/4/29		60 third
35	6	6345	4/7/25	23/6/28	111333	24 first 30 third
36	6	6346	10/7/26	20/4/29	111333	24 first 30 third

IWR 9 had a single first class coupé end compartment. IWR No. 15 did not have the round topped doors characteristic of Metropolitan Railway carriages.

Dimensions:

39 ft 6 in. long, 8 ft 2 in. wide, 7 ft 4 in. high. The tare weight was *circa* 17 tons.

IWR Goods Stock as at 1923

Type	Quantity	IWR Nos.	SR Nos.	Withdrawn
5 ton open wagon	1	60	27787	23/1/26
6 ton open wagons	34	various	27788-27821	1926-1928
9 ton open wagons	74	various	27822-27885	1927-1929
10ton open wagons	65	various	27886-27950	1929-1931
12 ton open wagons	21	various	27951-27971	1929-1933
15 ton open wagons	4	104, 205-207	27972-27975	1927-1928
Covered vans	12	57-62, 91-92, 113-115, 208	46975-46986	1927
Cattle wagons	3	24, 111-112	53377-53379	1927
6 ton timber & flat wagons	10	30, 53-56, 88-90, 93-94	59011-59020	1927-1930
9 ton timber & flat wagons	3	1-2, 6	59021-59023	1927-1930
Open carriage trucks	7	20, 37, 76-77, 87, 130, 136	4378-4384	1924-1928
Horse box	1	209	3368	6/6/25
Tar tank wagons	2	202-203	61381-61382	1947
Brake vans	2	1-2	56033-56044	1930 & 1932
Works crane	1	none	425s	1966
Travelling crane	1	none	426s	1969
Match truck for above	1	ex-9 ton open 107	426sm, later DS3138	1969

Several 10 and 12 ton open wagons became MPD wagons.

Bibliography

General
Rails in the Isle of Wight, P.C. Allen and A.B. MacLeod, George Allen & Unwin Ltd, 1967.
The Railways and Tramways of Ryde, A. Blackburn & J. Mackett, Town & Country Press Ltd 1971.
The Portsmouth - Ryde Passage. A Personal View, J. Mackett, The Ravensbourne Press, 1970.
Once Upon a Line (4 volumes), A. Britton, Oxford Publishing Co. 1983, 1984, 1990 and 1994.
The Signalling of the Isle of Wight Railways, Signalling Record Society 1993.
Ups and Downs (Funiculars and Lifts in Ventnor), F.H. Brown, Ventnor & District Historical Society 1999.
Wight Report and *Island Rail News*, magazines of the Isle of Wight Steam Railway.

Locomotives and rolling stock
A Locomotive History of Railways on the Isle of Wight, D.L. Bradley, Railway Correspondence & Travel Society, 1982.
Isle of Wight Steam Passenger Rolling Stock, R.J. Maycock & M.J.E. Reed, The Oakwood Press, 1997.
The Isle of Wight Railway Stock Book, R. Silsbury, Isle of Wight Railway Co. Ltd, 1994.
An Illustrated History of Southern Wagons (volume 2), G. Bixley & others, Oxford Publishing Company, 1985.

The locomotive shed at St Helens seen during BR days has changed very little since it ceased to be used for locomotive purposes in the 1920s. The water tank is supported by some unusually shaped ironwork.
R. Brock/R. Silsbury Collection

Index